THE
THEOLOGY
OF
FEAR

EMMETT COYNE

ISBN: 1468015648
ISBN-13: 9781468015645

1

DEDICATION

IN MEMORY OF . . . Anna Utenhove, a servant woman buried alive in 1597 after an instigation by her pastor on suspicion she was a heretic; Cayetano Ripoli, a schoolteacher who was the last victim of the Spanish Inquisition, in 1826, for refusing to take his pupils to mass and substituting *Praise Be to God* for *Ave Maria* in school prayers; and countless persons who tragically received death, not abundant life, while subject to the dark side of the Roman Catholic Church.

Also, priests John Hus, Giordano Bruno, and numerous "other Christs" executed because of their dissent.

And, heroic persons such as Ben Salmon (American) and Franz Jägerstätter (Austrian), both ordinary Catholics, dissenters against war, unsupported by their Church, with limited education yet able to reason to the immorality of war when popes, prelates, priests, and their fellow parishioners could not.

The tradition of Kingdom values is passed on more by individuals' faithfulness to the spirit than by popes' canonical claims. True tradition is an expression of the spirit, not the recourse to law.

ANY PROFIT . . . from this book will be contributed to the organization described below. Your purchase will not be totally in vain. For twenty-four years I raised money and consciousness on behalf of "the least ones" through two other organizations which unfortunately were more about building a business than creating an authentic ministry to the poor.

Therefore, all proceeds from this book will be donated to the non-profit organization Partners in Health (PIH). See www.pih.org

PIH reflects my ideal of an organization that systemically addresses the plight of the poor rather than simply providing Band-Aids. I feel PIH, though a public organization, does better than even many religious organizations in keeping before the public "the preferential option for the poor." Its mission is both moral and medical, based on solidarity rather than charity alone. PIH is transparent and practical, providing education to its supporters so they can understand the complexity of factors—including political and economic—impacting the world's most vulnerable populations.

DISCLAIMER . . . The opinions presented in this book are solely the author's and do not reflect in any way the mission or values of PIH.

SEE FR. COYNE'S WEBSITE . . . at www.emmettcoyne.net

TABLE OF CONTENTS

PREFACE

CHILDHOOD BELIEFS IN QUESTION: RETHINKING TRADITION

"Growth is the only evidence of life." – John Henry Newman

Why was Jesus always creating conflict, causing trouble, toppling convention?

It's right there in the four gospels. But this view is rarely emphasized to believers, in a seeming attempt to downplay a negative image of him as a disturber of religious tradition. Before his torture and execution, the charge would be made: "He is stirring up the people with his teaching all over Judea." (Lk 23:5)

Search the gospels yourself. The persistent drama in Jesus' public life involves his conflict with the religious leaders of his time, not with the simple folks under the burden of the Law. You'd be hard pressed to find a positive encounter with religious leaders.

Ultimately, the leaders handed Jesus over to the Roman authorities with this charge, and it got their attention. Romans represented a colonizing power and would not brook anyone perceived as a threat to the empire's order. But theological controversy wouldn't particularly move them to act. So the religious leaders upped the ante, claiming "anyone who makes himself a king defies Caesar." (Jo 19:12) This caught Pontius Pilate's ear, though *King* was a political word. You know the rest of the story. This is not the only instance of

1

trumped-up charges leading to execution. The leaders gave misleading evidence. Jesus never referred to himself as a king, and in one instance when people wanted to declare him a king, he fled to the mountains. But he *did* speak of the Kingdom of God. *Often.*

Prior to this run-in with political authorities, Jesus clashed constantly with religious leaders over their interpretation of the Law (Torah, Mosaic). He wasn't even an official *rabbi* (teacher), merely a layman, yet he dared to proclaim his broader perspective, preferring to err on the side of the person rather than the rule. And worse, he charged that these leaders didn't practice what they preached. Here was an upstart, a troublemaker, a Galilean bumpkin. They alone had the authority to interpret long-held beliefs and practices. Who was he to question them, openly and repeatedly? He didn't exactly warm the cockles of their hearts, if you believe the gospel stories.

Why wasn't Jesus simply an observant Jew, intent on obediently adhering to the letter of the Law? Why didn't he direct his energies to urge his fellow Jews to follow their leaders totally, unquestioningly? Why wasn't he concerned solely with his own observance of tradition? Why did he feel he could interpret this tradition freely? Is he a model for us in this regard—encouraging us to interpret our own traditions handed down to us?

Saul, later renamed Paul, would ultimately promote Jesus. But not before he ruthlessly attacked his followers. "I am a Jew, born in Tarsus of Cilicia, but brought up in this city, educated under Gamaliel, strictly according to the law of our fathers, being zealous for God just as you all are today. I persecuted the Way [followers of Jesus] to the death, bidding and putting both men and women into prisons." (AA 22:3)

Eventually, a personal conversion experience would create a 360-degree change. It would be no small thing to utter, "When I was a child, I used to speak like a child, think like a child, reason like a child; when I became a man, I did away with childish things." (1 Cor 13:11) When Paul heard the story of Jesus circulating orally, and learned of the freedom Jesus indulged in when interpreting his Jewish tradition, was he convinced to the point of putting aside childhood thinking?

2

Paul's change of course led to a profound change for the world. More than even Peter, he would make the Jesus story universal, catholic. Despite Paul's profound endorsement of Jesus of Nazareth, the overwhelming majority of Jews, then and now, have rejected Jesus as the messiah. Was Paul a Jewish deviant, or at least a religious one?

Paul was more of a religious deviant than Jesus. Jesus' questioning is not out of the mainstream of Jewish tradition. It is just that those in power differed with his interpretation. No less than Roman Catholic authorities today (who hold the power) resisting those who interpret their tradition. The genius of Judaism allowed vigorous questioning. But there was a downside—those who had power controlled the "official" interpretation. Yet, Catholicism doesn't have a questioning tradition like that of Judaism, and resisting such, is more reminiscent of a controlling empire that will brook no dissent.

If it weren't for Paul, the Jesus story might not have reached a wider audience, especially his proclamation of the Kingdom, which Paul seemed to ignore. But because Paul's promotion of Jesus enabled the gospels' wider circulation, the Kingdom proclamation was realized.

Paul's interpretation of the Jesus event was written and circulated about twenty to thirty years before any written gospel account. Paul's letters and perception of Jesus were considerably different from the Jesus of the four gospels. The gospel writers didn't even refer to Paul, or Paul to them. They seemed to be on parallel, independent tracks, offering different versions of the Jesus story. Paul never met Jesus in the flesh, yet this didn't prevent him from interpreting what he had heard about Jesus. All who subsequently received the Jesus story likewise learned it through hearsay from others, who also never knew Jesus in the flesh.

Paul took an extreme departure from his religious upbringing. Is he a model, a mentor, in reevaluating childish things?

Paul was not totally free from the indoctrination of his religious childhood even as he attempted to break new religious ground. He brought worn baggage from his past—"old wine"—and blended it with the revelations he shared—"new wine." Nonetheless, he clearly deviated from what he was taught and had held fervently for years.

3

Ought not everyone, then, reinvestigate interpretations of all traditions received—religious, political, cultural, and social? Should we hold fast to our traditions, or challenge and question them? The latter seems amenable even to the current pope, Benedict XVI, who wrote that "traditions were criticized in order that genuine tradition might be revealed." [1] Questioning any tradition, however, will not be without repercussions. Ask Jesus and Paul.

Nearly two millennia ago, Paul suddenly had a born-again moment on the Damascus road. More recently, many of us have had a born-again moment on the Roman road, or other religious, political, or cultural roads we journeyed after childhood schooling.

As adults, we've let go of some childish things. Jewish folk singer Theodore Bikel aptly noted, "I prefer to choose which traditions to keep and which to let go." While some things are valuable to pass on to the next generation, others need to be phased out.

Topping my list of childish things to jettison is belief in the Devil, my first to get the heave-ho. While we all know evil flourishes, attributing it to an independent agent is childish, essentially believing in a bogeyman. Yet the Roman Church tenaciously clings to maintaining belief in such a bogus character. Sadly, it is resurrecting the Devil when it should be exorcising it completely.

Recently in Peoria, IL, Bishop Daniel Jenky directed parishioners to revive *The Prayer to St. Michael the Archangel*, imploring him to "be our protection against the wickedness and snares of the devil." [2] Sadly, Jenky is not alone among bishops in promoting the Devil today. And where would multitudes of Christian sects be without the image of a restless Satan, always on the prowl? He is alive and well in many traditions, effectively terrorizing members.

It is easy to abandon childish things such as the Devil. But that's only a start. What other questionable or simplistic "answers," accepted uncritically in childhood, fail to weather life's revelations? What "beliefs" need to be examined anew in the search for truth, for the authentic tradition even Pope Benedict XVI seeks?

INTRODUCTION

WHEN IN ROME:
DEALING WITH THE VATICAN'S BOUNCER

"All roads lead to Rome." – Hilaire Belloc
"All roads lead from Rome." – Author

In 1957, at age eighteen, I traveled to Europe for the first time, with a high school classmate, Pat Broderick. The children of Irish immigrants didn't do "Grand Tours" of Europe, though ours wouldn't be quite grand. It cost us about $1,000 each for a transatlantic voyage that led to a three-month exploration and exposure to a world far beyond the confines of our Chicago Irish ghetto.

We were high school students at the minor seminary of the Archdiocese of Chicago, Quigley Preparatory Seminary, or *"Le Petite Seminaire."* As simple seminarians on the lowest rung of priestly formation, we received a free week of lodging through the influence of Msgr. Ernest Primeau, a Chicago priest. Little did I know then that he would subsequently become my bishop and I would be ordained by him in 1966 in Manchester, NH.

The Roman visit was an early introduction to the perks and privileges of clerical membership. A priest guest at the same residence forfeited two tickets to us for a semi-private audience with Pope Pius XII (1939-1958). For a class project, we had assembled a book on the pope's life, modeled after the then-popular TV program,

This Is Your Life. We had filled it with photo copies of the pope and added our fulsome commentary as a paean to our presiding pontiff. Naively, we thought we would be able to personally hand it to him. The unexpected tickets provided access to the front line in a Vatican reception salon at Castel Gandolfo, complete with a pope on a throne. After his presentation, Pius XII came down to greet those in the front line, where we were able to personally hand him our homey book of pirated pictures. Undoubtedly, he could hardly wait to peruse it.

Fifty-two years lapsed before I returned to Rome, in August 2008. This time, my classmate (who left the seminary) had been dead about twenty-five years, and my companion now was my German sister-in-law, Oda. In the interim, I had been ordained a Roman Catholic priest. According to Catholic teaching, a priest is an *"Alter Christus"* (another Christ). Ordination underscores the uniqueness of a priest in the Church. He is a man set apart.

At the same time, Catholic theology holds all members of the Body of Christ are equal, but as I would learn, some more than others, particularly priests—only one example of the multiple contradictions in Catholic theology. With ordination, a man becomes a priest forever. He is unique in having *three* indelible marks: for baptism, confirmation, and holy orders. The Roman Church has to be the biggest purchaser of indelible ink.

As if being an *"Alter Christus"* wasn't ennobling enough, John Paul II (1978-2005) further underscored priestly uniqueness above rank-and-file members by claiming priests act *"in persona Christi"* (in the person of Christ). Not enough to just be an *"Alter Christus"!* This was a theological attempt to undermine the theory behind baptism, whereby each person is equally incorporated in the person of Christ, forming the Body of Christ.

Ironically, it was under his pontificate, the second-longest on record, that the clerical sexual-abuse scandal erupted publically and universally. Countless priests, acting as both *"Alter Christus"* and *"in persona Christi,"* were sexually abusing the most innocent and vulnerable of the flock.

Unfortunately, this would become a truly "catholic" phenomenon.

Pressure mounted to defrock pedophile priests. John Paul was reluctant because a priest was a priest "forever" and had the indelible mark to prove it. Suddenly, "forever" seemed relative. In the core of a pedophile priest's soul, he remains a priest forever. Catholic theological hype about men called to be priests was attributed to Jesus: "You have not chosen me but I have chosen you." (Jo15:16) Evidently, Jesus had chosen a lot of pedophiles.

As a priest, one automatically experiences incredibly unmerited deference, especially within the Catholic community, but also outside of it. That is, unless you are a priest touring the Vatican, as I would learn on that 2008 trip. Membership doesn't *always* have its privileges. One would assume an *"Alter Christus"* visiting the home office would receive a little special treatment, as the hierarchy had instructed the lowly laity to show deference to its priests.

As a lowly seminarian I had gotten more respect than I now had as an ordained priest of forty-two years. I had never bought into the clerical hype (in truth, it made me uncomfortable) but I trusted the home office did. I would discover there was no Vatican deference to priests, not even a discount fee to enter its museums! I was now viewed as an ordinary customer filling the Vatican City coffers. A nod to the equality of all members of the Body of Christ? Yes, as long as they're paying pilgrims.

"When in Rome, do as the Romans do." Visitors to Rome's churches are expected to be "modestly attired" (showing minimal bare skin). Truth be told, burqas would be preferred. Some females are without the proper "wedding garment," so sheer clothing is benignantly bestowed on them. For males, pants need to be below the knees, though no sheers are provided for exposed thighs. Despite the heat of a Roman summer, modesty trumps comfort.

On a hot, humid August Sunday I attempted to enter the Church of the Holy Trinity atop the Spanish Steps, wearing black, but shorts that didn't reach the knees. I had visited the church in 1957 and had minimal interest in seeing it again. But due to the heat and my arthritic hip, I sought refuge, moved by my discomfort rather than religious fervor. (Historically, popes couldn't handle the heat either and sought a cooler clime in Castel Gandolfo.)

At the entrance I was stopped by a tall, well-built, intimidating male bouncer wearing dark shades, possibly a recent immigrant from Africa, reminding me of the Tonton Macoutes of Duvalier's regime in Haiti. He acted as the judge of human flesh, and may have been put into the occasion of sin by having to constantly check out bodies. My shorts wouldn't pass muster. At sixty-nine, I wouldn't think my legs would arouse anyone, but he refused me entry.

I proclaimed loudly, "But I am a *sacerdos*, a priest!" Evidently, Latin wasn't a prerequisite for the position. I tried to shimmy my shorts down to cover my knees, but he vehemently shook his head. I gestured to the sheer wrap given to women to cover bare shoulders, indicating I would use it, but to no avail. I tried my Latin again and again, "*Ego sum sacerdos!*" ("I am a priest!"), to the consternation of other tourists awaiting entry. Finally, he gave me the green light, begrudgingly.

Once inside, the first thing I saw was a soft-porn statue of a nearly naked Jesus, covered with the briefest loin cloth that exposed thick muscular thighs, as if he had been working out in some Palestinian gym. When I came out, I gestured to the bouncer to follow me back in. I pointed to the statue and asked, "How did *he* make it in?" My English perhaps escaped him, but I think he got my point.

What a waste of energy and expense, to have "modesty monitors" at church doors. Anyone wearing a thong would hardly be visiting churches on a hot summer afternoon. Perhaps the position gave the poor African employment. But why not hire him for something more constructive for the human community, like feeding Rome's homeless?

It is symbolic of the mistaken priorities of the Roman Church, which distances itself from the gospel message and shows more concern for dress codes of its museums than for desperate human needs of the multitudes.

Perhaps John XXIII (1958-1963) was struck by this great disparity, prompting him to proclaim that we are not on earth to guard a museum but to tend a "flourishing garden of life." The urgency should be in nurturing human beings, not maintaining buildings.

The fifty-two years that had zoomed by with unimaginable speed caused me to experience a frightening sense of time's relativity. In a half-century, Rome's inner core had changed only imperceptibly. It lived up to its moniker as the "Eternal City" and demonstrated a permanence that eludes humanity. Greek philosopher Heraclitus, long before the founding of Rome, observed that "nothing is permanent except change." Rome seemed to elude this truism. Despite even Vatican II, one needed a discerning clerical eye to identify any tweaking the Council had caused.

John XXIII made familiar the Italian word, "*aggiornamento*," a bringing up to date. In a sense, the II Vatican Council has been a failure because the Roman Church has never "updated" its theology. Despite the word *New* in its title, the so-called *New Catechism of the Catholic Church* published in 1992 basically reiterates pre-Vatican II theology, though in a less strident style. Roman Church theology sorely needs to be "updated." Otherwise, it will remain essentially unchanged, promoting what I think of as "the theology of fear."

Rome hadn't changed much, but I had changed radically. No longer the naïve, guileless, earnest seminarian who relished absorbing the grandeur that was our beloved home office, the Vatican, I finally understood what Heraclitus meant.

Nineteenth-century academics wanted to make the Church less insular to the scholarship fermenting in science, theology, and biblical studies. They advocated a rationalist approach to the Bible, the reasoning of the Enlightenment, the separation of church and state, and the synthesis of modern philosophy with Catholicism as the Scholastics had synthesized Plato and Aristotle.

Such revolutionary ideas were viewed as a threat to the Roman hierarchy. Pope Pius X (1903-1914, later sainted) ruthlessly squashed this "Modernist Movement," forcing loyalty oaths and excommunicating the noncompliant.

George Tyrrell, who openly supported the movement, was expelled from the Jesuits and suspended from the sacraments. He was allowed Extreme Unction on his deathbed in 1909 but was denied burial in a Catholic cemetery. One priest at Tyrrell's non-Christian burial compassionately made the sign of the cross over his grave, resulting in a bishop suspending him.

This new theological reign of terror shaped a Church that was more inward, neurotic, narcissistic, preoccupied with self. In essence, though, it merely represented a continuation of what I call "the theology of fear."

The Roman Catholic Church (which I'll often refer to as "the RCC" here) had been preaching this message of fear since it joined the Roman Empire and began enjoying the perks that come with power and control. In doing so, it ultimately deflected the Kingdom of God and its message of liberation and freedom.

The purges of Pius X led to a surge in outward signs of personal piety. Religious practices and rituals were stressed, emphasizing a vertical relationship linking the individual to God. Anything horizontal in scope, laterally affecting others in society, was suspect and eliminated. Followers were expected to read prayers, make novenas, receive sacraments, embrace miracles, become pilgrims, and seek out visionaries. Critical thinking was unthinkable.

As a young man, I was a product of the piety Pius X so vigorously promoted. A piece of saccharine religious poetry, its author unknown, touched my pious heart and soul, and inspired me to the priesthood:

> *Boyhood dreams of long ago*
> *Saw an altar fair,*
> *Consecrated, trembling hands*
> *Lifted there in prayer.*
> *And those dreams have led me on*
> *Dreamlike though they seemed,*
> *Now, dear friend, thank God with me*
> *I am what I have dreamed.*

But since then, like Paul, I have put away my childish things.

CHAPTER ONE

SECOND THOUGHTS:
FOLLOWING THE TRADITION OF DISSENT

"Among mortals second thoughts are wisest." – Euripides

Paul evidently had "second thoughts" about Judaism earlier rather than later in his life. For others, it's near the end of life. And some never have second thoughts. Intense indoctrination makes it difficult to think and act outside the box of religious programming.

In the decline of life, I've finally arrived at a plateau where I have second thoughts about practically everything that I once believed wholly, accepted unquestioningly, promoted dutifully.

At the beginning of the journey, answers abounded on all theories and beliefs and dogmas, before we even asked the questions. But now there are more looming questions and few certain answers. Those spoon-fed answers haven't stood the test of time, experience, and reflection. In the end, we become victims for having swallowed them whole without first chewing critically.

The poet Rainer Maria Rilke counseled loving the questions. But we wanted certainty—we were taught to *expect* certainty—and we drank the Kool-Aid served.

Visiting Rome can be hazardous to one's spiritual health. Fr. Martin Luther, the German Augustinian monk, was scandalized on his first visit. He assumed the experience would be healthy for his soul, but subsequently assaulted the city with a vengeance not unlike Alaric's sacking of Rome.

Fr. Ronald Knox, the English cleric who singlehandedly translated the entire Bible into exceptional English, once was asked if he had ever been to Rome. He quipped, "Just because I am on the *'barque'* [boat] of Peter, it doesn't mean I have to go into the engine room!"

Fourteenth-century Italian writer Giovanni Boccaccio, an early acerbic critic of the RCC, bestowed a positive spin on a most unlikely Roman visitor. He tells the tale of a Parisian Jew named Abraham and his Catholic friend. The friend thought Abraham would go to hell if he didn't become a kosher Catholic, so he relentlessly tried to convert him. Eventually, Abraham declared he would travel to Rome to see for himself the chief pastor and his court. But the Catholic was taken aback. "And if he goes to the court of Rome and sees the lewd and wicked life of the clergy, not only will he never become a Christian, but, were he already a Christian, he would infallibly turn Jew again." Despite the Catholic dissuading him, Abraham went to Rome. "There he experiences the filth of the papacy, from the top cleric to the least one, given to lust, not only in the way of nature, but after the Sodomitical fashion. He found the lot gluttons, drunkards and slaves to their bellies, covetous, greedy for money, buying and selling the offices of the Church."

Abraham returned to Paris and explained all this to his friend, who was sure Rome lost the last chance for his soul, while acknowledging that he saw there "no piety, no devoutness, no good work or example of life, but lust, covetousness, gluttony and the like and worse. And as far as I can judge, your chief pastor and consequently all others endeavor with all diligence and all their wit and every art to bring to nothing and banish from the world the Christian religion, whereas they should be its foundation and support. Despite the best efforts of churchmen to destroy Catholicism, it waxes and increases brighter and glorious, I manifestly discern that the Holy Spirit is verily the foundation and support thereof." Abraham was subsequently moved to be baptized forthwith.

Defenders of the papacy find Abraham's experience proof of the Holy Spirit's ongoing presence in the RCC, notwithstanding its decadent, immoral members, even if popes. Catholics have long taken comfort in the quote from Matthew that even the gates of hell shall not prevail against it. The argument attributes to the Holy Spirit an ecclesiastical insurance plan. But it is possible for any group to endure, despite deviations by members. Christianity is a relatively young religion compared to Hinduism, Buddhism, Shintoism, and Judaism. What "Holy Spirit" guides their belief systems, despite the failures of their adherents?

It is said Napoleon once threatened a seasoned papal aide, Cardinal Ercole Consalvi, claiming he would "crush" the Church. The world-weary Consalvi sighed, "If in 1,800 years we clergy have failed to destroy the Church, do you really think that *you'll* be able to do it?" [3]

Today, I would beg to differ with the cardinal. Clericalism *has* destroyed the RCC. The clerical sexual-abuse scandal is only the most recent manifestation. Over the centuries, Roman clergy in Europe lived as a privileged class. Rather than serving humanity, they largely lorded over their flock. The minority of clergy who truly served were outnumbered, often drawing resistance from the hierarchy, as in the French "priest-worker movement" of the mid-1900s.

The residual impact of this clericalism is a Europe where the RCC today is a collection of cathedrals and museums, rather than a vibrant and prophetic center of activism and intense participation.

INDOCTRINATION IN THE SEMINARY
"Keep your mouth shut and your bowels open!" – Anonymous

Seminarian formation for would-be priests is indoctrination rather than open-ended inquiry and examination. Priests are to pass on what is uncritically assumed to be an unchanging tradition, despite incredible shifts throughout Church history, unbeknownst to most.

The RCC would like its uninformed members to believe it was the same in the beginning, as is now, and always will be.

An ignorance—or dismissal—of history summarizes the "tradition" of the RCC. Well-meaning followers believe it is as it *always* was. In June 2011, progressive members gathered in Detroit, MI for a three-day conference advocating for increased institutional change. The Archdiocese had warned local Catholics not to attend and priests not to participate or face being defrocked. Some 2,000 attended anyway, though others balked. "The conference was not welcomed by Ralph Ascensio," the *Detroit News* noted, adding that outside the hall he carried a sign reading, *Don't Protest, Obey Jesus!* "These people are advocating change," said Ascensio, who reportedly got into a quiet debate with a Catholic seeking change in the Church. "It hasn't changed in 2,000 years." [4]

Poor Ralph. It's changed so much Jesus wouldn't recognize it.

Reinterpreting tradition was the issue that fingered Jesus as a marked man. He claimed fresh interpretations that clashed with prevailing beliefs. He offered "new wine." And human history shows that the old guard always vigilantly resists something new. Jesus shared a parable indicating a new patch cannot be sewn on an old garment without it pulling apart, and new wine cannot be poured into old wineskins without causing them to burst. Sometimes the old has to be totally jettisoned.

Priests are expected to promote and defend the RCC's official interpretation of doctrine and morality. To dissent publicly leads to swift reprimand, if not dismissal. The hierarchy is more tolerant of lustful and avaricious priests (and members) than any who question its theological proclamations.

Consider priests such as John Hus and Giordano Bruno, burned at the stake by the RCC because they questioned, like Jesus, its interpretation and practice of tradition. And English priest John Wycliffe so angered Church officials that, though unable to burn him at the stake, they angrily brewed and stewed for thirty-one years after his natural death. In 1415, the Council of Constance declared him a stiff-necked heretic. Pope Martin V (1417-1431) later commanded his remains be exhumed and burned and his ashes be cast into the river flowing through his hometown.

After making the case that a priest is an *"Alter Christus,"* then proceeding to burn a priest or his remains, the RCC had no qualms about once again sacrificing Christ to death.

14

These represent countless instances in which Church actions demonstrated its cognitive dissonance of the gospels. In this era of Church history dominated by the clerical sexual-abuse scandal, contemporary prelates defend themselves by claiming they didn't understand the nature of pedophilia. Considering the history of dissenters being sentenced to torture, death, and posthumous outrages, past prelates evidently didn't grasp the elemental teaching of the Fifth Commandment either. How much of a learning curve was necessary?

How many sexually intemperate or avaricious priests are historically remembered as being burned at the stake by the RCC? The institution is forgiving of such men, finding them a niche as long as they don't question its theology or tradition.

IRON RULE IN THE VATICAN
"An iron fist in a velvet glove." – Holy Roman Emperor Charles V

Unfortunately, through centuries of inquisition and suppression of books and ideas, the RCC successfully internalized self-censorship by dissenting members, largely clergy, and dutifully suppressed public opposition. Vatican II sought to open a window and let in fresh air to reexamine previously held interpretations, while acknowledging "the signs of the times."

It didn't take long for John Paul II and his chief inquisitor, Cardinal Ratzinger, to sniff the scent of nonconformity like bloodhounds, and close the window John XXIII had cracked open ever so gingerly.

Robert Bennett, a lawyer who served on the original committee to investigate the clerical sexual-abuse scandal, was recently interviewed on EWTN (Eternal Word Television Network), a conservative Catholic cable TV station, where he acknowledged favoring women's ordination. This provoked EWTN, when rebroadcasting the interview, to cut Bennett's favorable comment about female priests.

The non-ordination of women is apparently a settled issue as viewed by the Roman hierarchy, which will squash all attempts among any precincts or members who question it. New bishops are vetted for their loyalty to the pope on this issue (and other selective ones) before getting to wear the pointy hat. William Morris, an Australian bishop who simply raised the question in light of the shortage of priests, was summarily dismissed. Women who "attempt" ordination are not just slapped with a mortal sin, but excommunicated.

While dissenting priests were often tortured and burned at the stake, imprisoned, or banished, they were a minority compared to lay people tortured and subject to capital punishment for questioning the RCC's interpretations and practices. Civil law now restrains the hierarchy in its punitive punishments. Today, it can only internally punish a discordant cleric, usually by financially disenfranchising him.

But a bloodless inquisition operates today, sanctioned by Benedict XVI. He was not the first Grand Inquisitor to become pope, but upon becoming so, the theologian Fr. Hans Kung (Ratzinger's contemporary) commented he was "sweet, but dangerous!" In past times, Kung would have experienced severe repercussions. The Vatican had already rescinded his authority to teach Catholic theology, forcing him to leave the Catholic faculty at Tubingen, though he was welcomed by the ecumenical faculty there.

The public persona of Benedict XVI appears as a gentle, mild, even timid man. But behind closed doors, unsmiling, showing steely resolve and an apparent empathy deficit, he dismisses theologians who deviate from his interpretations.

Matthew Fox, prolific author and cleric who was censured and ultimately expelled by Ratzinger, kept a list. "In an appendix, [Fox] lists the names of ninety-two individual theologians and pastoral leaders who have been silenced, expelled, or banished under Ratzinger/Benedict, including about twenty Americans," one online reporter comments. "In my view, as long as there is an institutional church, there will probably be a church authority that will determine who is in and who is not in the church group. But Fox urges us to consider carefully what the people who have been silenced and/or expelled have said or done to deserve their punishment." [5]

In former times, bonfires may have awaited them.

16

Benedict XVI, who underscores tradition, acts as a descendent of Jewish leaders who constantly clashed with Jesus over interpretation of Torah Law. Ultimately, they would hand Jesus over to Roman authorities, who alone could impose capital punishment.

When a priest is promoted to the inner circle of the hierarchy as a bishop, he selects a biblical motto for his princely coat of arms. Benedict's motto ought to be non-biblical, the popular German mantra, *"Alles ist in ordnung"* ("Everything is in order"). His Germanic penchant for structure is a perfect fit with Roman control. One can only surmise how Jesus might fare before Benedict. His official motto is *"Cooperatores Veritatis"* ("Cooperators/Coworkers in Truth"). The implication is that "truth" is a settled matter. Why are most persons not convinced?

Deviation from doctrine is viewed by those in power as harmful to "the faithful," far removed from the subtleties of theological investigation. Pedophile priests and prelates, however, do more harm to the faithful, for the faithful more readily grasp the damage resulting from sexual abuse than from theological abstractions. Yet there is no rush to judgment of such pedophiles, and Canon Law is scrutinized to afford leniency. The "bugger bishop of Bruges" sexually abused even his nephew, yet continues to roam unsupervised, unchallenged. On the other hand, theologians like Bishop Morris (canned by Benedict) and Bishop Jacques Gaillot (canned by John Paul II) are given short shrift of any canons that might protect them.

In my travels to more than 1,300 parishes, some priests have privately shared their rejection of Catholic doctrines, but have indicated they will not publicly dissent. The lack of enthusiasm of many to promote issues the institution holds as priorities underscores their inner disbelief. While there is a fervent clerical minority who toe the line publicly, the silent majority of priests offer faint lip service. The increasing unwillingness of young Catholic males to embrace the priesthood is additional evidence that the life of a dogma enforcer or morality cop is hardly exciting these days. There are more interesting and creative ways of going to hell.

Nonetheless, most priests would not disavow their ministry, as it might indicate they had spent their lives in vain. No one wants to consider their life meaningless, or worse, having contributed to the furtherance of a repressive theology. Most take refuge in the idea that pastorally they tried to reach out to persons in their time of need and were part of important junctures of life's journey, e.g., births, weddings, deaths—hardly prophetic activities.

Some "street priests" have created, though not without hierarchical opposition, life-enhancing ministries. Fr. Greg Boyle, founder of Homeboy Industries, rescues gang members. For Boyle, salvation is about human life on the mean streets; for John Paul II and Benedict XVI, salvation is about the safety of the sanctuary. Fr. Roy Bourgeois, founder of SOA Watch (School of the Americas Watch), organizes public protests to stop U.S. complicity in military interrogation training. Fr. Michael Pfleger, the white Chicago pastor who has led an African-American parish for decades, galvanizes community protests against the exploitation of urban blacks.

Fr. Shay Cullen is an Irish priest working in the Philippines. In 1974 he created an organization to intervene on behalf of abused children, particularly those vulnerable to child sex trafficking. For his efforts, he has been twice nominated for the Nobel Peace Prize. But he is a cleric who spends his days in the streets, not the sanctuary.

These activists are often viewed as a threat by Church leaders and priests who prefer a secure and serene sanctuary.

On Good Friday 2005 at the Roman Coliseum, during Station IX of the Way of the Cross, Benedict XVI decried "how much filth there is in the Church." This has been widely interpreted as referring to his disgust over the sexual abuse of children by priests. Many apologists boast Benedict XVI has done more to resolve this crisis than anyone. That is tantamount to saying, "In the kingdom of the blind, the one-eyed man is king." Few have done *anything* about it. One who did, Fr. Thomas Doyle, O.P., sounded the alarm way back in 1985.

At that time, Doyle was a secretary at the Vatican Embassy in Washington, D.C., where he first learned of sexual abuse cases involving Catholic priests. This compelled him to author a prescient study ("The Problem of Sexual Molestation by Roman Catholic Clergy") that gauged the scope and consequences of an emerging pedophile scandal—including criminal, canonical, financial, and spiritual issues—which in time would be revealed as truly catholic. He estimated in 1985 that the financial cost (of minimal importance compared to the lives destroyed) would surpass $1 billion. As of 2010, it was nearly $3 billion. [6] Not only did his scathing report and advocacy on behalf of victims fall on deaf ears, but the hierarchy turned on him with a papal full-court press. Ultimately, after years of service as an Air Force chaplain, Doyle was stripped of the position in 2004 by Archbishop Edwin O'Brien, head of the Archdiocese of Military Services, who also blocked his retirement benefits.

O'Brien became a cardinal in 2012. He will hardly be a champion of victims' rights concerning clerical abuse. If Benedict XVI were serious about cleaning up "the filth" and dealing with the sexual abuse of children in the RCC—as well as preventing further horrendous crimes against the most innocent—Thomas Doyle should have been appointed cardinal. He could have acted as a protector, an advocate, an ombudsman for the abused, while pressing for a moral and institutional upheaval in the RCC.

But the papacy seems not to be about enacting reform, but coalescing power. Promotions go to clerics who lack credibility and credentials, who reinforce the status quo, who act as cheerleaders for an institution obsessed with control, not service. It is a narcissistic system rewarding those driven to self-promotion no matter what it takes, rather than pursuit of truth no matter where it leads.

Meanwhile, Fr. Doyle is vetted as a *persona non grata.* He remains a moral voice, a genuine threat to "the filth."

Most clerics would shun these activist priests, perceiving them as a threat in leaving the secure confines of the sanctuary and getting into the trenches, becoming incarnational. Seminary training emphasized "confecting" (making) sacraments and acting as dogma enforcers and morality cops.

The first pastor to whom I was assigned was indignant over "new breed" priests, those who advocated involvement in social issues in the wake of Vatican II. In exasperation he once exclaimed, "We are not ordained to be social workers!" He was the product of his

19

indoctrination. Apparently, the Jesus who was constantly on the road, intervening in response to the human needs of the masses, was not *his* Jesus. Why wasn't Jesus spending time in the synagogue or Temple? Why was he always out among the ordinary people?

Most priests cling to the comfort of confecting sacraments in a church building, effectively restricting themselves to a cultic role. They resemble the cultic priests of the Roman Empire, entrusted with the correct ritual of prayer and sacrifice for the well-being of the state. They were not inclined to intervene in social concerns that might affect a community of citizens, non-citizens, slaves, and foreigners. Their domain was restricted to the Temple and did not extend to the marketplace.

Exceptions do not make the rule. Most priests are enforcers of the hierarchy's doctrines. Some have an epiphany after years in ministry but find it difficult to leave an institution that provides a comfortable lifestyle. "To beg I am ashamed; to dig I am unable."

Furthermore, religious training doesn't provide skills for the secular workplace, and priests are keenly aware of their lack of occupational expertise. An Irish seminarian left in his year before ordination. To console him, his pious mother reminded him that with all his Latin and Greek training, he should have no problem finding employment. To which he replied, "The only thing I'm trained for is the Roman Empire, and that went out of business." Actually, it didn't.

The RCC is the Roman Empire reincarnated, preserving much of its language and some of its practices. *Help Wanted: Latinists!* The RCC still uses many Roman terms adopted long ago: *alb*, *bulla*, *cathedra*, *chasuble*, *cincture*, *collegium*, *consistory*, *curia*, *diocese*, *nuncio*, *ordo*, *sacerdos*. The pope is the "*Pontifex Maximus*," the high priest of the Empire's "*Collegium Pontificum*." On public monuments, "*PM*" is chiseled after a pope's name. Interestingly, few biblical terms are as actively employed, and among all the titles given to the pope, the biblical title of "shepherd" is absent.

The "Roman Curia" is the administrative apparatus of the Holy See and the seat of entrenched power. When John XXIII announced the II Vatican Council, he was met with fierce resistance from the Roman

Curia. When asked how many worked there, he rejoined, "About half!" The Curia was threatened, afraid that it might lose power. Interestingly, the Curia has its origins in the Roman Empire, which was a governing body. And every diocese has a local curia. So the administrative model for the RCC is based on an empire, not a pastoral council of cooperators for the Kingdom.

Power, not service, is the message.

The Church also adopted "statuary," commonplace in the religion of the Empire. Roman temples housed the cult statues of the deities, as did homes, gardens, and parks. Judaism and Islam prohibit statuary as a representation of divinity. The RCC claims statues are no more than the material they are made of, but in the souls of many members, they are revered as much more.

Personally, my life as a priest contributed little to the human condition. Few people will admit their life wasn't worth a tinker's dam. Leonard Woolf, husband of Virginia Woolf, served most of his life in the British Parliament. A candid soul, he reflected on the ineffectiveness of it all, noting that he might as well have played ping-pong all those years, because life on the human anthill had improved imperceptibly through his efforts.

It is painful to realize how inconsequential our lives have been, or to honestly determine what, if any, personal contributions have improved the lives of others. Billions have lived and died; only a few—famous and infamous—are remembered.

There are those who claim God has an individual plan for each person. The evangelical preacher Rick Warren made a bundle from his universally popular book, *The Purpose Driven Life*. By 2007, more than 25 million copies had been sold in over fifty languages. Warren's forty-day program to find purpose in life is based on the forty days Jesus spent in the desert, where Jesus evidently conducted his own personal seminar to find meaning in life.

You won't find many "purpose driven" study groups in Darfur or Haiti or Afghanistan or other hellholes here on earth. The masses of humanity have neither time nor energy to speculate about the meaning of life, being preoccupied with speculating about whether there will be daily bread for their family.

Warren is not the first religionist to promulgate that every life has a divinely driven purpose. Cardinal Newman wrote, "God has created me to do Him some definite service; He has committed some work to me which He has not committed to another. I have my mission—I never may know it in this life, but I shall be told it in the next." [7] What was he smoking? He has his mission, but will not know it in this life, only in the next?

Hungering for purpose in human existence isn't new. The old song lyrics "What's it all about, Alfie?" question the purpose of life. Humorist Art Buchwald mused on this during his last days: "I have no idea where I'm going but here's the real question: What am I doing here in the first place?"

To keep the beasts and wild demons at bay, we create our own meaning and purpose. Viktor Frankl, in his philosophical recollection of life in a concentration camp, *Man's Search for Meaning*, probed the application of Friedrich Nietzsche's observation, "He who has a *why* to live for can bear with almost any *how*." Developing our own purpose in life relieves us from being driven mad by human existence. For billions, meaning in life is not unlike the daily routine of the lower animal species—the search and struggle for food, water, and shelter.

The meaning that absorbs and consumes much of human activity revolves around the family. But the RCC denies this to its priests, leaving them prey to their own worst inclinations. Ironically, among Eastern Catholic priests, where marriage has been an unbroken tradition from apostolic times, there is little sexual abuse of children.

Religionists favor a divine plan foreordained by God and tailored to the individual, who only needs to discern it, like a sleuth looking for a hidden clue. Frankl underscores that the individual alone creates meaning.

Not everyone discovers God's special plan or fashions one, however. Many live their lives subject to the events of time, more victims than agents. Philosopher Thomas Hobbes claimed that for humanity, life is "solitary, poor, nasty, brutish, and short." This description of life is confirmed daily, much more than a "purpose driven" life.

No one asked to be born, but everyone is forced to die. This encapsulates the ultimate fear and dread of human beings. If we didn't die, would there be a need for religion and its comforting myths of resurrection and rebirth?

CONSOLATION IN TRUTH SEEKING
"Many of us saw religion as harmless nonsense. Beliefs might lack all supporting evidence but, we thought, if people needed a crutch for consolation, where's the harm? September 11th changed all that." – Richard Dawkins

At the twilight of life, what consolation do I have for an existence that has little to say for itself, that has offered nothing singular or unique to the human condition? To paraphrase T.S. Eliot, my life ends not with a bang but a whimper. What is my Last Will and Testament? It is totally subjective and miniscule, meaningful only to me.

For self-satisfaction, I find purpose in seeking to witness to truth, as I know it—that elusive abstraction that remains more question than answer.

Pontius Pilate's question, "What is truth?" is one all of us ask and answer according to our individual lights—our intuition, our insight, our experience.

Jesus claimed the truth will set you free. "But," observed President James Garfield, "first it will make you miserable!"

Brian Hall writes of a young poet encountering Robert Frost on a train and discussing poetry. "He sees a chance to offer up a line of Philip Sidney's: 'Good poetry always tells the truth.'" Frost agrees. That's a good one, he says. "But it makes us fall back on the stock phrase, 'What is truth?' Age-old. Take Keats's 'Beauty is truth, truth is beauty.' A fine phrase, as far as it goes. But we know well that truth is not always beautiful. Ugliness is truth. We must remember that." [8]

In my youthful idealism, a line in John's gospel caught my attention, attributed to Jesus: "For this was I born, and for this I have come into the world, to testify to the truth." (Jo 18:37) Interestingly, Jesus didn't say he came to testify for God. The Jesus story is reassuring, as his brief life was incomplete, unfinished, and even mistaken. He thought the Kingdom of God would come in his lifetime, but it didn't. Nonetheless, he did seek to witness to truth.

In John's gospel, love and truth are metaphors for God. Jesus declares, "I am the truth." (Jo 14:6) Literalists interpret that Jesus does more than testify to truth, he *is* "the Truth." While including questionable grammar, that statement may indicate others see him as a way to truth.

Bearing witness to truth is different from claiming to have truth. Having the truth can mean using it as a club to beat up others, an apologetic assault on all those who are not Christian, or are but adhere to a different interpretation. Testifying to the truth is being a servant in the pursuit of truth, knowing it is elusive and never fully acquired. This keeps one humble, open to the new and the unknown, and to change. Again, as Heraclitus said, "Nothing is permanent except change."

However, intolerance has been a human staple in rejecting others' perceptions of truth. Author Cullen Murphy documents this in *God's Jury*: "Inquisitions invite members of one group—national, religious, corporate, political—to sit in judgment on members of another: to think of themselves, in a sense, as God's jury. Fundamentally, the inquisitorial impulse arises from some vision of the ultimate good, some conviction about ultimate truth, some confidence in the quest for perfectibility, and some certainty about the path to the desired place—and about whom to blame for obstacles in the way." [9]

John Locke reportedly held that human beings can't know for sure which truths are actually *true*, "and in any case, attempting to compel belief only leads to trouble." [10]

Living with uncertainty is like living with the unknown—it's unbearable to many, hence their desire to accept the comforting certainty that authorities offer even if that "truth" is questionable.

Retired Australian Bishop Geoffrey Robinson writes, "The constant search for truth and the constant openness to truth are more important than the possession of truth. The constant and genuine search to find moral goodness is more important than the possession of particular moral truths. The search for answers to questions of evil and suffering is more important than any answers we come to. And the search for God is more important than any ideas of God we may have. The Bible is a search, the spiritual life is a search, life itself is a search, love is a search and God is a search. There will never be a time in this life when we can stop searching because we are in possession of all that we need to find. We must move from a God we can possess to a God of infinite surprise. We must never forget the necessity of profound humility." [11]

Because of public thoughts such as these, and his outspokenness on the clerical sexual-abuse scandal, Bishop Robinson is currently yet another *persona non grata* to the Roman hierarchy and the Roman Congregation of the Doctrine of the Faith (formerly the Holy Office of the Inquisition). Robinson advocates questioning, probing, rather than accepting certainty that the RCC believes it possesses. In former times, if he didn't recant, he might have been subjected to a bonfire.

Leonardo Boff, who studied under Joseph Ratzinger (later to become cardinal, then pope), eloquently writes, "Christianity was reduced, in its pathological Catholic understanding, to a simple doctrine of salvation: it became more important to know the truths 'required for salvation' than to be converted to a '*praxis*' (practice) of following Jesus Christ." [12]

The RCC asserts that it *alone* has the truth. Under John Paul II and especially Benedict XVI, it aggressively insists it possesses, with certainty, the way to God through Jesus Christ. Benedict XVI was alarmed theologians were relativizing the Christian message, seeming to present Catholicism as "one among many" equally important and authentic religions. His is an absolute position, maintaining antagonism between religious groups, putting them on the defensive, creating conflict. Benedict is uncomfortable in simply being a truth seeker, like others of goodwill, humbly pursuing the fullness of truth. Instead, he affirms that he alone *has* it.

Jack Valenti, longtime president of the Motion Picture Association of America, often quoted an old Texas saying: "Give me the company of those who are seeking the truth, but please spare me the company of those who think they've found it."

Many are attracted to Benedict's certainty, and unfortunately, some are quite nasty toward those who think otherwise. They are not content to "live and let live," but continue the worst part of the RCC's tradition—rooting out those deemed heretical.

Fortunately, most civil societies now ban bonfires.

Dawkins, quoted above, is a proud public atheist who shares valuable insights. Through the centuries, religions collected a lot of questionable notions and practices. They need to be reexamined for any instruction or doctrine that might lead a member to condone or advocate violence. Each of us must examine our own tradition.

The RCC has an insightful truism: *"Ecclesia semper reformanda est"* ("The church is always being reformed"). Would that reform were held high as a top priority rather than viewed as a threat. Instead, the current leadership is in high gear to silence and suppress anyone questioning tradition and practice.

Such lively reexamination is a form of truth seeking. And truth seeking is a comforter on one's old-age bed.

CHAPTER TWO

RELIGIOUS ILLITERACY: REDISCOVERING THE KINGDOM

"Who do you say that I am?" – Jesus of Nazareth

"Canada is the only country in the world that knows how to live without an identity." – Marshall McLuhan

Stephen Prothero's book, *Religious Literacy*, describes how members of today's religious tribes are *illiterate* regarding their own belief systems. One could give a pop quiz on basic concepts and most believers would probably flunk. [13]

This was substantiated by the *U.S. Religious Knowledge Survey* recently conducted by the Pew Research Center. Ironically, atheists and agnostics scored highest in correctly answering questions on world religions. White Catholics scored about average and Hispanic Catholics scored below average. [14]

It's no secret that atheists and agnostics tend to be critical and skeptical regarding what they accept or reject, while religious believers often take on "faith" whatever they are fed.

Fr. Benedict Groeschel, a conservative apologist for the RCC, once bluntly asserted, "I'm going to write a book about why Catholics are so stupid before I die." [15] To be fair, he claimed Catholics are "stupid" because they don't understand or appreciate chastity. If so, perhaps they can be called "stupid" for not understanding more basic beliefs.

Most Catholics, like Jews and Muslims, were born into their religion and indoctrinated while young with answers to questions they weren't asking. To remain in the religious tribe, members need give only nominal assent, so they may have no reason to explore their belief system. Unfortunately, they frequently retain some of the most damning elements of their indoctrination, those most detrimental to their wholeness as human beings.

The questions posed by the Pew survey were simple and generic—the biblical figure who led the exodus from Egypt, the religion of Mother Teresa, and so on. They were multiple-choice questions. If they were open-ended or theologically challenging, most participants would have flunked altogether. How many know the *Hypostatic Union*, *Shekinah*, or *Aqeeqah*? Most believers would struggle if tested on substantive concepts of their own religion and would flunk miserably on those of other religious tribes.

Many adhere to a particular religion, even minimally, because its mythological tenets provide a meaningful structure on which to shape their lives, as well as an explanation of what might happen at the end. Once accepted, these beliefs are rarely questioned by those within their religious tribe, but more likely by those free of such constraints, particularly when living in open, pluralistic, and democratic societies.

For Christians, tremendous solace is found in believing in a resurrection, particularly involving an ultimate reunion with loved ones. But infinite consternation is caused by believing in a place of eternal torture and punishment—also part of the Christian message as currently packaged. Some tribes deemphasize it, others keep it in the forefront as a cautionary tale, but few eliminate it altogether.

The RCC contends that its theology is derived from the Jesus story of the New Testament. But there's a catch. It relies on a very selective interpretation—*suppressing* the primary proclamation of the liberating Kingdom of God while *emphasizing* the oppressive fear of retribution for a life of sin. Most Catholics have only a vague idea of what Jesus purportedly said or did in the scriptures. All they know is what was filtered to them as children. The Church has never had an adult catechesis. Its primary emphasis has been the debilitating fear of punishment, not the liberating *"praxis"* of love. The Letter to the Hebrews advises, "Let us fix our eyes on Jesus, the author and perfecter of our faith." (Heb 12:2) Keeping our eyes on Jesus, rather than the Vatican, may allow us to let go of that fear.

With time, experience, and reflection, I began to see that the RCC mirrors the Roman Empire more than the Kingdom. As Boff notes, "The Church's exercise of power followed the patterns of pagan powers in terms of domination, centralization, marginalization, triumphalism, human *hybris* (sic) beneath a sacred mantel." [16] *Hubris* is a mix of arrogance, unrealistic imaginings, and overestimation of one's own importance. It is the opposite of the meekness enjoined in the Beatitudes.

Irish Prime Minister Enda Kenny, in his widely reported response to the clerical sexual-abuse scandal in his country, was outraged by the hubris of the Roman Church, by "the dysfunction, disconnection, elitism, the narcissism, that dominate the culture of the Vatican to this day." [17]

COGNITIVE DISSONANCE AND HYPOCRISY
"I hope you have not been leading a double life,
pretending to be wicked and being really good all the time.
That would be hypocrisy." – Oscar Wilde

Human existence is fraught with inconsistencies. Author Frantz Fanon comments on the fallout from daily affronts on cherished beliefs: "Sometimes people hold a core belief that is very strong. When they are presented with evidence that works against that belief, the new evidence cannot be accepted. It would create a feeling that is extremely uncomfortable, called *cognitive dissonance*. And because it is so important to protect the core belief, they will rationalize, ignore and even deny anything that doesn't fit in with the core belief." [18]

The term *cognitive dissonance* refers to the tension created by two conflicting thoughts held simultaneously in the mind. St. Paul acknowledged this dilemma. "For what I am doing, I do not understand; for I am not practicing what I should like to do but I am doing the very thing I hate." (Rom 7:15) Jesus' teaching to love one's enemies is unique to the Christian message. It is in direct opposition to seeking revenge, getting even. Cognitive dissonance is the awareness of opposing forces within, and as long as this tension is maintained, it is healthier than when no tension is perceived at all. The *lack* of tension is the problem—holding one thing in the abstract but doing the opposite thing without any sense of conflict or incongruity.

Analogously, an "immoral" person (who has *some* bar or norm by which to measure behavior) is healthier than an "amoral" one (who has *no* such ethical standard). The RCC, in many instances, seems acutely unaware (or blissfully in denial) of the widespread conflict created when it simultaneously holds one principle or belief but in practice demonstrates the opposite.

Much of American history reveals the absence of mental discomfort in light of extreme personal conflict. Some Founding Fathers, while espousing equality, nonetheless lived comfortably possessing slaves. Many Americans, while affirming equality, nonetheless denied civil rights to other citizens—some even *worked* to deny them—unaware of any contradiction.

The Jewish religious tribe received from Yahweh on Mount Sinai the commandment, "Do not kill." Yet this didn't prevent members from proceeding to initiate a pogrom of ethnic cleansing in the Promised Land. It was the prophets of Israel who dared to point out this "disconnect" between Yahweh's command and their actions. For these gentle reminders regarding cognitive dissonance, their fellow Jews often killed the messengers. (Even Yahweh jettisoned any cognitive dissonance—and apparently violated his own commandment—in ordering the Israelites to cleanse the land of its inhabitants.)

The RCC effectively disavowed and undermined Jesus' and Paul's teaching on equality of the person by structuring and maintaining a hierarchy of *inequality*—based not on sanctioning different tasks in a community, but on assigning different levels of status. This lack of cognitive dissonance indicates that membership in the Body of Christ is *not* based on equality. This disparity is particularly acute in the treatment of women. Even putting aside the argument for ordination, the RCC denies women equal governance within its community, with no acknowledgement of cognitive dissonance. The RCC remains the world's most well-known (and last?) male power bastion, yet it continues to mindlessly preach human equality.

Dissenters to Church practices are conveniently pegged as the problem. Yet they are more closely aligned to the Jewish prophets—and like them, are often eliminated. They are the guileless children who are aware that the emperor is naked—and tell the truth about it. Cognitive dissonance remains a conflictive tension within that compels them to act.

Over the centuries, the RCC persistently sanctioned killing—of pagans, Jews, Protestants, even its own members—while preaching love and forgiveness. Benedict XVI is alarmed at the lack of absolutes today, contending everything is reduced to relativism. The commandment "Do not kill," which the Church adopted from Jewish tradition, was never considered absolute. It was made relative by tolerating—even encouraging—massive slaughter, as in the Albigensian Crusades. If cognitive dissonance were present, the RCC might be closer to embracing the commandment as an absolute.

But dissenters within the Church *do* experience cognitive dissonance, aware of the gap between professed belief and actual practice. In 2011, Bishop Robert Finn, ultraconservative and ardent pro-lifer in Kansas City, MO, was told of a priest friend with similarly conservative views who was photographing young girls from the bottom up. Rather than calling the police, the bishop kept quiet about the sordid situation. When it was made public months later that he had violated state law and church procedure, he tried to explain it away. A vocal minority of diocesan members supported him, most were silent, and only a few disavowed the shepherd who had failed to protect the most vulnerable members of his flock. Jim McConnell, who had spent considerable time and capital preparing to become a deacon, responded by declining to proceed with his ordination. He could not offer his unqualified obedience to a bishop who had lost his moral legitimacy. Unfortunately, other candidates had no problem in submitting their obedience, recognizing no cognitive dissonance in doing so. In September 2012, Bishop Finn will become the highest-ranking U.S. Roman Catholic official to be criminally tried for failing to report suspected child sexual abuse. (A high-ranking monsignor, William Lynn, was found guilty of child endangerment in June 2012.)

Before the psychological concept of cognitive dissonance was developed, there was good old hypocrisy. Say one thing and then do another. As Jay Livingston said, "Cognitive dissonance is a close cousin to hypocrisy."

Hypocrisy was a favorite charge of Jesus. He tossed it frequently as a verbal hand grenade toward religious leaders, which didn't endear him to them. "You hypocrites! You know how to analyze the appearance of the earth and the sky, but why do you not analyze this present time?" (Lk 12:56) He chided leaders for clinging to past traditions, making conventions absolute, refusing to see their irrelevance to the present. So with the Roman hierarchy's attempts to answer present conflicts, especially regarding human sexuality, by clinging to the past, resisting new information.

Jesus warned the crowds and his disciples about these hypocrites. "The teachers of the law and the Pharisees sit in Moses' seat. So you must obey them and do everything they tell you. But do not do what they do, for they do not practice what they preach." (Mt 23:1) "Not practicing what we preach" is the very definition of *hypocrisy*. But who can be truly consistent in all words and actions? As English novelist William Thackeray noted, "Man is an animal consistent only in his inconsistencies."

But does not true hypocrisy occur in the opposite order—in first *doing* one thing and then *saying* the opposite? It is arguable whether Jewish leaders were *always* hypocritical. But when Jesus called them on their actions, and afterward they claimed otherwise, they could be tagged hypocrites.

If we *say* one thing yet *do* another it is more likely we will be forgiven. We humans *say* things all the time. We might espouse the permanency of marriage but eventually divorce. We might proclaim an ideal but be unable to live up to it. And we're absolved.

We're less likely to be forgiven when we *do* something and then *say* something contrary. In the contemporary political climate, Republican politicians have aggressively promoted family values, especially pertaining to sexuality. Senator Larry Craig was cited for soliciting sex from an undercover cop in an airport bathroom. He responded, "I am not gay, I don't do these kinds of things." [19] He appeared hypocritical from supposedly professing one thing and then doing another, and even more after being caught in a sex sting and then insisting it didn't happen.

Cognitive dissonance regarding love and fear is the great fault line. Despite Jesus' last command—"Love one another"—the RCC has enforced fear. Despite John's development of Jesus' teaching, unequivocally stressing that "perfect love casts out fear" (1 Jo 4:8), the Church has kept fear alive. The preponderance of the scriptures depict a Jesus who confronts the issue of fear in his followers and challenges them to "be not afraid" and to love, even the enemy. Scripture and tradition were embedded in the Jewish experience. The early followers of Jesus maintained the importance of both.

And today, empires still impose fear. Roman Catholic leaders express no cognitive dissonance when they, like the Pharisees, do not practice what they preach. What charge might Jesus hurl against them today—hypocrisy, or lack of cognitive dissonance?

THE EMERGING JESUS STORY
"We know something of the history of the spread of Christianity, but much passed from recorded memory and much was transmitted by tradition whose accuracy has been repeatedly questioned." – Kenneth Latourette

If the real Jesus is elusive, so are the teachings attributed to him. Sorting and scrutinizing is necessary to sift the old from the new. Scholars universally agree that Jesus wrote nothing.

The great divide is over the interpretation of scripture—with the Romans, Orthodox, and mainline Protestants on one side, and the fundamentalists and evangelicals on the other. The latter are literalists. They wouldn't be who they are without an adamant insistence on the literal interpretation of the entire Bible.

Paradoxically, one of the few passages the Romans and the Orthodox take literally—the teaching that bread becomes the real body of Jesus—is one that fundamentalists and evangelicals roundly reject. Even religionists are consistent in their inconsistencies.

Biblical translator Ronald Knox offers this view of scripture and community: "What did our Lord leave behind him at his Ascension? An example, certainly, to the human race; but you need not be a Christian to inherit that. He left behind him no writings; the Scriptures of the New Testament were composed years later, and it is the Church, not our Lord personally, that guarantees to us their authenticity and their integrity. He left behind him a body of moral precepts, and something, at least, of a theology. But all these, be it observed, have only been handed down to us by the agency of a society which he originated; a society which consisted in the first instance of his own immediate followers. That society is primarily his legacy to the world; he left us, not Christianity, but Christendom." [20]

Roman and Orthodox Christians understand that a community of believers wrote the "Jesus story" after his death, ultimately becoming responsible for recording what Jesus said and did, eventually producing the Christian scriptures. They insist that not only the scriptures, but also a group of believers, filtered and shared the memory of Jesus. (This extra-biblical source of the community is referred to as *tradition*.)

Knox is cautious, hardly a Roman partisan, in accepting the Orthodox as among Jesus' immediate followers. Unfortunately, the Romans muscled in and pushed the Orthodox aside, claiming that they alone made up that original community, that they alone were executors of the scriptures.

This is why I believe the RCC mirrors not the Kingdom of God but the Roman Empire. The Empire was about dominance and control, while Jesus claimed the greatest is the one who serves, not dominates. (Lk 22:26) The RCC acted in sync with the Empire's spirit when it willfully suppressed Orthodox legitimacy as historically part of that first community and aggressively controlled how the Jesus story was to be interpreted. It waged a war for religious hegemony—and became more "Roman" than "Catholic."

Consider Knox's statement that Jesus "left behind him a body of moral precepts, and something, at least, of a theology." In time, this would morph and evolve until it metastasized into the theology of fear, forming tumors of anxiety in every part of the Body of Christ. It was not a welcome liberation from fear, which Jesus challenged his disciples to embrace, but an unsettling imposition of fear, which defines the tradition today.

REVISITING THE JESUS STORY
"Pontius Pilate was the first great censor and Jesus Christ the first great victim of censorship." – Ben Lindsey

The RCC claims Jesus, the Christ, as its founder. It creates its theology from gospel accounts of him, along with letters of Paul and several others. Jesus, unlike Mohammed, never wrote anything; a gospel passage said he once scribbled something in the sand—hardly a medium for posterity.

The issue, then, is how one interprets New Testament texts versus non-biblical sources such as ritual and tradition. And gospel writers were not all on the same page. New Testament scholar Bart Ehrman addresses this issue: "And so we have to have an answer to our ultimate question of why these gospels are so different from one another. They were not written by Jesus' companions or by companions of his companions. They were written decades later by people who didn't know Jesus, who lived in a different country or different countries from Jesus, and who spoke a different language from Jesus." [21] If Jesus had just written his own diary, we wouldn't be second-guessing him now.

The gospels are, at best, secondhand information. In its 2011 coverage of the clerical sexual-abuse scandal in Philadelphia, the *Inquirer* reported Cardinal Anthony Bevilacqua was questioned by a grand jury regarding why he failed to remove a priest who had raped a ten-year-old girl. He insisted he needed "evidence in order to ask someone to step down," but not "secondhand information," which he said lacked credibility. The prosecutor continued to press him, noting that the New Testament was written by people born well after Jesus' time. "It's the jurors' understanding that the gospels of Matthew, Mark, Luke, and John were written many years after the actual events." Bevilacqua agreed. So, the *Inquirer* article concluded, using the cleric's own logic, wouldn't that make the gospels "secondhand information"? [22]

Christianity became extremely fragmented largely because of differences in interpreting the New Testament, and control over interpretation was critical. Martin Luther's translating the Bible into a vernacular language, German, allowed those who could read to interpret it personally. This was the Church's worse nightmare, as it alone claimed control, in effect bridling the Holy Spirit, not allowing it to blow where it will. So the Church tightened control over the interpretation, claiming exclusive rights. The Council of Trent (1545-1563) reasserted that the Roman Catholic Church was *solely* responsible for the true interpretation of the Bible, and it hurled anathemas to anyone countenancing otherwise. "*Anathema sit!*" In plain English, "Go to hell!"

It is this theological tradition of the RCC, formulated over centuries, with which I differ. It took time, experience, and reflection to understand and parse the theology passed on to me, particularly how it is applied and practiced. Now in the autumn of my life, I perceive this theology primarily as one of fear and anxiety rather than liberation and love. As a priest, I experienced too many members distraught over the possibility of going to hell, or having their loved ones do so. The theology of fear overshadowed their lives.

While the New Testament is strong on love, a powerful current of fear also runs through it. Old and new wines are comingled. It is necessary to strain old additives from the new.

The New Testament departs from the Old in giving greater emphasis to love. In the King James version, the word *love* appears only 126 times in the Old Testament (which contains 602,585 words), but 184 times in the New (which contains only 180,552 words). Love is not absent in the Old Testament, but is brought to a deeper awareness and greater challenge in the New. The nature of love in the New, though, is singular and remarkable among historical texts. The challenge to love inclusively, particularly the enemy, pushes humanity toward an unprecedented summit in its existence.

36

Opinions differ as to the opposite of love—is it hate, or fear? Minimally, they are interrelated. The RCC has not directly advocated fear but its theological implications give priority to fear in the lives of its members, as I seek to show. As a priest, I uncritically enforced the theology of fear rather than advocating freedom and love. I was too fearful to do otherwise, lest I be reprimanded.

The teaching of fear is not always overt, but it is the dominant thread woven through a theology the RCC fashioned from its arbitrary interpretation of the Jesus story. Jesus is to have said, "You shall know the truth, and the truth shall make you free." (Jo 8:32) But Roman theology seldom emphasizes freedom. Instead it advocates an ever-prowling and devouring Devil, keeping the flock in a constant state of fear. Humans are already fearful, and easily frightened. We don't need a theology reinforcing fear, but one freeing us from it.

Franklin D. Roosevelt was closer to the spirit of Jesus in his 1941 speech, "The Four Freedoms" (freedom from fear being one of them), delivered in the midst of war, a time of high anxiety. The idea originally surfaced in his 1933 inauguration speech, when he uttered perhaps his most memorable line: "Let me assert my firm belief that the only thing we have to fear is fear itself—nameless, unreasoning, unjustified terror which paralyzes needed efforts to convert retreat into advance." [23] Roosevelt reasoned we need not be victims of fear, as it only hampers our maturity and courage. Fear paralyzes the creativity to imagine otherwise. His words have a universal resonance, as fear is part of our human DNA. Who would not want to be freed from the pervasive and countless fears plaguing humanity?

What pope could come within miles of Roosevelt in unequivocally exorcising fear and promulgating freedom? Rather, the papacy continues to enforce fear, despite even John Paul II's frequently quoting Jesus, "Be not afraid!" (Mt 14:27) He didn't exorcise fear when he identified the Devil as real.

In the gospels, Jesus takes on the issue of fear and seeks to liberate people from its grip. True, the New Testament doesn't exorcise *all* elements of fear. Yet its focus on overcoming fear is unique among historical records. Unfortunately, unfaithful to Jesus' admonition, the

RCC seized on fear as an effective pedagogy to oppress people rather than emancipate them.

Belatedly, I've realized how devastating and destructive the Church's theology of fear is to the human psyche—and why it needs to be exorcised if the testament of Jesus is truly to be consumed as "new wine."

Throughout the centuries, the RCC tightened its grip on the lives of members through a catechesis of fear. Fear controls people; freedom and love lead people out of bondage. Ultimately, fear trumped freedom and love.

I sense most Catholics think in sync with the Vatican, rather than have "the attitude which was in Christ Jesus." (Php 2:5) Their only understanding of Jesus is largely mediated by Rome's interpretation, since they have little biblical knowledge. The Protestant Reformation clamored to return to the original source of Christianity, the story of Jesus. This led to a battle over interpretation. Though Protestantism was not totally free from employing fear as a catechesis either, it did open the door to fresh interpretation, new emphasis.

THE ELUSIVE, ENIGMATIC JESUS
"Where would Jesus be if no one had written the gospels?"
– Chuck Palahniuk

Did Jesus exist?

The very question riles many Christians, especially fundamentalists and evangelicals. If asked to prove his existence, most would default to the authority of their particular brand of Christianity. In more than sixty years, I had never even *considered* the question, not until I read about others pondering it. In my younger years, I would have scandalized myself to even *think* of questioning his existence.

Others look at this issue more dispassionately, as when questioning the existence of Buddha, Moses, Mohammed, or any revered religious figure. It isn't a controversy that consumes much attention or energy—unless it involves one's *own* leader. Usually, one can be dispassionate about the existence of *other* religious founders, but just don't get too close to home! For many Christians, questioning the existence of Jesus can be contentious.

Interestingly, Hinduism, the world's oldest formal religion, doesn't consider any particular person as instrumental to its origins. It emerged through group consciousness rather than a single person.

Jesus left no writings and had no family, unlike Mohammed, who bequeathed posterity both. This marks Jesus as a more elusive figure, especially given the brevity of years attributed to him and his miniscule public life (some think less than a year, others as long as three). Moses led his people for forty years, Buddha taught his disciples for about forty-five years, and Mohammed about twenty.

If Jesus had married and had a family, at least a bloodline would have provided a trail. Dan Brown's widely attacked but widely read novel, *The Da Vinci Code,* sought to create a genetic path for Jesus by joining him in marriage to Mary Magdalene. If this were incontestable, there would be DNA traceable to the many relics claimed to be his mementos, thus establishing some viable historical record, debunking superstitious frauds, and freeing the faithful from dubious "miraculous" attractions.

Jesus was a highly unusual male Jew in not having married, as far as current evidence allows. "Increase and multiply and fill the earth" (Gen 1:28) was the first command of Yahweh. An observant Jewish male who ignored this would be questioned regarding his orthodoxy. Jesus' short life and shorter public ministry underscore his belief in the eminent coming of God's Kingdom, where marriage wouldn't be necessary. "The sons of this age marry and are given in marriage, but those who are considered worthy to attain to that age and the resurrection from the dead, neither marry nor are given in marriage." (Lk 20:34)

Those who reject an historical Jesus argue that the evidence about him is based on hearsay, and hearsay evidence is not allowed in a court of law to establish a fact. Paul clearly acknowledged he never met Jesus in the flesh, but that didn't prevent him from waxing eloquently on the mystery of the Christ.

Jesus remains an enigma, though innumerable writers throughout history have written his biography, filtered through their own devotion, imagination, or skepticism.

The evidence of the historical existence of Jesus from non-Christian sources is wafer thin. Some Romans—notably Flavius Josephus (a born Jew and Roman citizen), Pliny the Younger, Tacitus, and Suetonius—offered obscure references that believers cite to prove Jesus existed. None were even remote eyewitnesses, as all were born after the timeline attributed to Jesus. And their information came to them from believers.

The Jewish writings in the Talmud referencing Jesus stem from the third through fifth centuries, not exactly eyewitness accounts. But if Jesus was truly a thorn in the side of the religious leaders and the Temple hierarchy of his time, they would have documented the life of this upstart, as they did others—particularly since his death took place little more than a generation before the fall of Jerusalem and the destruction of the Temple.

In the gospels, Jesus praises John the Baptist (his cousin) as most unique. "Truly I say to you, among those born of women there has not arisen anyone greater than he." (Mt 11:11) He figures prominently in the Christian testament. I once asked a rabbi if he had ever heard of John the Baptist. He responded, "Only from Christians!" Christian evidence is largely drawn from its own sources.

For centuries, the Christian faithful were encouraged to venerate the "Shroud of Turin" as the burial cloth of Jesus. Only in recent times, with the assistance of atomic testing, a sample of the shroud revealed pigmentation from the medieval era. Despite this scientific debunking, the shroud draws millions seeking a fleeting glimpse and possibly some miraculous intervention. Science has had little impact. "My mind is made up! Don't confuse me with the facts!" Faith and facts mix like oil and water.

What Franz Werfel attributed in his book, *The Song of Bernadette*, to the visionary of Lourdes is applicable here: "For those who believe, no explanation is necessary; for those who do not believe, no explanation is possible."

Some Christian scholars distinguish between a Jesus of history and a Jesus of faith. Some argue he is both; others argue for one or the other. If even the scholars are divided on the historicity of Jesus, how do the average blokes in the pews determine the truth? Usually, they default to what their religious leaders teach them.

To this day, Catholics have far less direct experience with the Bible than other Christians do. (While filming his epic movie, *The Bible*, director Dino De Laurentiis told an interviewer, "Five years ago I had never read the Bible, because in Italy we learn everything about religion from priests." [24]) One notable scripture scholar advised not to accept the Jesus presented in dogma, but to seek the Jesus hidden in scripture. Alas, typical believers have neither time nor skill to find a hidden Jesus, instead accept the pronouncement of the parish priest. The more skeptical, if they have time and interest, may prefer the probing of religious authorities. But most people will take a pass on both pronouncement and probing. Life's too short. They have more immediate and demanding personal problems and precious little time to speculate.

"Got Jesus?" is a popularized evangelical slogan, mimicking the "Got Milk?" advertising campaign. But the true question remains: What Jesus do you "got"?

Innumerable biographies of Jesus, the Christ, have been offered by scholars and non-scholars. Personally, I have been particularly moved by Oscar Wilde's little biography tucked in his *De Profundis,* written in prison at Reading Gaol while doing time for gross indecency. Fr. Robert Barron wrote and hosted *Catholicism,* a ten-part documentary series. His interpretation, according to one reviewer, "presents Jesus as divinely self-aware, a veritable Yahweh striding into human history to fulfill the law and the prophets." [25]

Benedict XVI recently published his two volumes titled *Jesus of Nazareth.* In them, he claimed that Jesus was *not* a revolutionary. Benedict wrote not as a biblical scholar but as a theologian; the two are not synonymous. John Dominic Crossan *is* a biblical scholar and author of about twenty-five studies. He asserted that Jesus *was* a revolutionary and titled one of his works *Jesus: A Revolutionary Biography.* To date, the pope hasn't pronounced infallibly that Jesus was not a revolutionary; he has merely speculated like others who interpret the Jesus story through a personal lens.

It is in Benedict's interest to downplay the whole idea. To now accept Jesus as a revolutionary would reveal how the RCC since Constantine accommodated itself to the status quo, rather than acting as a persistent, prophetic, thorn-in-the side to power. I titled my first homily in the seminary, "The Catholic Church Is the Largest 'Non-Prophet' Organization." In its alliance with Constantine, the Church forfeited its prophetic birthright, more interested in *profits* than *prophets.*

Of the two biographers, Benedict and Crossan, which should be considered more authoritative? Why select one over the other? For orthodox members of the RCC, it is a non-question. Benedict is pope and that settles it. But he is a theologian, not a biblical scholar like Crossan. A plastic surgeon cuts a face to remove surface wrinkles, and a brain surgeon cuts a cranium to remove interior blockages. While both work on the human head, who would want a plastic surgeon to do brain surgery, or a brain surgeon to do plastic surgery?

The papacy under Pius IX (1846-1878) claimed the pope infallible in faith and morals, using its infallible power only twice, with reference to Mary the mother of Jesus. But if the modern papacy indeed has the power of infallibility from the First Vatican Council, and asserts it alone has the true interpretation of scriptures, why is it hesitant to put an infallible stamp of approval on what it considers to be the authentic biography of Jesus gleaned from the scriptures?

While hesitant to intervene *biblically* by referring to the scriptures, the RCC has aggressively intervened *theologically* by defining the nature of Jesus, interpreting the scriptures to create dogma, regulation, and an entire belief system to its advantage. If Benedict XVI truly believes Jesus wasn't a revolutionary, what's holding him back from making an infallible statement, as popes in these latter days boast they are endowed?

The haunting "Who do you say that I am?" continues to be an open-ended, unanswered, unresolved question. Evidently, no pope wants to take a stand.

Historical evidence supporting the existence of Jesus inside and outside Christianity is negligible. He was hardly dead when doubters already had second thoughts about this Jesus of Nazareth. Emerging as early as 50 CE, the teaching of Docetism (from the Greek, "*to seem*") held Jesus' physical body was an illusion.

Of course, this was condemned by dominant Christian communities.

That apparently put the question to rest until the seventeenth century, when a new breed of questioners emerged, including Hermann Reimarus (1694-1768), considered the Father of the "Quest for the Historical Jesus."

In recent times, intense probing of historical sources has forged on with new tools of investigation. Today's scholars particularly look to the historical and social contexts of Jesus' era. Today there is a concerted effort to enlist demonstrable scientific criteria, considered more objective and reliable than personal observations.

Believers are particularly besieged today by non-believers who are quite public and assertive in questioning an historical Jesus. Perhaps because of advanced methodology and open discourse in pluralistic societies, the question is pursued more rigorously—which may put believers on the defensive, especially if they think this is a settled issue. In truth, many arguments they put forth are subjective and therefore open to challenge.

Objective evidence, as mentioned, is thin but not altogether lacking. A recent investigator of the enigmatic "Who do you say that I am?" question is Bart Ehrman. He offers believers convincing data in his book, *Did Jesus Exist? The Historical Argument for Jesus of Nazareth.* It is safe to say that, being an agnostic, he presents a distanced, unemotional, objective explanation in the quest for the historical Jesus of Nazareth.

For the sake of this analysis, I proceed with the assumption Jesus existed historically and the Roman Church subverted his revolutionary impulse, particularly his proclamation of the Kingdom of God.

IT'S ALL IN THE HISTORICAL INTERPRETATION
"All things are subject to interpretation; whichever interpretation prevails at a given time is a function of power and not truth."
– Friedrich Nietzsche

Born in 1939, I became a member of two societies—the U.S. government and the Roman Church. Neither was of my choosing, and both immediately began subjecting me to their histories, laws, rules, and values. About a month after birth, I was brought to the parish church to be baptized. At that moment, an indelible mark was stamped on my soul, branding me a Roman Catholic. To my knowledge, no other Christian church asserts that the soul is indelibly imprinted at baptism.

It would take years to understand what it meant to be part of these two societies. After all, we are not automatically programmed with a microchip in our psyche, providing instant understanding of their histories and traditions. The degree to which we grow in understanding largely depends on our life circumstances, our personal motivations, and our interest in revisiting the tradition.

Both state and church provide some sense of history through their educational endeavors. But only through self-study does it become evident what was presented was largely a gloss, a biased interpretation accentuating the positives, burying the negatives. Both indoctrinate.

Americans are not keenly interested in history, and many would flunk a simple history test. Consider these troubling statistics offered by author Morris Berman, who quoted a 2011 Marist poll: 42 percent of American adults (and 69 percent under age thirty) "are unaware that the U.S. declared its independence in 1776," and 25 percent "don't know from which country the United States seceded." [26]

The insight of George Santayana, "Those who cannot remember the past are condemned to repeat it," is acknowledged by few. (Well, first they'd have to *know* the past in order to *remember* it.) One might assume people would be naturally inclined to devour history, as it is primarily a collection of stories. Both children and adults love stories. Novels and TV shows and movies are constantly created and consumed. The public can't get enough. Strangely, when it comes to historical stories, the public falls asleep.

History was the only study in which I excelled, and, for the most part, had an interest. In pursuing it, I came to have a broader perspective of the two societies into which I was born. It is this historical inclination that has sensitized me to cognitive dissonance within both church and state.

Growing up on the Southside of Chicago in a dominantly Irish enclave, I became aware of racism. Our neighborhood was bordered on two sides by black communities. There was great hostility toward black people, viewed as a threat, as an unwelcome tribe that might move in and take over our domain. We felt superior, and assumed that they were—somehow—inferior. I recall a black man once straying onto our block. We children chanted, "Eeenie, meenie, minie moe. Catch a n----- by the toe. If he hollers, make him pay, fifty dollars." Though he was a grown man, he quickened his steps; we were fearless in our taunt.

While racism was apparent in neighbors' and parishioners' speech, it was not discussed in the parochial school, or addressed from the parish pulpit. Pastors were seen as pivotal in maintaining our lily-white communities. A code of silence kept teachers and clergy from discussing the issue (and sin) of racism, let alone promoting integration. Upon the death of a prominent Irish pastor in 1953, it was rumored that the well-known newspaper covering the regional black community, the *Chicago Defender*, reported his demise with the headline, "The Boss Is Dead." Of course, none of us would touch the *Defender* to verify whether what was being circulated orally was indeed verified in print.

Leo O'Donovan, a former president of Georgetown University, wrote a *Washington Post* op-ed piece in the aftermath of 9/11, relating an experience as a parochial student in New York City after the Japanese attack on Pearl Harbor. A Dominican sister had the children draw the Nativity with the Holy Family as Japanese. I could only imagine that if a Dominican sister in our parish school had instructed us to draw the Holy Family as black, our pastor would have demanded that she be immediately reassigned.

45

At the time, I didn't understand the source of the Irish people's animus toward black people. Little did I know that part of the hostility was a matter of economics. Both were blue-collar groups trying to move up the ladder. Rather than uniting in their struggle, they were antagonistic toward mutual best interests. In Memphis after the Civil War, there were riots between the blacks and the Irish. The local newspaper editorialized that if the Irish killed the blacks, the Irish should be hanged, and the city would be rid of both.

(Our history lessons in Chicago revealed little about the Civil War. Years later, living in the South, I was struck at how alive the Civil War was to southerners. I slowly became aware that history is often a selective memory, a subjective interpretation.)

In 1969, I had an opportunity to be part of the first class in African-American Studies at Boston University. By then I had been assigned to a parish in New Hampshire, and the racial issues that had roiled the 1960s were still causing aftershocks in white communities. I needed to delve into this critical issue affecting the entire fabric of American society. When I mentioned my pursuit to family members, relatives, and white friends, most couldn't fathom why I would waste time studying something of interest only to black people.

To me, African-American Studies benefited white people, whose ignorance of American history—myself included—was second only to our ignorance of the demise of Native Americans. I had one semester in a Ph.D. program, *The History of New England and American Studies*. That brief interlude exposed me to the fate of native people in Puritan New England. When King Philip's War (1675-76) and King William's War (1689-97) ended, native people signed treaties with colonists. In short order, the colonists violated the treaties. This became the pattern while the United States expanded. Treaty after treaty was repeatedly broken as ethnic cleansing swept across the land.

This was not considered something for youngsters of the mid-twentieth century to ponder. Our knowledge of Native Americans came from popular "Cowboy and Indian" movies and TV shows of the time, produced in abundance, successfully terrifying us with images of savages who needed to be eliminated.

Even with an historical inclination, it took me years to grasp the true history of the land grab from the native peoples, and the free labor afforded by slaves—as the saying goes, "250 years without a paycheck!" Capitalism had great footing here—free land, free labor! Injustice was a concern for only a few true patriots.

The exposure to the founding documents of this country—the Declaration of Independence, the Constitution—contrasted with the lived reality of millions of persons here. Though the country was founded on the words, "We hold these truths to be self-evident, that all men are created equal," they came with asterisks. "All men" actually referred only to white male landowners. It took a long struggle for the inclusion of all white men, longer for women, and even longer for people of color.

The Pledge of Allegiance, repeated in schools since the late 1800s and officially adopted by Congress in the 1940s, ends with the words, "with liberty and justice for all." Those words represent the more difficult part of the American ideal, resisted by millions of fellow citizens who remain unwilling to treat all as equal. In the latest struggle, gay Americans fight to have their relationships treated equally by their fellow citizens. Most citizens cannot afford to pay for "equal justice before the law," and so are incarcerated, while the wealthy often find the law lenient on their behalf. The powerful few with incredible economic resources are able to unduly influence politicians to hamper any equitable distribution of wealth. Our American ideals represent an ongoing struggle to be true for all.

The documents of the government I inherited by birth are quite impressive. They represent an accumulation of long-fought ideas and ideals, a tumultuous and complex history of democracy. I might have been accidentally born in one of any number of countries where daily existence provides little freedom or justice.

The Preamble to the Constitution begins, "We the People of the United States, in Order to form a more perfect Union ..." The struggle for "a more perfect union" has continued since those words were written. The crux of this founding noble document rests on its interpretation. Ultimately, a power struggle ensues over whether the interpretation will be narrow or wide. Presidents backed by powerful interest groups select candidates for the Supreme Court on the basis of ideology, who in turn ultimately decide how inclusive or exclusive this experiment in democracy will be.

Those with the power to interpret the founding documents for the rest of us do not always render a decision in harmony with American ideals.

In 1857, the Supreme Court's "Dred Scott decision" (in *Dred Scott v. Sandford*) provided a dreadful example of how far the interpreters had strayed, ruling that as a slave, Scott could not claim citizenship since he was the property of another. And in 1896, the Court ruled in favor of separate-but-equal schools for blacks and whites (in *Plessy v. Ferguson*), though this would be undone in 1954 (in *Brown v. Board of Education of Topeka, Kansas*).

Sometimes the Supreme Court is supremely wrong, undermining the nation's ideals. Japanese-American citizens were forced into concentration camps during World War II—yet German-Americans were not—with the approval of the Supreme Court. The cognitive dissonance failed to be felt by so many "patriotic" Americans.

This American experiment in democracy is an ongoing struggle. It took a Civil War to implement some of its principles. Some still seek a narrow interpretation of the founding documents. The rights of workers and particularly of women and children have been won only through fierce efforts. Muslims and atheist citizens battle to be accepted and respected equally. Those who prefer the status quo often denounce fellow citizens seeking change within the country, demanding that they "love it or leave it!" Those who criticize it need not "leave it" in order for it to be "a more perfect union." Once aware of the cognitive dissonance, they love by remaining, by resisting the subversion of society's ideals.

This singular issue of equality in both my societies—secular and religious—has affected my understanding of their histories. In essence, equality remains unequal.

The link between the government I involuntarily joined at birth and the religion I involuntarily joined at baptism is the issue of *interpretation.* Both state and church have their common documents; how they are interpreted determines whether the original vision becomes realized or not.

My interest in history primarily involved church history, and secondarily American history. As a priest, it is difficult to make personal decisions. The nature of the Roman priesthood is that of a "kept man," an indentured servant. At ordination, one has to pledge obedience to one's bishop, and his successors. Unfortunately, this implies blind obedience. A bishop would make the major decisions affecting a priest's life—where and with whom he would live, the pastoral work he would do. A priest was to be "on duty" twenty-four hours a day at least six days a week. (Much like a firefighter assigned to a station for twenty-four-hour shifts. But a priest has a vocation, while a firefighter has a job.) It is difficult for a priest to undertake a course of studies unless assigned by a bishop, who selects those to be groomed. To study for a degree on one's own is a stealth endeavor. The majority of priests are sent to study Canon Law. Very few obtain a degree in scripture, let alone church history.

When living in Washington, D.C., I approached the retired dean of church history, John Tracy Ellis. He invited me to lunch, where I shared with him my desire to pursue a doctorate in church history at Catholic University. He enthusiastically encouraged me to apply. When I did, a French-born faculty member dissuaded me, as I was in my forties then. To this day, I feel I should have applied. The population pursuing a doctorate in church history is so minuscule that one would think any warm cadaver would be welcomed.

The RCC's founding documents are the collections of gospels and letters in the New Testament. The Jesus story is given more prominence than the letters of Paul, which were in circulation before the gospels. It is the narratives and images from the Jesus story that are most deeply etched into the psyche. The Church developed its theology from the New Testament, although it maintains, unlike Protestants, that it is not "scripture alone" (*"sola scriptura"*) but also tradition that has shaped its doctrine.

Tradition, though, is more nebulous, and is often invoked arbitrarily. And tradition, far from edifying, raises the most problems.

49

While the Jesus story has often been presented to be interpreted literally, Roman hierarchs, unlike fundamentalists and evangelicals, have never unequivocally held to a literal interpretation (although in practice, they have). The question then becomes: What should be taken literally? What is metaphorical, allegorical, or historical? The answer: In matters of interpretation, the Church has all rights reserved.

The challenge is to distinguish what is "new" from "old" in the New Testament, because a lot of the Old Testament found its way there. Marketers often push products as "new," but often there is nothing qualitatively new about them—just the packaging.

What, if anything, in the Jesus story is truly and qualitatively new? What is unique, fresh, and distinctive?

Of course, what might be considered "new" is a matter of interpretation. Jesus is depicted as saying, "You have heard it said, but I say to you..." The main clash between Jesus and his contemporaries, the religious leaders, was the interpretation of Torah Law. Jesus is portrayed as offering a wider rather than narrower interpretation, and a more compassionate one. Yet, Jesus was not part of the official Jewish religious hierarchy. While his disciples referred to him as *Rabbi*, it was more honorary than real. As a simple layman, he was daring to interpret Jewish texts and traditions.

In time, this would be the Protestant Reformers' position, with greater freedom for individuals (and lay persons) to do the interpreting. Reformers like Calvin, however, had a very definitive interpretation, one that would not tolerate dissent. Historically, the Church developed a theology by emphasizing various parts of the Jesus story and dismissing others. And like Calvin, it did not treat kindly those dissenting from its version. Those who didn't abide by its interpretation were denounced with its customary, *"Anathema sit!"*

Most Catholics now seem to exist on the fringes of the institution, or participate only minimally. As a clergyman, it is difficult to take the institution lightly, particularly when what it has emphasized from the

Jesus story has had profoundly negative effects, creating the wrong kind of guilt in its followers. It has had, and still seeks, a powerful impact on governmental policies. It aggressively exerts political pressure, particularly to implement its interpretations of morality in the personal and sexual areas of human activity, even when the majority of its members reject these interpretations.

The Jesus story offers new insights into the possibilities for humanity. It offers challenging ideals that seem almost impossible to achieve—to love one's enemies, return good for evil, forgive without limit, include all in one's love, give priority to the poor, have pure intentions. Mere exposure to these ideals can have a positive effect in living one's life.

As an insider, I've become sensitive to the RCC's emphasis and de-emphasis. Priests are expected to enforce its interpretations even when they disagree. Many resolve conflict by minimizing what is expected, or passively complying while internally dissenting. But this confronts some with a conflict of conscience. Certainly, many who have left couldn't be enforcers. There are those who are enthusiastic supporters, continually demonstrating their trustworthy mettle, eyeing promotions. There are prostitutes, accommodating themselves for a power surge. And there are those who genuinely agree with the RCC's interpretations.

While an outsider might develop an objective view of things, it takes immersion within a tribe to grasp its hidden depths. And it takes courage to confront one's own. Most want acceptance from the group and are willing to pay the price for conformity. Until recently, it has been difficult to distance oneself without great personal cost. It is in the scriptural portrayal of Jesus confronting and challenging his own religious tribe that I find a prototype in the pursuit of truth. For him, dissent came with a steep price.

One need not "love it or leave it." One can remain, willing to speak truth to power, express a different interpretation of the Jesus story, and take the consequences. The greatest suffering comes from one's own. Some members are extremely hostile to others who dissent, telling them to get the hell out. Not that easy! Not with the way the Church has structured things. Because of baptism's indelible mark, *once* a Roman, *always* a Roman! (That's why the RCC can insist it has more than 1 billion members—because once marked, always marked, even if lapsed, agnostic, or atheist.)

Since Constantine, the RCC has rejected the Gamaliel Principle. Jesus' followers were dragged before the Sanhedrin, the highest Jewish court of law, for deviating from traditional Judaism in their beliefs and practices. Some Sanhedrin members wanted to put them to death, but a sage among them, Gamaliel, intervened. "Let them go! For if their purpose or activity is of human origin, it will fail. But if it is from God, you will not be able to stop these men; you will only find yourselves fighting against God." (AA 5:38) His words allowed them to escape death.

Unfortunately, the Roman Church forgot this key part of its origins, and in centuries to come it would act as self-appointed god, sending others to death who questioned its interpretations.

SUBVERTING THE JESUS STORY
"For some years I deserted religion in favour of Marxism. The republic of goodness seemed more attainable than the Kingdom of God." – Lionel Blue

If you take Interstate 95 North, on entering the state of Maine you'll see a sign proclaiming, *Maine: The Way Life Should Be!* It is an apt description of Jesus' proclamation (*"kerygma"*), the Kingdom of God. *The Kingdom: The Way Life Should Be, Here on Earth!* The RCC's obsession with the afterlife subverts this proclamation.

And upon returning from his desert experience, Jesus immediately announces, "The Kingdom of God is at hand!" His great error was his belief that its ultimate reality would happen in his lifetime. "Truly I say to you, there are some of those who are standing here who will not taste death until they see the kingdom of God after it has come with power." (Mk 9:1) It didn't come. How did he get it so *wrong*?

Jesus' identification and definition of the Kingdom is not immediately clear. Serious scholars differ in deciphering its meaning. Perhaps that is why the RCC devised the Seven Sacraments as a religious framework for an institution, rather than accepting this ambiguous concept as one that would need to be continually reinterpreted through "the signs of the times," one that was incipient in Jesus but not fully realized then or now.

The Kingdom is often viewed as synonymous with *Apocalypticism*, a belief that the world will come to an end very soon, a result of confrontation between good and evil. John the Baptist and Jesus were affected by a current of Apocalypticism within Jewish tradition. Many contemporary Christians expect an "Apocalypse Now."

But in the Kingdom proclamation there is less an indication of *the end of the world*, more a sense of *the end of things as they are*.

Some hold that for Jesus, the end of the world meant an end of life as it was, a new imperative for those on earth. *The Catholic Catechism for Adults* teaches that the coming "Reign of God" will be a kingdom of love, justice, and peace.

The gospels are unanimous in depicting Jesus as hardly satisfied with the status quo, hardly urging conformity. Rather, he is a contrarian, inciting people to reject fatalism, to see beyond the way things are, to have faith to imagine otherwise. So, his urging is to seek the Kingdom first. The necessity to have faith is paramount, "then faith in this kind of kingdom can change the world and achieve the impossible." [27]

The Kingdom was not fully realized in Jesus' life but was present in his words and deeds. "Thy Kingdom come" represents the insistent hope for the community of Jesus, that it be eventually fully realized "on earth as it is in heaven."

Jesus erred in thinking the Kingdom would arrive in his lifetime. Or, like Moses before him and Martin Luther King, Jr. much later, did he visualize a promised land aware he would not personally experience it? Why did he err? After all, the RCC and others hold Jesus was true God (divine) and true man (human).

It wasn't immediately and unanimously acknowledged Jesus was both. It would take centuries to develop what many Christians hold today. The war between Roman and non-Roman Christian churches was protracted, and at times bloody battles were waged over the nature of Jesus. Scores would lose their lives to acknowledge whether Jesus had only a divine nature (Monophysites) or both a divine and a human nature (Dyophysites). The Roman position (two natures) prevailed in the West after centuries of theological conflict, while the opposite position (one nature) survives today in the Copts of Egypt.

My seminary training explained little of the intense, violent conflict over the nature and person of Jesus. The "argument" whether Jesus was human and/or divine was presented as if all reasonable persons calmly come to the conclusion that Jesus *of course* had both divine and human natures. The conflictive history was minimized. But I seriously doubt if the teachers knew any better, as their training had been similar. The institution passed on its own non-critical theological interpretation.

In *Jesus Wars*, Philip Jenkins details the internecine warfare the disciples of Jesus waged to impose their interpretation of this enigmatic, elusive figure. One would think that theological quibbling would not be movie material, but Jenkins demonstrates otherwise. His book has all the stuff of an intense drama, complete with a cast of dubious characters, mob scenes, murders, and enough blood and guts to give it an X rating. "Each side persecuted its rivals when it had the opportunity to do so, and tens of thousands at least perished. Christ's nature was a cause for which people were prepared to kill and die." [28] (Think Muslims killing others who desecrate the Koran.)

How could they be so passionate about the nature(s) of Jesus that they would not only fail to practice his teaching to love one another, but actually slaughter one another? Was this early evidence of what was to come for the RCC—the priority of *orthodoxy* (true teaching) over *orthopraxy* (true practice), with a refusal to see any cognitive dissonance in this issue?

Today in the West, many denounce the violence they contend is inherent in Islam. Ignorantly, many commentators who present themselves as Christian fail to see the violence beam in their own historical eye. Says Jenkins: "Horror stories about Christian violence abound in other eras, with the Crusades and Inquisition as prime exhibits; but the intra-Christian violence of the fifth- and sixth-century debates was on a far larger scale and more systematic scale than anything produced by the Inquisition and occurred at a much earlier stage of church history." [29]

Benedict XVI has been among those highlighting violence in Islam. He once quoted an obscure reference by a Byzantine emperor who questioned the founder of Islam: "Show me just what Muhammad brought that was new, and there you will find things only evil and inhuman, such as his command to spread by the sword the faith he preached." [30] Besides the fact that this outraged Muslims worldwide, this was disingenuous of the pope, who demonstrated massive historical amnesia regarding Christian violence, which had also spread "faith" by the sword.

In the aftermath of his speech, a simple religious woman witnessing to the gospel of service was killed by Muslims incensed at the pope's inflammatory reference. He who had been a scrutinizer of theologians' words knew well his incendiary commentary.

If one believes Jesus is both divine and human, Jesus' error in thinking the Kingdom of God would be realized in his lifetime reveals his divinity was of absolutely no assistance to his humanity. Makes one question his "divinity"! How would this divinity fail to inform his humanity that the Kingdom of God was *not* imminent but a future reality?

Jesus acknowledges that only the Father knows. "But of that day and hour no one knows, not even the angels of heaven, nor the Son, but the Father alone." (Mt 24:36) Yet elsewhere, the scriptures have Jesus boasting, "I and the Father are one." (Jo 10:30) And that intimate bond is intensified. "No one knows the Son except the Father and no one knows the Father except the Son." (Mt 12:27) If he is one with the Father, why wouldn't he also know the day and hour? Did he forget to press the "Default-to-Divinity" button when his human side was uncertain? Roman theology teaches God is omniscient (knows all), and Jesus is God. Why was Jesus wrong? Where was the weak link in the Hypostatic Union?

The bloody battles to ensure Jesus had a solidly divine nature raise many questions. Why didn't he anticipate future conflicts in providing unequivocal teaching? (By definition, his divine nature meant being omniscient.) Presently, the RCC is taking a hard and absolute line on abortion, yet Jesus never refers to abortion, which was common then. Why not? Where was his omniscience to anticipate the violent battles waged over abortion today? Who can discern when his humanity is operative, when his divinity is operative, when both in tandem are operative?

Those who continued to believe in his dream and his vision after his demise had to reorganize the community. The Kingdom was preached as proclaimed by Jesus but yet to be fully realized. The use of the word *kingdom* was politically subversive, and Roman authorities in Palestine would quickly remove anyone seen as a potential threat to Caesar and the Empire.

The arrival of the full realization of the Kingdom—the Second Coming, the end of the world, the end of time, the Rapture—became particularly emphasized in latter-day American Protestantism. (Not all these terms are synonymous with *the Kingdom*, but have become so by careless usage.) It remains a highly debated issue today. In early 2011, Harold Camping, a preacher on Family Radio Network, had billboards erected around the USA claiming the end of the world was coming on May 21, 2011. When that didn't happen, he said he miscalculated and predicted October 21 instead. (At least he's persistent—he had previously targeted September 1994.)

Despite Jesus' erring when the Kingdom would be realized, followers who later wrote the gospels picked up the pieces and promoted the proclamation of the Kingdom of God as a future reality. The Kingdom of God was Jesus' goal, just as racial equality was the goal of Dr. King's "I Have a Dream" proclamation. King didn't realize in his lifetime the fulfillment of his dream, anticipating he would never enter the Promised Land of freedom and equality—and indeed, like Jesus, assassinated shortly after articulating the dream.

You can kill the dreamer (as we do continually), but not the dream.

Richard Westley writes, "Carl Sandburg, the American poet, wisely observed, 'Nothing happens unless first—*a dream!*' How true. For many of us, the dream of Christianity has traditionally been to instill in people a desire for salvation. To help us acquire that desire, many who taught us leaned on scaring us with the horrors of the alternative—eternal damnation. That works rather well, up to a point, because when the dream is presented in that 'religious' way, it capitalized on the natural dynamism of self-interest. This, after all, is the engine of most of our actions." [31]

Westley continues: "As we have seen, put most simply, the dream is the coming of the Kingdom of God. Until recently that hasn't meant much to Catholics, but that is itself very instructive, since the coming of the Kingdom is the central theme in the whole of the New Testament. I sometimes get angry when I reflect on that fact. Having gone to Catholic schools all my life, why did I have to wait until I was approaching mid-life before I came to understand the importance of the Kingdom? It is nothing short of scandalous." [32]

Gerard Goldman strikes the same chord: "I was jolted recently with my teenage daughter about Jesus' proclamation of the Kingdom of God. My daughter was struggling to remember what the Kingdom of God was, and was surprised to learn it was the central message of Jesus' mission. There may be many reasons for this, including that the language of 'Kingdom' is quite outdated in today's postmodern world. However, I suspect my daughter's lack of recall may not be uncommon and may point to a fundamental failure in family and parish (including school) catechesis on focusing on the Kingdom of God as the heart of Jesus' challenge to us today." [33]

As a Roman priest, it was not until about age sixty that I, too, understood this should have been the central focus of the Christian proclamation.

In Jewish scripture, the *Kingdom of God* appears only once and in a section not accepted by many, while the word *kingdom* appears 160 times in the New Testament. The part of Jewish tradition that Jesus embraced particularly was the prophetic. The prophets of Israel witnessed to the original vision of the Covenant, an egalitarian society in which justice reigned as testified in Amos 5:24: "But let justice run down as waters, and righteousness as a mighty stream." The word *church* appears but five times in the New Testament, in Matthew's gospel only. Yet most Catholics assume Jesus was focused on inaugurating *the Church*, thinking he had *Roman Catholicism* in mind, insisting on an unbroken line of popes starting with St. Peter. This thinking dismisses the fact that Orthodox Christians have no less a link to the original communities and tradition of Jesus' believers.

Catholics have only a vague understanding of the Kingdom of God, because in a kind of religious narcissism, the Roman Church has emphasized *itself* as the focal point. So most members automatically think "the Church," not "the Kingdom."

Fr. Alfred Loisy, considered the Father of Biblical Modernism in the RCC, is famous for his comment, "Jesus came preaching the Kingdom, and what arrived was the Church." Not surprisingly, he was ultimately excommunicated by the Church-as-Empire.

Theologians, writers, and scholars have expended incredible time and effort to write about Mary, who was *not* at the center of Jesus' proclamation (she is mentioned more frequently in the Koran), while failing miserably to clarify the Kingdom of God, which *defined* his central proclamation.

The Kingdom teaching, not Mary, ought to be the object of ongoing investigation and discovery. Author Walter Brueggemann rightly underscores this: "The church has no business more pressing than the re-appropriation of its memory in its full power and authenticity." [34] It needs to re-appropriate the centrality of the Kingdom.

A clear separation of the Kingdom and the Church is sorely needed. They currently are *not* one and the same—thank God!

One of the few who has explored this distinction is John Fuellenbach. In his work, he quotes K.E. Skydsgaard: "The Church owes its existence to the Kingdom of God and both conceptions belong closely together, so that it is hardly possible to reach a clear understanding of the nature of the Church without relating it to the basic New Testament conception of the Kingdom of God." Fuellenbach further writes, "The Church is not the Kingdom now, because the Kingdom makes itself present outside the Church as well. Her mission (church) is to serve the Kingdom and not to take its place. Vatican II states clearly: 'While helping the world and receiving many benefits from it, the Church has a single intention: that God's Kingdom may come, and that salvation of the whole human race may come to pass.' This text replaces what was perhaps the most serious pre-Vatican II ecclesiological misunderstanding; namely, the identification of the Church with the Kingdom of God on earth. This misconception accounts in many ways for the kind of ecclesial triumphalism that regards the Church as beyond all need for institutional reform and conceives her mission as bringing everyone within her fold in order to assure salvation." [35]

At the base of St. Peter's dome in the Vatican is the quote from Matthew 16:18: "And I tell you, you are Peter, and on this rock I will build my church." This text is the RCC's assertion that Jesus intended Peter to be the foundation of his Church. This text alone is pure triumphalism. It needs to be balanced by what Jesus said almost immediately afterwards to Peter: "Get behind Me, Satan! You are a stumbling block to Me; for you are not setting your mind on God's interest, but man's." If the two tandem texts in Matthew were inscribed together, it would be a constant humble reminder that the Church is always capable of being both a rock and a stumbling block, that it is constantly in need of being reformed (*ecclesia semper reformanda est*).

When one reviews the tradition, the historical reality is clear—the RCC continually acted in opposition to the Kingdom of God. The most serious rupture is its active and passive acquiescence in the use of violence and coercion against any perceived disagreement with its positions, both inside and outside its confines. Too many examples reveal the Church as outwardly antagonistic to the Kingdom, with effects still causing universal turmoil. Initiating inquisitions and promoting the Crusades are the more obvious examples of its deviation from the spirit of the Kingdom.

Unfortunately, these are only the tip of the theological iceberg. If members of the Church grasp little of its theology, they know even less of its history. Ignorance is not liberating. Rarely are prospective members ever presented with its history, and if so, it is probably a highly sanitized version, skipping the dark side of its tradition. Even seminary preparation offered few courses, so priests themselves would not fare well in an exam on church history. Does historical amnesia come with one of the sacraments?

One can gain more insight through modern-day media, which offer a trove of suspenseful and salacious materials awaiting resurrection from the RCC's extensive archives. The Dan Brown phenomenon whetted the public's curiosity about much that is opaque in Catholicism. People want to draw back its mysterious veil and pierce its hidden center. Fictional accounts continue to be popularized. But fact is stranger, still, than fiction.

I venture most members have an extremely simplistic version of RCC history, believing the Church as it is, it was, and always will be. When Vatican II dropped the Tridentine Mass many were upset, assuming this is how mass was *always* offered. The RCC did little to dispel historical ignorance, instead allowing for historical amnesia. This is in the best interests of the RCC, because if it encouraged members to review its true history, it would open a can of nasty worms.

Analogously, many Americans know little American history. An idealized country has been glorified in history texts. The appalling truth—the treatment of native peoples and black slaves, the devastation of millions of lives within a society boasting liberty and justice for all—has been released for public consumption only within recent generations. The sins of the Founding Fathers have been visited upon the children.

In similar fashion, Catholics must face the truth about their church's history. Tragically, over the centuries, in making the Seven Sacraments its central focus and the theology of fear its tradition, the Roman Catholic Church managed to subvert the Kingdom of God.

This sabotage prevails today. In many ways and on so many levels, the Church doesn't pursue truth. It doesn't stress liberation and creative love. It doesn't offer "new wine." It only promotes itself and spreads more toxic fear, the plague of the human condition.

CHAPTER THREE

THE EMPIRE IN DRAG:
REINFORCING THE REIGN OF FEAR

"Jesus died to forgive our sins. Dare we make his martyrdom meaningless by not committing them?" – Jules Feiffer

In rural Oklahoma in 1959, while visiting two elderly sisters, both deaf, a sudden burst of thunder and bolt of lightning caused me to jump. One sister placed her frail arm on mine and calmly reassured me, "Perfect love casts out fear."

Did she have perfect love?

I believe she did. She'd sensed the incredible thunder, and even in her frailty was most tranquil. She seemed to say she had exorcised fear from her life, and she certainly calmed me.

St. John said, "Perfect love casts out fear." (1 Jo 4:18) What is this so-called "perfect love" that has the power to eradicate fear from our hearts? Unexplained, the whole idea remains something relegated to a motivational poster.

St. Paul proclaimed, "There remains but faith, hope, and love, but the greatest of these is love." (1 Cor 13:13) Unfortunately, the overriding human impulse is fear, which the RCC has made its primary pedagogy instead of the "*praxis*" of love.

61

Fear is the tool of power, which an empire employs as a means of control. Are we more hard-wired for fear than love? To transcend fear and be motivated to live by love is an extraordinary human feat.

THE ONLY THING WE HAVE TO FEAR . . .
"The whole secret of existence is to have no fear. Never fear what will become of you, depend on no one. Only the moment you reject all help are you freed." – the Buddha

Who wouldn't like to "have no fear," to "never fear," to "be freed" as the Buddha suggests—to live by love? Fast-forward to the twentieth century and Roosevelt's "the only thing we have to fear is fear itself" pinpoints the pervasive plague. Certainly, some fear is necessary as a precaution, alerting us to avoid dangerous situations and resist volatile confrontations. But when fear is the unconscious motivator of our *entire* human existence, we are victims of fear itself.

Overcoming fear is not an easy human endeavor. Years ago I saw a motivational film in which a woman committed herself to work on a different personal fear each year. She identified her fear of heights as her "fear of the year" and to overcome it, took skydiving lessons. With training and practice, she succeeded. How many people would be that self-disciplined to work on a tick list of fears?

I have a fear of heights, too. I would rather drive long distances than fly, though in fact driving is statistically more dangerous. In an effort to psychologically overcome this fear, I have flown well over 500 times, and I've forced myself to venture up high precipices. I am still not at ease, and the fear of heights definitely remains, but it is constrained. It has not immobilized me.

There is hardly a letter of the alphabet that doesn't identify with a phobia. One website lists 530 phobias, with new ones continually surfacing. The overarching phobia is the fear of death. It permeates all our experiences and looms as the dark side of everything we do. Christianity is attractive because of its story of resurrection and heaven. But an afterlife of hell *also* comes with the package.

"*Amor vincit omnia?*" ("Love conquers all?") is a more accurate version of the quotation, a question rather than a statement of fact.

For "*Timor vincit omnia!*" ("Fear conquers all!") more clearly expresses the fact of human existence.

Institutions and individuals resort to fear as pedagogy to control others, mindful of the deep, scary well within the human psyche. Leaders readily use fear, and people easily succumb. Niccolo Machiavelli in *The Prince* advised the political leader to consider fear in governance: "Upon this a question arises: whether it be better to be loved than feared or feared than loved? It may be answered that one should wish to be both, but, because it is difficult to unite them in one person, it is much safer to be feared than loved, when, of the two, either must be dispensed with ... but fear preserves you by a dread of punishment which never fails." [36]

George Orwell's *1984* depicted a police state in which Big Brother is watching and will swiftly intervene with punishment, causing citizens to look fearfully over their shoulders. Orwell wrote this well aware of the police states where Stalin and Hitler produced reigns of fear, pacifying countless citizens. Few had the courage to resist, fearing harsh consequences.

Spreading political fear didn't stop with Stalin and Hitler. In its most horrifying forms, it still dominates volatile regimes, violent dictatorships, and troubled nation-states worldwide. In its more subtle forms, it clearly thrives in the USA, in underlying propaganda techniques and media control.

George W. Bush effectively used fear to scare Americans into supporting his war on terror, invading Afghanistan and Iraq. The terrorist became the bogeyman of the American public, which in turn acquiesced to Bush, providing him *carte blanche* the monies and policies to beat the bogeyman "over there" rather than "right here." Bush was no dummy, aware of that deep well of fear underpinning our American insecurity. He essentially paraphrased Roosevelt, with a new stomach-churning twist: *The only thing we have is fear itself.*

Meanwhile, "the world spends more than $1 trillion a year on militarism, with no curb in sight." [37] Fear is the engine supporting such spending, as nations and their people continue to seek refuge and safety in the primitive use of force and violence. We haven't emerged far from the doorway of the cave with a club—we've just found a nuclear club. We have to be better armed than our neighbor. The veneer of civilization is thin. The slightest pressure cracks it, and primeval fear emerges. We have reached the historical point of authorizing what Thomas Merton called "the unspeakable" in developing and investing in weapons of mass destruction, and seeing them evolve also in unstable nations.

FEAR AS THE MODUS OPERANDI OF THE ROMAN CHURCH
"If people are good only because they fear punishment, and hope for reward, then we are a sorry lot indeed." – Albert Einstein

While the political realm employs fear as an arrow in its quiver to shoot into the hearts of ever-anxious citizens, one would think religiously inspired institutions would be at the forefront of exorcising fear rather than nurturing and reinforcing it.

Not exactly. The early 1900s *Dictionary of Catholic Theology* (in French) had this to say: "From a pastoral point of view, one must ask whether it is useful to preach on hell in our day, and human wisdom tends to respond, no. True traditional wisdom has thought otherwise. Certainly, it is always better to come to Jesus because of love, but fear is capable of leading to love, even fear of hell. It is necessary to temper that fear with love, but it is also necessary to engender love of God through fear of chastisements, and to avoid sin by the thought of the divine sanction, i.e., hell. Fear is just as necessary today as it was of old, because human nature is always basically the same." [38]

The "old wine" depicted Yahweh as pummeling the Israelites back in line when they deviated from his commands. In uncorking the "old wine," it's like the mosquito surveying the nudist colony: "I know what to do but I don't know where to begin!" The Jewish scriptures provide numerous accounts of this fear-mongering Yahweh. Chapter 26 of Leviticus alone records enough material to lose faith in this God. No need to swamp the reader with multiple excerpts to substantiate this claim—one suffices: "But if you do not obey Me and do not carry out all these commandments, if instead, you reject My statues, and if your soul abhors My ordinances so as not to carry out all My commandments, and so break My covenant, I, in turn, will do this to you: I will appoint over you a sudden terror, consumption and fever that will waste away the eyes and cause the soul to pine away; also, you will sow your seed uselessly, for your enemies will eat it up. I will set My face against you so that you will be struck down before your enemies; and those who hate you will rule over you, and you will flee when no one is pursuing you. If also after these things you do not obey Me, then I will punish you seven times more for your sins." (Lev 26:14)

Fear is also a motivating factor in Islam. The Prophet Mohammed was familiar with the Jewish scriptures and could have been influenced by them, if only subconsciously. "It is only Satan that suggests to you the fear of his votaries: Be not afraid of them, but fear Me (Allah), if you have faith ... fear not men, but fear Me." (Koran 3:175) Mohamed Atta, who was on board American Airlines Flight 11 on 9/11, counseled fear in his Last Will and Testament, dated 4/11/96: "I want my family and everyone that reads this will to fear Almighty God and not be deceived by what happens in life. Fear God and follow his prophets if you are a real believer." [39]

Inculcating fear into little ones can only be viewed today as abusive. We know from modern psychology that fear need not be the overriding pedagogy in raising children. Psychology, unlike religion, enables greater effort to lessen or contain fear rather than reinforce it. But many find it hard to swallow the new wine.

Ironically, Christian fundamentalists reach back on the shelf for the old wine of the Jewish Scriptures, subscribing to corporal punishment: "Do not withhold disciples from a child; if you beat him with a rod, he will not die. If you beat him with the rod you will save his life from Sheol." (Pr 23:13) In doing so they bypass the kinder, gentler new wine of the Christian scriptures right in front of them: "Fathers, do not exasperate your children: instead bring them up in the training and instruction of the Lord." (Col 3:21)

Christians still serve the Kool-Aid of fear, as it gets people to comply immediately, just as parents default to fear tactics to get instant compliance from children. Paul says "love is patient."

But fear is *impatient*. It demands prompt results.

Drive through America's Bible Belt and you'll be hit with a barrage of urgent, fearful billboards: *Go to Church on Sunday or the Devil will get you!* Or, *Do you want to spend eternity in Hell?* Frightening signs are more numerous than those proclaiming unconditional love. It seems the subtext is that you can experience God's "unconditional" love— but only if you get right first. And the underlying lesson? If you talk love, people will do whatever the hell they want, but if you talk fear, you'll keep them in line.

As cited above, "human nature is always the same." This is a static, fixed view of humanity rather than a fresh, dynamic perspective. Jesus offered new wine in overcoming the static view. The Old Testament cites *fear* 270 times, while the New only 70. While the former overwhelmingly enforces fear, the latter more often challenges one to overcome it. Jesus said, "Be not afraid." He asked, "Why are you fearful?" He knew that fear immobilizes us. We can't think straight, become paralyzed, can easily resort to violence. As an antidote to fear, Jesus brings the new wine of faith—not as dry dogma, but as dynamic imagination.

Faith imagines other possibilities and alternatives besides fear, which freezes the mind from even considering other options. Faith rejects fatalism, the capitulation to the way things are. Faith imagines the dynamic of love as a motivator, pointing to the way things *could be*, *may be*. Love liberates us to see creative possibilities.

On an English countryside a parson came upon a weathervane with the inscription below it, *God is Love*. The parson asked the farmer, "So you think God's love shifts with the wind?" The farmer replied, "Not at all. Whichever way the wind blows, God is still love." More often, the God of fear is felt with every wind by God-fearing folk.

Jesus never directly said "God is love." It appears in the Letter of John. It is the distillation of the new wine Jesus pressed and poured out in his short life. His new interpretation would be expanded by his disciples. But the proclamation of love would reach its high point in Paul's statement of 1 Corinthians 15, that "the greatest of these is love." Like us, Paul was a work in progress. Even he still had to shake off some fears, not fully grounded in perfect love just yet.

Education, not religion, has been instrumental in lifting unnecessary burdens of fear from people's psyches. Education examines more rationally our human actions. Religion has more often chosen to enforce fear, to control members. Yet education, too, can default to using fear to gain compliance. It was found by government policymakers that in the push for citizens to comply with rules of the road, the soft approach was not as successful as the hard approach.

A recent study found people conformed more quickly when they realized violations would lead to punishment. As the *Washington Post* noted, "The campaign against distracted driving has provided another illustration that American drivers are more likely to respond to safety initiatives when they carry the threat of punishment." One official concluded that "combining strong laws with strong enforcement can bring about a sea change in public attitudes and behavior." [40] So the fear of a penalty, of a ticket, curtails bad behavior on the road. But is it possible to respond without the threat of punishment? "There is no fear in love; but perfect love casts out fear, because fear involves punishment, and the one who fears is not perfected in love." (1 Jo 4:18) Since governmental entities don't tout a gospel of love, they can't be faulted for threatening punishment.

It is the mission of an institution that believes it has an inspired, revealing message to enable people to be "perfected in love." If the RCC's catechesis was the *praxis* of love, it would nurture persons to treat others as others wish to be treated. But its theology of fear instead focuses on punishment, which leads to ongoing recidivism.

AND THE GREATEST OF THESE IS . . . FEAR
"Do the thing you fear most and the death of fear is certain."
– Mark Twain

If Paul proclaims that only three things matter—faith, hope, and love—and that the greatest of these is love, then why is so much emphasis put on the *other* three—fear, sin, and hell? Even Paul contradicts himself in advising followers to "work out your salvation in fear and trembling." (Php 2:12) Paul uses the phrase *fear and trembling* a number of times. But shouldn't we live confidently in love, since our salvation has been secured in the sacrifice of Jesus? Well, Paul is only human. He has yet to work out his own guilt—and has yet to deal with his own religious conversion, from being the persecutor of the followers of Jesus to the biggest promoter of Jesus.

Paul writes effusively about an abstract gift of God, which he calls "grace." The word *grace* is mentioned only eight times in the much longer Jewish scriptures, but 114 times in the Christian scriptures. Paul is developing a theological concept that remains mysterious today. Preachers now casually cast about the word *grace* without providing any empirical way of understanding or measuring it, leaving it an undefined concept that sounds nice but can mean anything to anyone.

Grace and freedom from the Law were promoted by Paul, but not by the RCC. It created its own extensive and oppressive laws to control members. It outdid the 613 Jewish commandments with a code of Canon Law that once swelled to more than 2,400 canons (now slimmed down to a mere 1,752).

Martin Luther was representative of Christians of his time, plagued with guilt and anxiety about his personal salvation. Indeed, he worked it out "in fear and trembling," which led to his bout of constipation. Could there be a better metaphor for being uptight about one's salvation? As a Roman priest, Luther had the contagious virus of fear. But he was exceptional in his grasp of Latin and Greek and could read the scriptures for himself. His reading of Paul on grace and freedom liberated him and led to a movement that broke the monopoly of the RCC in the West. Luther, of course, succeeded in lessening the emphasis on fear, not exorcising it completely.

Few people today are driven with anxiety about their personal salvation because coping with modern life is all-consuming. Having to factor in an unknown afterlife is overwhelming. They'll deal with that when they come to it, if they *ever* come to it. Yet contemporary Catholics are still conditioned to experience continual angst about their future status in some vague afterlife.

The RCC (and Christianity in general), in conditioning people to be anxious over every thought and deed in this life, and to fear what might come in the next, creates a dread of dying that causes most to avoid even thinking about it. Modern culture, also, aids and abets this denial of death. The RCC holds the only real life is the one to come, tormenting humans by itemizing sins that can send them to hell, by reminding them of the ever-present possibility of a fiery eternity with no exit.

What a different institution the RCC would have become if from its beginning it had centered exclusively on the *praxis* of love. Jesus planted the seed of inclusive love, but its application and practice could only be expanded in a community engaged in a dialogue on this expansive concept. The Church is not an enabler of open-ended dialogue. It fears losing control. It doesn't openly engage, but sternly dictates from the top down.

"THE POWER OF THE EVIL ONE"
"Man's nature is not essentially evil. Brute nature has been known to yield to the influence of love. You must never despair of human nature." – Mahatma Gandhi

John 3:16 is a favorite verse of evangelical Christians, often brandished at ballparks with digital lights flashing the text reference. "God so loved the world that he sent his only Son, so that everyone who believes in him may not be lost but have eternal life."

Ah, but then the cold threat kicks in. "Whoever does not believe in him is already condemned." Eternal death—not eternal life—is the trump card. Evidently God *doesn't* "so love the world," as his penchant for punishment ultimately outweighs his offer of love.

The First Letter of John is an extended treatise on love, amplifying seminal ideas of love found in the gospels. But, alas, it is full of contradictions. It has wondrous things to say about love, but then introduces chilling, dreadful elements. The boast that "perfect love casts out fear" is overshadowed with judgments and warnings.

Particularly unsettling is the emphasis that these are the "last days," the time of the anti-Christ, reinforcing the most fearsome force in the history of human imagination. It is embodied in the figure of the Devil, a.k.a. the Evil One, the Prince of this World, the Father of Lies, Beelzebub, Satan, Lucifer—we've heard them all.

69

Rather than exorcising this negative force, which first appears in the Garden of Eden, the New Testament allows the Devil to become a looming power "going about like a roaring lion" to devour others. Fallen angels dispelled from heaven—now devils—have an everlasting life of their own, both on earth and the beyond, able to rise up from the netherworld to lure people into choosing evil. The writer of First John reaffirms fear while expounding on love. "We know that we belong to God, but the whole world lies in the power of the Evil One." (1 Jo 5:19)

Similar contradictions exist throughout the Christian scriptures. John 3:16 says "God so loved the world," but 1 Jo 2:15 advises, "You must not love this passing world or anything that is in the world." How is a simple believer to reconcile this? Most religious leaders will gloss over it, or reinforce the more negative revelation.

Such sentiments understandably led level-headed Christians to flee this world, or move to its remote deserts and mountaintops, cutting themselves off from the civilization they believed Satan controlled. They got the message: *Only the afterlife matters. This life doesn't count. It is merely an anteroom. The least contact with this evil secular world, the better.*

The entire Bible is woven with the threatening thread of *Apocalypticism*—a divine rescue from evil and suffering on earth, noted earlier. The "end of the world" was being predicted almost as soon as the world began. Noah and his crew experienced intervention when corruption and evil flooded humanity. Old Testament prophets through to Jesus and Paul cited the imminent end to the Evil One's reign.

This fear-laden image still works today—it terrorizes the hearts of simple, sincere people.

Those who have undeveloped visions of an afterlife (or see no point in speculating) tend to become more engaged with *this* life, and work to change it, so that humankind may be truly *human* and *kind*. But if this world is held hostage by "the power of the Evil One," the best response is to disengage from it, as advised by the Church, correct? One problem—this abandons the world to the most hateful power imaginable. The RCC is not sincere about pursuing justice here. It counsels those "heavily burdened" to look to the life to come for relief. Does it not then, by default, simply hand over this weary old world to "the power of the Evil One"?

John Paul II strongly reaffirmed the Devil, lest the Devil become a casualty to Vatican II. As cited by a Roman news service, when Vatican exorcist Fr. Gabriele Amorth was asked if the Devil exists, he answered by stressing the pope's belief: "I respond with the words of John Paul II, who was once asked this question: 'Your Holiness, I find many bishops who don't believe in the Devil.' And John Paul II responded, 'One who doesn't believe in the Devil doesn't believe in the Gospel.'" Amorth added that the Devil has "a very large intelligence, immensely bigger than ours," and is okay with the "ridiculous" way he is portrayed "with wings and tail and horns" because this tricks people into dismissing his existence. [41]

But, as Tina Turner sang, "What's love got to do with it?" If the Devil and his fearful minions have free reign, then what? "*Timor vincit omnia*" (Fear conquers all)?

Believing in a God who is everywhere is difficult enough, but believing in a Devil who is lurking around each corner taxes the limits of human credulity. The reluctance of the RCC to incinerate Satan once and for all reaffirms its commitment to terrorizing people. It rejects exorcising the diabolic from its own body. Rather, John Paul II and Benedict XVI have reaffirmed the power and presence of the Devil, roaming freely about the earth to scare the hell out of people. Would that this truly scared the hell *out* of people rather than injecting it *into* people.

In a recent trend, the Vatican is training more exorcists to dislodge the Devil from the grip on victimized human beings. And it reinvents the Devil with a vengeance and a hard sell in the new *Catholic Catechism*. Children must be instilled with horror stories of the Devil's powerful prowling and trolling for souls. This maintenance of a robust belief in the Devil only dampens the power of love.

If perfect love casts out fear, yet the Devil remains the most active agent in this world, then perfect *fear* casts out *love*.

So the Devil is alive and well in Catholic theology. As Tony Equale notes, "The most damaging belief is the personification of evil in 'Satan,' imagined to be the god-like ruler of an evil empire. Not only has the existence and function of Satan, the 'Devil,' never been repudiated by the Church, it was actually reaffirmed as recently as 1992 with the publication of the Vatican Catechism. In Number 391 to 395 the Catechism speaks about the 'fall of the angels' as an event in which Satan and other devils were supposedly spawned." [42]

While contemporary popes train more exorcists, will any exorcise Satan from the RCC? "To fear is to expect punishment," and the Devil continuously seeks souls to torture eternally. If so, then Paul is correct; we need to work out our salvation in fear and trembling. The Kingdom teaching frees people from fear.

The RCC continues to incarcerate people in fear—with a little help from the Devil.

AN OBSESSION WITH SIN
Eskimo: "If I did not know about God and sin, would I go to hell?"
Priest: "No, not if you did not know."
Eskimo: "Then why did you tell me?" – Annie Dillard

The centerpiece of the RCC is obsession with *sin*, not *evil*. The Confucian approach asks the question, "Who can say what is good and what is bad?" The RCC asserts that it can, with absolute clarity.

Essayist Sue Cox illustrates this: "I was brought up with all the horrific fear stories of hell fire and damnation. In that Catholic world everything, apart from breathing, was sinful. Aged five I was told to pray for a cousin to die because he was about to marry a divorcee; his mother's priest told her that he would be better off dead than living in sin, so we should all pray for him to have a 'happy death.'" [43]

The moral theology courses I endured in seminary did not examine in any depth the nature of evil. We were presented with inventories of primarily proven and reliable mortal and venial sins—essentially readymade "checklists" for the confessional. Evil was a given, needing no serious concern or curious investigation. The complex and universal problem of evil—*theodicy*—should have been an engaging exploration of moral theology.

But there was no need to speculate about evil. The provided lists covered it; they presented and certified all sins necessary for the confessional. This was simpler and less challenging or threatening than the alternative—to lift the rock of human experience and peer into the dank underside of humanity. We were trained to be "morality cops," able to differentiate mortal from venial sins, and to determine how far estranged from God the faithful were. We were empowered to revive languishing or dead souls, to save the sinners from themselves. We had the power!

Preoccupation with sin lives at the dark center of the RCC. It focuses on policing potential incidents of sin rather than engaging in an ongoing dialogue on the nature of evil. It is universally accepted that there is a negative side to human existence. But the RCC mimics a scientific approach to sin (genus) and its multiple possibilities (species). It reinforces categories and degrees of sin. The big whopper is *original* sin, which baptism alone could wash away. Then there are *actual* sins (of commission and omission), *mortal* sins, and *venial* sins. Other religions speak more vaguely about generic sin, lacking the refined categories the RCC devised.

"Original sin" is a clever invention, an inescapable trap, originally manufactured. The Church says it is the sin that everyone—believer or not—automatically inherits at birth. "Behold, I was brought forth in iniquity. And in sin my mother conceived me." (Ps 51:5) So from our first burp, we are all damaged goods. Though innocent, we start life with a huge strike against us. It's nothing personal, it's just that we had bad first parents—Adam and Eve. Wow, that's a good one. Scholars may debate whether Moses or Jesus ever truly existed, but Adam and Eve would be their unanimous first choice as nonexistent. Nonetheless, through these imaginary first parents, we were branded. Did the Devil have his hand in this?

Genesis claims that God looked at all that he created and saw it was good—not just good, but *very good*. But that sentiment needs a theological footnote, as the RCC later saw that we were all born bad, *very bad*.

73

"Actual sin" is, well, "actually" committed by people, not just arbitrarily stained on their souls. It comes in two sizes—small or extra-extra-large, venial or mortal. Catholic theology says only two persons refused an actual sin—Jesus and Mary.

"Mortal sin," depending on the translation of 1 John 5:16 can be considered the sin that leads to death. *Mortal* is synonymous with *deadly*, and other adjectives describing this egregious offense— *grave, serious, eternal.*

"Venial sin" is okay, since it carries no eternal sentence, and it doesn't have to be confessed. Unfortunately, this has not been made clear to most Catholics, who still itemize each one, along with the number of times, though often stumbling over the precise amount. This is a comically tedious exercise for both priest and penitent. Who cares if someone was impatient ten or fifteen times, swore thirty or thirty-five times?

The Sacrament of Penance is *itself* penance. Confession for the scrupulous is pure torture. And this sacrament encourages scrupulosity.

The good news is that multiple venial sins do not add up to even one mortal sin. So, the curious mind wonders, how far can one go in the venial area before moving into the mortal area?

In time, the RCC offered official lists of sins—the "Penitentials," supposedly the most commonly confessed sins—with the appropriate penance noted to guide priests in getting people right with God.

While the Penitentials were detailed manuals that assisted clergy in identifying a wide range of sins and assigning penances, you can easily imagine the hottest topic, the one that heaped the most guilt on Catholics. The Penitentials identified *good* sexual activity (intended for procreation) and *bad* sexual activity (everything else), enabling clerics (often celibates) to determine the appropriate penance.

Effectively, they were porn manuals for clergy.

And the compilation of detailed sexual activities in these manuals could be problematic for the priest. The newly released *Sex and Punishment* explains: "One eleventh-century guidebook required that men be asked: Have you coupled with your wife or another woman from behind like dogs? The same book required that women be asked about aphrodisiacs, lesbianism, bestiality, masturbation, abortions, oral consumption of semen, and the use of their menstrual blood as a love charm." [44]

Early on, some priests were alerted to the moral dangers of these manuals: "In 821, Theodulf of Orleans warned confessors not to put ideas into people's heads with such detailed questions: There are many vices recorded in the penitential which it is [sic] not proper for a person to know. Therefore, the priest ought not to question him about everything, lest, perhaps, when he goes away he be persuaded by the devil to fall into one of the crimes of which he had been previously ignorant." [45]

Ironically, the Penitentials never made the RCC's hit list, the *Index Librorum Prohibitorum* (*List of Prohibited Books*), published in 1559.

Contrast the Penitentials of the RCC with the *Kama Sutra* (400 BCE– 200 CE) of the ancient Hindu tradition. The oldest known self-help sex manual, it sought to enhance sensual experiences, emphasizing the multitude of sexual positions and techniques that heightened pleasure. While the *Kama Sutra* was perhaps the first "how-to" manual, the Penitentials were a "how-*not*-to" manual.

Though sex acts *outside* marriage are mortal sins, it's the activity that leads up to them that might be mitigated. Therefore, it was often asked, how far could one go in "petting" or "necking" before it became a mortal sin? Yet sex acts *within* marriage can also be mortal sins.

I remember as a freshly ordained priest in 1966 finding a newly married couple at the rectory door. The young wife dragged her husband in and asked me, a naïve virgin, what could they do sexually without committing a sin? I was totally unprepared and managed to mutter that whatever was compatible was okay with God—and me.

A frequently debated question regarding Sunday mass was, how much of the mass can be missed before it becomes a mortal sin? This evidenced a quite common desire to participate as *minimally* as possible. But logic says that if one were to commit a mortal sin, it may as well be in the sexual arena—at least it's a more pleasurable way of going to hell than skipping a few prayers on Sunday.

Lest one thinks these issues don't count as matters for confession, Holy Mother sternly counsels, "The Church strongly recommends confessing venial sins, though this is not strictly necessary." [46] For a moment, it seemed a little window of mercy had opened, freeing people from confessing sins that don't rise to the immoral hall of infamy. But the new *Catechism* delivers a dire warning: "Deliberate and un-repented venial sin disposes us little by little to commit a mortal sin." [47]

So if one tells or listens to too many dirty jokes, one might end up masturbating—a mortal sin. Unfortunately, this caveat makes people susceptible to extreme scrupulosity, forever prisoners of their delicate consciences. Sadly, they will never know when their venial sin has morphed into a mortal one.

Jesus is depicted as a lover of children: "Let the children come to me, and do not hinder them." (Mk 10:14) One would think the RCC would give children a direct, unrestricted access to the Eucharist. Why not? But no, before children receive their First Communion, they *must* first go to confession. One would hardly think seven-year-olds capable of committing mortal sins; nonetheless, they have to first confess at least one venial sin before they are allowed to "come to Jesus" in the Eucharist. Interestingly, at baptism in the Orthodox Church, children have direct access to Jesus via the express lane— they bypass confession and go straight to communion. Better for kids to take the Orthodox route?

I've endured the torture of hearing confessions of little children. One of the blessings of the parochial school decline is that fewer children are dutifully marched into church for mandatory confession. They're coaxed and forced through the interrogation of adults who, like detectives, are determined to find *something* to confess. In practice, it's a form of abuse.

Another translation of Jesus' "Let the little children come to me" is "Suffer the little children come to me," and the RCC gladly fulfills *that* request by continually finding ways to make "the little ones" worry and fret. Inculcating fear at an early age has life-long negative consequences. Sadly, the RCC is afraid to offer them the largess of love, keenly aware that control of the adult ultimately begins with control of the child.

Leaders and supporters like to refer to *Holy Mother the Church*, but she is one strict disciplinarian who demands her children do as she says—or else! In an era when the majority of people were illiterate and fearful, the RCC could forge ahead unchecked. But as people became more educated and part of democratic and pluralistic societies, they became less fearful and more assertive. Contemporary believers are increasingly becoming more conscious, more self-motivated, internalizing their own *modus operandi* rather than submitting to external institutional pressures. Nonetheless, they remain sensitive to the ongoing presence of apparent evil and confrontation of it outside the confessional box.

Still, Holy Mother the Church continues to treat her adult sons and daughters as if they are still wide-eyed children. As a result, more and more of her grownup kids are having less and less to do with Holy Mother.

MORTAL SIN, IMMORTAL CONSEQUENCES
"I think my sexuality was heavily repressed by the church, by the, you know, the design of the mortal sins." – Thomas Keneally

The greatest tragedy of the RCC is its history of maximizing, not minimizing, the number of mortal sins a person can commit, and its insistence that unless repented, they lead to a sentence of an irrevocable hell with no exit but only unremitting, eternal torture. Mortal sin—it's the sin that keeps on punishing. How many persons, perhaps billions, have had this heavy millstone placed around their necks?

The RCC's clerics with too much time on their hands parsed the genus of sin into various species, but mortal sin was the top category. Catholics walk on endless fields of landmines where multiple mortal sins could explode at any time. Rather than reducing the number of sins members could commit, the RCC expanded them into unlimited possibilities.

When we were kids, the good sisters told us some bad stuff. If we committed mortal sin, God would be offended, would wince in pain, as if we were sticking pins into an imaginary voodoo doll. Apparently, we could hurt God the Almighty. So it seemed *we* were the almighty. But no, God had the last word—hell. Mortal sin would cut us off from God for all eternity and we'd be sentenced without any hope of parole once we were cast into that fire "where their worms die not, and the fire is not quenched." (Mk 9:48)

My frightening religious exposure was hardly unique—it was the norm for children schooled within the RCC's vast educational system. Author Carlos Eire eloquently describes a similar fear he absorbed at the earliest age: "Every desire is forbidden. Is this harsh or what? That's how the Christian Brothers explained it to us. In order to get to heaven, your soul needs to be pure. Think of it as pure whiteness, that's what they told us. Blazing, blinding white, that's how God wants your soul to be. Just one large stain is enough to land you in hell for eternity. One stolen toy, that's all it takes. One covetous glance at a pair of nice new shoes, or the person wearing them, or whatever belongs to someone else That's all it takes to be plunged into a sulfurous burning pit, where you will be horribly tortured by hideous demons for eternity." [48]

We too were given images of how long eternity was. One nun had us visualize a little sparrow trying to chip away at a gigantic iron ball. The "good sisters" were essentially good people who had been indoctrinated in poor theology, a system that abhorred critical thinking or reflection or feedback. Good people can be dangerous. (And anyway, what was it about birds that made them a favorite model in religious pedagogy for conveying deeper things?)

Again, Eire depicts similar instruction: "Hell they emphasized lasts forever. And what did *forever* mean? 'Ah, Carlos, good question. Infinity is beyond comprehension. The best we can do is employ images to convey a sense of infinity. You want to know what *forever* means in terms of hell and the suffering that awaits us there? Well, answer this question first: if all of the oceans on earth were to be filled with sand, and a bird were to remove one tiny grain of sand every million years, how long would it take for all of the sand to be removed?' We gave all sorts of answers, but all were wrong." Then Carlos suggests an answer. "'All right, you want to know the right answer? The right answer is this: ridding the earth of all that sand, grain by grain, in one-million-year increments would take only a fraction of the time one would spend in hell. The whole process would be only an infinitesimally insignificant fraction of the eternity that is hell. So small a fraction as not to count at all. Almost the same as zero. Eternity has no end.' And one sin would take you there. Just one." [49]

Abusers, we know now, tend to abuse others. They may not even think of what they do as abuse, but as simply continuing a pattern they had once experienced. When abuse is mentioned, we tend to think of sexual or physical abuse. But mental abuse perhaps is more devastating because it promotes lifelong fear. There was no promulgation by the "good sisters" (or even the "good fathers") of one of St. Augustine's best thoughts: "Love, and do what you will. If you keep silence, do it out of love. If you cry out, do it out of love. If you refrain from punishing, do it out of love."

The upgraded *Baltimore Catechism*, the present *U.S. Catholic Catechism for Adults*, describes what happens if we have a mortal sin on our soul: "Mortal sin destroys the loving relationship with God that we need for eternal happiness. If not repented, it results in a loss of love and God's grace and merits eternal punishment in hell that is exclusion from the Kingdom of God and thus eternal death." [50]

We can deduce from this statement that we, not God, have the power to sever the relationship, correct? If the RCC decided we weren't right with God, didn't it automatically follow that God acquiesced to its dictation? Is God then forced to cut off the love bond between parties? If so, then there are humans more magnanimous than God, humans who don't staunch the flow of love even when grievously offended.

A neighbor from youth had one son. As a young man he was heavily into drugs and alcohol. According to Catholic morality, choosing to abuse drugs and drink is a mortal sin. Even to deliberately "tie one on" is a mortal sin. In one of his many stupors, the son blinded his mother. He was sentenced to life in prison. But his mother never stopped loving him.

In June 2011, a news channel featured a woman whose only son was murdered by another young man, and she forgave him. Going the extra mile, she visited him in prison. Going another mile, when his sentence was completed she convinced her landlord to rent him the apartment next to hers.

Why can't God love like this, unconditionally? Is God incapable of forgiving as fully as some humans? Or, is it that the RCC controls how we *think* God acts?

Many people forgive individuals who murdered their loved ones, lacking any special requests or expectations. They don't demand a demonstration of worthiness first. A poet wrote, "Though I cannot be loved, let me love." Altruistic love doesn't hinge on an expected response, only on the willingness of someone who freely loves even when unloved, rejected. Cannot God love accordingly?

While the letter of John proclaims "God is love," the RCC slaps countless conditions on this love.

John Paul II was infatuated with a Polish nun, Sr. Faustina Kowalska. She kept a diary of her love trysts with God and promoted his mercy (as well as her horrible visions of hell for those separated from him). [51] This has been institutionalized on the Sunday after Easter, as "Divine Mercy Sunday." It is also the Sunday that features the gospel story of Jesus' first encounter with his disciples after they denied and abandoned him in his hour of need. Jesus is presented not as coming to settle the score with them, but blessing them. His first words were "Peace be with you!" He breathes on them and instills in them the power of forgiveness. "If you forgive others sins, they are forgiven them. If you hold them, they are held bond." (Jo 20:23)

The RCC calls this *the power of the keys*. The common interpretation is that priests have the authority to keep people in bondage to their sins if they do not show sufficient contriteness. But the context suggests another interpretation. The disciples who willingly cut themselves loose from Jesus were not cut loose by *him*. He doesn't return to keep them in bondage until they demonstrate worthiness to be forgiven. He returns to reiterate his unbroken bond with them. So, what is the point of keeping people bound to sin rather than loosening them from its grip? Only the theology of fear.

Later in John's account there is the touching encounter, again post-resurrection, where Jesus shares a meal with the disciples and says to Peter, "Do you love me?" (Jo 21:15) Note that he *doesn't* say, "Aren't you sorry for what you did to me?"

Pre-resurrection, Jesus told the most beloved of his parables, *The Prodigal Son*. After cutting himself off from his father, a contrite son squanders his unearned inheritance and reluctantly returns. As he babbles a scripted apology, his father abruptly shuts him off and embraces him, calling out to get a party going for the son who returned. This is the new wine Jesus offers, sent by a God who loves even when spurned, rejected, denied.

But this is not the God of the RCC. It still believes in Yahweh, a God keen on retribution. The RCC is not going to offer any new wine at an unbelievable bargain-basement price. You still have to pay heavily to get a drink. If you commit mortal sin, you have to confess to a priest and show a firm "purpose of amendment" before the priest will unbind you. If not, he has the power to keep you in bondage, the saving act of Jesus notwithstanding.

It is a fascinating *Catch-22* situation. God is all mercy—*but only under certain conditions*. One has to beg and groan and grovel first to get back into God's good graces. If not sufficiently repentant, he's fine with allowing hell and eternal torture to beckon.

The new *Catechism* puts it this way (though nothing new here): "In considering sin we must always remember that God is rich in mercy. 'Where sin increased, grace overflowed all the more.' (Rom 5:20) God's mercy is greater than sin. The very heart of the gospels is the revelation of the mercy of God in Jesus Christ. 'For, God did not send his Son into the world to condemn the world, but that the world might be saved through him.' (Jo 3:17) To receive this mercy, we must

81

be willing to admit our sinfulness. Sorrow for sin and confession of sin are signs of conversion of heart that open us to God's mercy. Though we can judge a given offense to be the occasion of mortal sin, and thus an act of objective wrongdoing, we must always entrust the judgment of the person to the mercy and justice of God." [52]

Unfortunately, even if contrite, one might have the misfortune of an unlucky draw, a demanding priest who takes seriously his power of binding and loosing and may not think one sufficiently repentant. He might well be angry, judging one's demeanor isn't impressive enough, believing one might commit the sin again if given the opportunity. Maybe a woman was raped, maybe a sonogram detected a dangerous medical situation for her, maybe she lived in poverty. Either way, she did the best she could and procured an abortion. "The quality of mercy is strained!"

To advocate a God serving the new wine of unilateral forgiveness is offering a libertine of a deity. When, then, will people stop sinning? The RCC believes only fear of eternal death will induce people to get right with God. Fear, not love, is the corrective. The sweet aphorism of St. Francis de Sales, "You can attract more flies with a spoonful of honey than with a barrelful of vinegar," is a bit sticky. It was intended for a convent of cloistered nuns, not a world of profligates. Only the threat of punishment will protect one from eternal torture. The masses respond best to the lowest human denominator—fear.

Obvious contradictions appear in the Good News. Jesus is depicted as sharing the intoxication of the old God, Yahweh. At times, he is dispensing the old wine of divine retribution. At the judgment scene where he separates sheep from goats, he declares to the goats, "Depart from me, accursed ones, into the eternal fire which has been prepared for the devil and his angels." (Mt 25:41)

While Jesus came with "Good News" for the poor, he was also moved to intervene for them, not out of fear but solidarity, despite religious authorities who frowned on his looseness with the Law. Association with a sinner contaminated him. If he was fearful, he wouldn't have put his life on the line in challenging the Law that had become a burden on the backs of the people. He came to lift that burden at personal cost. It seems love for others motivated him to act fearlessly, and take the consequences from those who didn't quite buy into his interpretation.

"If not repented, it results in a loss of love and God's grace and merits eternal punishment in hell that is exclusion from the Kingdom of God and thus eternal death." [53] If it were merely eternal *sleep*, it would involve some mercy for the condemned. Adolph Hitler's secretary claimed that when Hitler was in his bunker, ready to take his life, he looked forward to eternal sleep. But to be condemned to eternal *death*, one will need to be drugged, put on amphetamines that cause everlasting insomnia, forced to experience relentless torture.

One un-confessed mortal sin is enough to keep the punishment going forever. "We must confess all our mortal sins in kind and number." [54] If just one single solitary mortal sin totally separates a person from God, staunching the flow of love and grace and judging the person dead, how much more dead can two or two thousand mortal sins render a person?

This ultimate silliness underlies the "theology" of mortal sin. If a body is dead with one bullet, can it become "more dead" with a hundred bullets? If someone drops a bomb on a town and kills hundreds, does it count as one mortal sin or one for each person killed? If one masturbates every day, is it considered one continuous sin or does each act constitute a new mortal sin?

Retired Bishop Geoffrey Robinson voiced his opinion on this during a March 2012 symposium on sexuality and the Church: "For centuries the church has taught that every sexual sin is a mortal sin. The teaching may not be proclaimed as loudly today as much as before, but it was proclaimed by many popes, it has never been retracted and it has affected countless people." He stressed that "the teaching fostered a belief in an incredibly angry God, for this God would condemn a person to an eternity in hell for a single unrepented moment of deliberate pleasure arising from sexual desire. I simply do not believe in such a God. Indeed, I positively reject such a God." Robinson ultimately called for "a new study of everything to do with sexuality," which would ultimately have a "profound influence on Church teaching" concerning both homosexual and heterosexual relationships. [55]

Confession itself can be an occasion of sin, particularly for the priest who doesn't check his curiosity. Says the new *Catechism*: "It is also in confession that a priest and penitent can work together to find the direction needed for the penitent to grow spiritually and to avoid sin in the future." [56] Sexual issues are the overwhelming reason people confessed back in the day, at least until *Humanae Vitae*. The blowback of this papal broadside finally liberated most members from confessing their sexual acts.

For priests with a predisposition for sex with minors, however, the confessional became an opportunity for sexual assignation, not the occasion to grow spiritually.

Donald McGuire, a Jesuit and confidant of Mother Teresa, currently doing time for sexual abuse, found the confessional a venue for victims. As reported, "McGuire seemed to revel in the elaborate torment of his victims, perverting the sacraments into vehicles of abuse and turning vulnerable boys against their parents. One of his more notorious practices was to coax admissions of masturbation out of his victims under seal of confession—and then massage their genitals as part of the process of penance." [57]

Canon Law 979 expects the priest to question the penitent: "The priest in posing questions is to proceed with prudence and discretion." But no one monitors the questioner. An unscrupulous priest can probe as he pleases because he is protected by the "seal of confession." He will eternally be given the benefit of the doubt.

Some seventh- and eighth-graders in St. Petersburg, FL were made uncomfortable during confession when a priest allegedly asked whether they looked at pornography or masturbated, a local newspaper reported in 2011. He refused to meet with concerned parents, and the bishop backed him, citing the seal of confession. The article also reported on a local teacher fired after pushing for an investigation of a visiting priest who allegedly pressured teenage girls during confession "to give him details about whether they had masturbated or had sex." If they refused, he reportedly "would not grant them absolution." Administrators said the questions were appropriate and the school had no authority to intervene. A professor of Catholic studies disagreed, stating that confession is "not an interrogation" and most confessors avoid asking about sins the penitent hadn't brought up. [58]

Priests have free reign to probe according to their prurient interests, and bishops will back them with the "seal of confession." But this is only to be applied to what a penitent *tells* a priest, not what a priest *asks* a penitent. Bishops are not inclined to separate the two, however, so the confessional becomes a convenient venue for unscrupulous clerics who know they have episcopal immunity.

McGuire wasn't the first cleric who found the confessional an ideal "trysting" place. Laws are generally enacted after a crime has been committed. Canon Law 1387 acknowledges priests have solicited penitents to sin against the Sixth Commandment. The most severe penalty for a priest is dismissal from the clerical state. Canon Law verifies the historical precedence of a present-day cleric like McGuire. The RCC, however, is more concerned with protecting the seal of confession; victims are unlikely to have their day in Canon Law court.

St. Charles Borromeo (1538-1564), one-time archbishop of Milan, is credited with inventing the confessional box, commonplace in Roman churches till post-Vatican II, which created the open reconciliation room. Andrew Graham-Dixon writes that Borromeo had it created to "avert any danger of unclean thoughts, polluting their (priest and penitent) necessarily intimate relationship." He evidently was aware of sexual assignation that sometimes occurred during the process. "The archbishop's suspicious view of human nature extended to his own priests and confessors. In the late 1570s, when a woodworker named Rizzardo Taurini was commissioned to build five confessionals for the new Jesuit church of San Fedele in Milan, he provoked Borromeo's rage by curtailing one of the partitions at the bottom of the standard double sentry-box design. The Jesuit provost of San Fedele recalled the archbishop's outraged protest: 'the confessor can easily touch the woman's feet with his own.' Borromeo repeated the objection several times, to the evident exasperation of the provost, who found the archbishop's insistence on the moral dangers inherent in a proximity between two people's feet more than faintly absurd. 'He greatly insisted on this,' the provost remembered, 'as if lust enters the body through one's shoes, and he is unaware that in his confessionals the woman's mouth is close to the confessor's ear.' The Jesuit knew a truth that Borromeo did not want to acknowledge: no matter how strong the grilles and walls of any confessional box, nothing could absolutely prevent priests and penitents from harbouring feelings for one another. The partitions might even enhance the illicit thrill of such emotions. This exchange between the worldly provost and the archbishop reveals the paranoid fear of sinfulness—and the corresponding desire to close off almost every avenue of human sensuality—that lay at the heart of Borromean piety." [59]

Even the open confessional of Vatican II allows for the same preying behavior. A New Jersey newspaper documented such an incident in 2012: "In a candlelit room at St. James School in Basking Ridge, Brian Kvederas remembers confessing the overwhelming fears of his adolescence to Rev. Luke Travers some twenty-five years ago ... As Kvederas spilled his innermost anxieties, the two sat knees to knees, candles flickering, in a secluded corner of an office or small classroom, Kvederas recalls ... After the emotional talk, Kvederas said Travers hugged him, then whispered a request: 'Kiss me.' Stunned, Kvederas nonetheless went to give Travers 'a peck on the cheek.' He says the monk swung his head around, kissed him on the lips and 'tried to stick his tongue in my mouth.'" [60]

EXCOMMUNICATION, A SENTENCE TO HELL
"If forgers and malefactors are put to death by the secular power, there is much more reason for excommunicating and even putting to death one convicted of heresy." – Thomas Aquinas

Rather than rescuing people from hell, the RCC sent people to hell by hurling excommunications, censures, interdicts, and anathemas throughout history, all damning sentences to the fiery pit. It would defend these tactics of terror and fear as medicinal, as attempts to save individuals from perdition, but of course these practices became counterproductive. While they succeeded in creating external conformity, the hearts of humans were far from motivated in the long run.

In excommunication, the RCC instantly consigns the person to hell, unless the individual repents and does appropriate penance. It designs its own batch of mortal sins to which members may be subjected. If one becomes an apostate, heretic, or schismatic, one automatically incurs excommunication.

Sarah Palin and Glenn Beck would be categorized as apostate because they were baptized Catholic but joined other religious sects. Millions of once-baptized Catholics fall into this category, grievously wounding God, though often unaware of it. Ignorance of RCC law is no excuse—they are hell-bound. They may wonder why when they wake up in hell some day, but will be clueless.

Procuring an abortion means *"latae sentential"* (excommunication) of the woman, automatically, without a competent authority having to impose it. The difficulty of extricating oneself from the theology of fear is revealed in a letter to a priest columnist, Fr. William Saunders: "Many years ago, I had an abortion. After many years as a lapsed Catholic, I returned to the Church and to confession. Although the priest said something about abortion carrying with it an excommunication, he gave me absolution. I gave it no additional thought and continued to receive the sacraments. It wasn't until recently that I read something about the 'rite' of removing an excommunication that I began to fear what I had done and continue to do something wrong. Can you help by setting my mind at ease or instructing me in the way to proceed?" (Wikipedia)

In his response, Saunders discusses how many others incur mortal sin and are bound for hell. "Any Catholic accomplice in the act of procuring an abortion, even though not specifically mentioned in Canon Law 1398, receives the same penalty of automatic excommunication. Here an accomplice is one who assists in such a way that the heinous act would not have been committed without his assistance." (Wikipedia) The cab driver who drove the woman to the doctor? If Catholic!

Why would the abortion of a fetus ("the purposeful murder of an innocent, unborn child," according to Saunders) automatically excommunicate a person, but the cold-blooded murder of an innocent grandmother would not? Some lives, evidently, are more precious than others, even among murdered innocents.

In Phoenix, AZ, Sr. Margaret Mary McBride, a Sister of Mercy, received no mercy from her local shepherd, Thomas Olmsted: "McBride was an administrator and member of the ethics committee at St. Joseph's Hospital and Medical Center, which is owned by Catholic Healthcare West. In November 2009, the committee was consulted on the case of a 27-year-old woman who was eleven weeks pregnant with her fifth child and suffering from hypertension, her doctors stated that the woman's chance of dying if the pregnancy was allowed to continue was 'close to 100 percent.' McBride joined the ethics committee in approving the decision to terminate the pregnancy through an induced abortion. The abortion took place and the mother survived." (Wikipedia) Sr. Margaret Mary McBride did not. Under pressure from the bishop, she was publicly excommunicated.

Bishop Olmsted has publicly excommunicated more people in the twenty-first century than any other hierarch. He holds the ecclesiastical Guinness record of twelve. Of the twelve, four lived in the Phoenix diocese, under his "pastoral" care.

Many categories exist whereby people are automatically excommunicated without public notice, such as clergy who leave without permission and "attempt marriage." The latest one the RCC has dreamed up is imposed upon any woman who "attempts" to simulate being a priest. The poor, banished daughter of Eve is assured a ticket to hell unless she repents appropriately—and surely not to another so-called "female priest."

In effect, the RCC *creates* situations that instantly—and often permanently—break off a relationship with God. Most religious organizations use some form of banishment or "shunning" of members who deviate from the group's norms. But the RCC is intent on sending those individuals to hell. It acts on the premise that punitive fear is more efficacious than unconditional love in winning over the minds and hearts of sinners.

Think of how ineffective Jesus would have been as a bureaucratic leader of the institutionalized Church. Rather than calling his disciples *away* from fear, he would have been forced to draw them more deeply *into* fear, so they could "get right with God."

"LOVE IS PATIENT" BUT THE ROMAN CHURCH IS NOT
"If suffering alone taught, all the world would be wise,
since everyone suffers. To suffering must be added mourning,
understanding, patience, love, openness and the willingness to
remain vulnerable." – Anne Morrow Lindbergh

The RCC is impatient with Paul's idea that "love is patient." Parents obtain quick results by threatening their children with harsh consequences if they do not behave. The penalty acts as a deterrent, enforcing a code of conduct. To guide children without pressure of punishment takes extreme patience. If they want strict obedience, they will employ fear. If they want personal growth, they will endure long-suffering love.

Totalitarian regimes are founded and maintained on a pervasive reign of fear. Externally, order and conformity prevail. Internally, people are seething. For dissent, there is swift punishment. Democratic and pluralistic societies are sloppy, noisy, and seemingly disorganized, people pulling in all directions. But given the choice, humans will overwhelmingly embrace chaos over order. Much of human history has been written by various forms of dictatorships employed to control people, who in turn pushed the boundaries to be free, no matter the cost. The fight for freedom can become a long nightmare. The 2011 "Arab Spring" in the Middle East demonstrated the risks unarmed persons take to throw off the yoke of state-imposed subservience and suppression.

Before the fall of the wall, Berlin was a metaphor of fear versus freedom in its two contrasting societies. In East Berlin, conformity was essential. The streets were eerily quiet, with omnipresent military personnel maintaining order. Shops and restaurants offered limited selections, cars all looked the same. People were muted in speech, clothes were minimal in style and color, facial expressions were almost unalterably similar. With the fall of night, anxious citizens scurried indoors. In West Berlin, life was chaotic and vibrant. The streets seemed brighter by night than by day. Noise from traffic and pedestrians made it difficult to sleep. Color was everywhere in the variety of clothing, buildings, vehicles. Abundant offerings awaited consumers in stores and restaurants. Chaos seemed to take over. The few police brought out the worst in some.

Who would have freely chosen East Berlin over West? The colorful chaos of the West seemed more life-inducing than the drab order of the East. How many sought to flee West Berlin for East? Which side built the wall to trap its people?

In a parable of Jesus, weeds are found growing among the wheat. The field hands ask the master if they should pull up the weeds. The master tells them not to, lest they also pull up the wheat. Let it go till harvest time, he directs them, when harvesters will separate the two, throwing weeds into the fire and bringing wheat into the barn. Some misinterpret this parable, latching onto the reference of throwing weeds into the fire, warning of the looming hell. That subverts the main point of the parable, don't preemptively dig up what may look like weeds but indeed is wheat. Jesus offers liberating new wine here. Don't be in a rush. Love is patient.

But the RCC preferred to follow the instruction of Augustine, who held that "error has no right to exist," taking his teaching as a green light to root out and burn all those it judged to be weeds. It wouldn't tolerate diversity of opinion or action. And it did so with gusto when it sanctioned inquisitions that took countless lives. With those very acts, the RCC itself became "the weeds." While there may be a human limitation for tolerance, violence is not the solution. Love is patient, Paul claims, adding that love is not provoked; it bears all things, endures all things. The Church itself regularly failed Paul's love test.

Jesus said, "I have come to cast fire upon the earth, and would that it was enkindled." (Lk 12:49) The *fire* here is a metaphor not for the fire of hell but for the fire of love. The Roman Church has worked tirelessly to smother the fire Jesus cast, with its reigns of terror, its creation of new mortal sin opportunities, its bondage of members, its enforcement of the sacraments. Being the largest Christian sect, it has a long history of subjecting the masses to unnecessary suffering, to its theology of fear. But *most* Christian sects have used fear to some degree. Their members should exorcise their own theology of fear and replace it with the new wine of unconditional love.

Otherwise, what is the point of *any* Christian sect? It becomes simply a religious tribal club, keeping anxious believers in bondage.

CHAPTER FOUR

THE AFTERLIFE:
LIVING IN FEAR OF THE FUTURE

"Fear not for the future, weep not for the past."
– Percy Bysshe Shelley

Is the afterlife a figment of the collective human imagination? Is it all make-believe? The idea certainly challenges our faculties. Norwegian painter Edvard Munch (best known for "The Scream") admitted this: "I find it difficult to imagine an afterlife, such as Christians, or at any rate many religious people, conceive it, believing that the conversations with relatives and friends interrupted here on earth will be continued in the hereafter."

Not so in RCC folklore. Many saints were privy to visions of what lay beyond. He is not exactly a household name, but Drithelm of Northumbria (now northern England) supposedly died and experienced a powerful vision of heaven, hell, and purgatory—then was found to be alive. Following this astonishing experience, he gave up all his wealth, divided his possessions among his wife and children, and became a monk, spending the rest of his resurrected life in austerity until his actual death (700 CE).

These types of tales were circulated by the RCC to inspire an illiterate people to keep before them the encroaching afterlife and the looming possibility of either eternal blessing or eternal damnation. The RCC has a penchant for stirring things up, promoting unconfirmed accounts, allowing superstitious interpretations to flourish. It keeps the faithful interested in (and worried about) the afterlife.

EXISTENCE BEFORE LIFE AND AFTER LIFE
"Being religious means asking passionately the question of the meaning of our existence and being willing to receive answers, even if the answers hurt." – Paul Tillich

Attempts by some to contact their beloved dead through séances stem from a desire to continue relating to loved ones, but also a hope there is life after death. Others seek to regress to a former life through hypnosis. Take the case of a Colorado woman, Virginia Tighe, who believed she was another Irish woman, Bridey Murphy, in a former life. Some groups (Hinduism, Jainism, Sikhism, and Buddhism) as well as some Greek philosophies believe humans have previous lives. Mainstream Judaism, Christianity, and Islam reject this idea but some offshoots (Kabbalah, the Cathars, the Alawi, the Druze, and Rosicrucians) dissent, as do many tribal societies that believe in reincarnation.

The Roman philosopher Pliny held there was neither a life after death, nor a life before this life. "The period after your last day is precisely the same as the period before your first day: neither body nor mind has any more sensation after death than it had before birth." [61] Pliny noted we don't extend an afterlife to animals, so no need to think there is one for humans, "as if man's method of breathing differs in some way from that of other animals." [62]

While Jews tend to be nebulous about the afterlife, Christians and Muslims offer quite colorful and detailed visions, their imaginations at times spinning out of control in their zeal. Now on my last lap of life, those scenarios once inculcated into me are more frightening than comforting. Bloodcurdling ideas I glibly believed in younger years now take their place in a horror show about to commence. Even if I were to make it to heaven, knowing that somewhere there is also a purgatory full of "temporary" torture (for centuries perhaps?), plus a hell full of eternally relentless torture, would be far from consoling as a catastrophic climax to my existence.

I have to debrief myself. It is hard to divine a deity who would orchestrate a perpetual "house of horrors." Such a monster god, alas, would get support from some who relish the notion that *others* will have an eternal sentence of nonstop anguish and agony.

Conversely, Universalism, an offshoot of Congregationalism, envisioned reconciliation between the divine and human. It's the RCC's permanent sentence to hell that's disturbing. A Pequot Indian who became a Methodist minister reasoned, "If [sinners] repent, why will God not let them out again?"

Of course, to the RCC such notions equal heretical thinking. It teaches that the sentence to hell is irrevocable. So while preaching God's unconditional love, it holds, in tandem, that hell's torment will be without end. Doesn't it see the cognitive dissonance there?

Heaven is much more difficult for Catholics to access than hell. The opportunity for endless mortal sins, the anxiety over obtaining and retaining grace, the need to work out salvation in fear and trembling—despite the insurance policy created when Jesus died to save all—keeps them on edge, wondering what's behind the curtain. Many lapsed Romans fearfully capitulate to the refurbished "Last Rites," the Anointing of the Sick. But since the number seeking deathbed solace has declined, does this indicate more are putting aside childish things?

A Church that maintains belief in hideous devils and everlasting torment conditions members to remain continually anxious. Earthly existence creates enough anxiety without religious institutions piling on more angst. In 2010, more than 46 million Americans were taking anti-anxiety medications such as Xanax and Ativan. In a *New York Times* op-ed on our age of anxiety, author Daniel Smith notes that fourteenth-century Europe was an era of "psychic torment," possibly "even more jittery than ours," with devastating famines, pillaging mercenaries, peasant revolts, a plague that wiped out half the population—and, religious turmoil. "Nor did the monolithic presence of the Church necessarily help; it might even have made things worse. A firm belief in God and heaven was near-universal, but so was a firm belief in their opposites: the Devil and hell. And you could never be certain in which direction you were headed." [63]

Sounds like contemporary Catholicism. Six centuries later, the II Vatican Council attempted to respond to "the signs of the times," but this threatened the old guard of the Curia. Lest anyone think the RCC has changed in any way at all, a quick read of the *Catholic Catechism* will prove otherwise. It states that members must believe in God *and* in Satan. Both are equally eternal. Satan rules the domain of the damned, and God, the realm of the blessed. Nowadays, belief in a god or gods is rejected by a hefty portion of humanity. It would be more significant if a good portion rejected belief in the Devil and his unholy terror squad.

Many already do. One 2009 study found that 40 percent of Christian participants said they "strongly agree" that "Satan is not a living being but is a symbol of evil." And 19 percent said they "agree somewhat" with that perspective. A minority (35 percent) disagreed with the statement, indicating they believe Satan is real, and the remaining 8 percent were not sure what they believe. [64] The RCC insists on steadfast belief in this dastardly character. Check out the *Catholic Catechism for Adults*, page 55.

Millions of Catholics who use birth control commit mortal sin in doing so. Hence, the *Catholic Catechism* labels most adult members as hell-bound, the Council notwithstanding, and schedules their personal appointments with the Devil.

In its recent healthcare legislation, the Obama administration mandated that religious institutions must provide participants access to contraceptives. The RCC responded with a thunderous roar that this was a denial of religious liberty. The law does not *force* people to use contraceptives, just *gives access* to contraceptives. Meanwhile, a near-universal acceptance of contraceptives is seen in Catholic couples as well as sexually active Catholic women. And countless Catholic males regularly wear condoms. They are not rushing to confession, though, to plead guilty. Besides, they would not receive absolution if they intended to keep using birth control methods, due to "the power of the keys." For a little fleeting pleasure, eternal torture and fire await the many.

Despite "the signs of the times," which we know provide greater understanding of human psychology and biology, the RCC asserts its one-and-only interpretation, and trumps informed understanding achieved by the secular world. The *Catechism* reinforces the ever-present chance for mortal sin and eternal damnation. While Jesus saved everyone from the grip of the "Prince of this World," those who fail to cooperate with this saving grace are damned nonetheless. Ultimately, we have to save ourselves.

Would not Pliny's assertion that no sensation will occur after death be more consoling and gracious than the overwrought scenario the RCC has imposed upon the hapless faithful through the centuries? The message is clear—fear permeates this life and defines the one beyond.

Given the approaching apocalypse, one can only shudder at a horrific future. No wonder people cling to life here, even with its endless suffering, and, in the words of Dylan Thomas, "rage, rage against the dying of the light." For, the Devil you know here is better than the Devil you don't know there.

This life is of no great interest to the RCC. It is only a stepping stone to the next, the afterlife being the only "real" life. That is the institution's ultimate priority, continually badgering members to anxiously ask themselves, "Where will I go?" Then it conveniently spells out three clear and distinct options (in order of importance): hell, purgatory, or heaven. A fourth, limbo, is now crossed off the list.

HELL
"To judge from the notions expounded by theologians, one must conclude that God created most men simply with a view to crowding hell." – Marquis de Sade

In Judaism, the concept of hell was murky, vague, and ill-defined. In time, Catholicism provided graphic details than would outdo the imagination of a Stephen King. Catholics have a penchant to be visionaries (contending with UFO observers), more frequently involving sightings of Mary, but also eyewitness accounts of hell.

The latest, Sr. Faustina Kowalska, provides a vivid report: "Today, I was led by an Angel to the chasms of hell. It is a place of great torture ... The kinds of tortures I saw: the first torture that constitutes hell is

95

the loss of God; the second is perpetual remorse of conscience; the third is that one's condition will never change; the fourth is the fire that will penetrate the soul without destroying it, a terrible suffering, since it is a purely spiritual fire, lit by God's anger; the fifth torture is conditional darkness and a terrible suffocating smell, and despite the darkness, the devils and the souls of the damned see each other and all the evil, both of others and their own; *the sixth torture is the constant company of Satan*; the seventh torture is horrible despair, hatred of God, vile words, curses and blasphemies. These are the tortures suffered by all the damned together, but that is not the end of the sufferings. There are special tortures destined for particular souls. These are the torments of the senses ... There are caverns and pits of torture where one form of agony differs from another. I would have died at the very sight of these tortures if the omnipotence of God had not supported me. Let the sinner know that he will be tortured throughout all eternity ... I am writing this at the command of God, so that no soul may find an excuse by saying there is no hell, or that nobody has ever been there ... *I, sister Faustina, by the order of God, have visited the abysses of hell so that I might tell souls about it and testify to its existence.* I cannot speak about it now; but I have received a command from God to leave it in writing ... What I have written is but a pale shadow of the things I saw. But I noticed one thing: that most of the souls there are those who disbelieved that there is a hell. When I came to, I could hardly recover from the fright ... Consequently, I pray even more fervently for the conversion of sinners. I incessantly plead God's mercy upon them." [65] (Emphasis added)

The Church's promotion of her writings—which are even more authoritative since it sainted her—upholds its tradition of terrorizing simple, sincere souls. Many lampoon her words as utter claptrap, but the greater legion are unquestioning, uncritical persons from whom fear has not been exorcised.

Faustina claims when she came to, she could hardly recover from the fright. She evidently did, continuing in the mundane life of a religious sister. After such an experience, how could one go back to any form of "normal" life, mundane or marvelous? Hard to imagine her returning to light housekeeping in the convent. It would seem, rather, that the experience would have driven her mad.

Preaching on hell was a favorite of Catholic teachers, but their imaginations conjured up a place they had never visited. This motivated sorry souls to continually return to confession in order to (once again) be rescued from the fate of the fiery pit.

James T. Farrell captured the Catholicism I was exposed to growing up. Particularly vulnerable were the impressionable young. His character, Studs Lonigan, describes one preacher: "Alas, my dear young friends, you must move down the hard and stony paths of life ... the primrose path to the everlasting bonfire; sown with the flowers and fruits of the Devil, bounded by beautiful rose bushes behind which hides old Nick and his fallen angels; the foxy, the sly and foxy hordes of hell. You must beware of old Nick, and you must not allow him to snare your souls. Old Nick, the Devil, is tricky, full of the blarney, as they say in the old country ... He will always make false promises to you; he will seek to deceive you with all the pomp and gold and glory of this world. He is a master of artifice, and he will pay your price in this ... if you will pay his price in the next world; where Hell hisses and yawns, and the damned suffer as no earthly being can or has suffered." [66]

Lonigan's depiction was almost humorous, but more fearful descriptions were the norm, as seen in Merrie Ann Nall's book about a religious order: "At that time, Catholic revivals were common and often specifically targeted children with graphic accounts of the plight of unrepentant sinners burning in the fires of hell for all eternity. Thoughts of suffering souls condemned to eternal damnation affected Mary deeply, and she eventually became scrupulous—ultrasensitive to even the possibility to sin...she maintained no good Catholic could use a frying pan for fish that had been used for meat. Years later, her own experience of the detrimental effect that such a great fear of sin and punishment could have on the hearts and minds of young children led Mary to write that instead of emphasizing the fear of God, children should learn of Christ." [67]

A prayer the RCC recited at the Mass for the Dead provided little comfort to those in the pews. "Deliver me, O Lord, from eternal death in that tremendous day when the heavens and the earth shall be shaken, when thou shall come to judge the world with fire. Seized am

I with trembling, and I fear that approaching trial, and that wrath to come. O that day, that day of wrath, of calamity and misery, that great and bitter day indeed, when Thou shall come to judge the world with fire." [68] Blessedly, the prayer was in Latin, so most were unaware of its intended apprehension.

Vatican II toned down scare tactics. Preachers and teachers no longer subject captive audiences to this nonsense—except among traditionalist groups revived by John Paul II and Benedict XVI. For them, hell is still harrowingly real, and they are not embarrassed to return to the fiery rhetoric of old. They promote Faustina to restore what Vatican II downplayed. They claim the world has lost its sense of sin, and they would be remiss in their pastoral duties if they failed to regularly remind members of the unquenchable fires of hell.

In the movie *Groundhog Day*, Bill Murray plays a weatherman assigned to cover the Groundhog Day event in Punxsutawney, PA. He's been living a selfish and hedonistic life, has even attempted suicide. He suddenly finds he is forced to repeat the same day over and over again until he gets his priorities right. This sounds like a narrative of reincarnation as found in Hinduism, Jainism, and Sikhism, and of rebirth in Buddhism. This universal concept is found in cultures from Australia to Siberia, supporting the notion that humans can rejuvenate themselves to get their priorities right.

This image is certainly more merciful than the RCC's hell, where there is no escape, no recourse, no higher appeal—where all decisions are final. Teaching hell, especially to children, effectively injects terror for lifetime. It is difficult to extract the roots of this horrific concept. If mercy and love were motivating factors, the archaic idea of spending eternity with the Devil and his minions in a blazing underworld would have been exorcised by the RCC long, long ago. But its sinister imagination adds fuel to the fire and conjures up the worst possible scenario, with the goal of manipulating rather than consoling, beginning with impressionable children.

Richard Westley describes how disturbed his eight-year-old daughter was one evening as they prepared dinner. Tears streamed down her face. "Oh Daddy, I'm scared," she cried. He took her into her arms and asked solicitously, "Now, Ruth, what are you so scared about?" Still sobbing, she managed to say, "Daddy, I'm scared I am going to hell!" [69] She had been introduced to hell by her religious school teacher that day. And the RCC would heartily approve, since the desired response was obtained. It wouldn't think of reprimanding the teacher for mentally abusing an innocent child.

Westley refers to philosopher/theologian Søren Kierkegaard's observation that a wrong perspective from youth can lead to a life of distortion. This warning should be applied to all children indoctrinated by any ideology before their critical faculties have developed. Rather than frightening the most vulnerable, we should be inoculating them from terror. Civil societies have finally condemned sexual activity with minors. They haven't matured physically, emotionally, intellectually, or legally—they are not consenting adults. Shouldn't societies condemn mental abuse of minors when they are indoctrinated with theological horror stories?

Scaring vulnerable children with tales of the Devil can only be a form of child abuse. Children are susceptible listeners and gullibly believe what adults say. It is beneficial to begin at an age-appropriate level in explaining the nature of evil. But tying it to a free agent who prowls around tempting and seducing mere babes represents just one more harrowing lesson from the theology of fear. Yet this has been the standard catechesis for Catholic children.

Mario Valentini, writing of his childhood in Italy, describes how in preparation for First Communion, his uncle, a priest, informed him and his classmates of an even greater fear. "'Next week I will you tell about something worse—something more dangerous and more powerful than *Lucifero*,' my uncle repeats." Mario and his little classmates are overwhelmed: *"Something worse than the devil? How could it be?* What he has said throws into confusion everything we've been taught. What could be worse than the worst of all the demons?" The kids badger him to reveal what could be worse than Satan. He won't relent except to say, "Next week." [70] (Rest assured the answer will be given in an upcoming chapter!)

Hell, devils, eternal fire, unimaginable pain—this was the stuff of the elementary classroom. In Mario's case, he and his classmates were preparing for their First Communion. One would think the orientation would be entirely focused on this positive encounter with the Jesus, on this faith in the Eucharist. But no—the theology of fear permeated and dominated even such a joyful occasion.

Becki Ianni was effectively indoctrinated into the terror of hell at the tender age of eight when her parish priest, Fr. William Reinecke, began to sexually abuse her. An online account reported that "during her testimony last January in Richmond, Ianni recalls telling the lawmakers how Reinecke told her, 'I would go to hell if I told anyone.' She said she thought it was her fault. 'I thought I was a bad, silly little girl and I was being punished.'" [71] Ianni suppressed these memories for forty years, so fearfully did Reinecke convince her. (He subsequently committed suicide.)

Westley offers a solution: "We must have or acquire the courage and strength to tear ourselves out of the error." We need to "somehow find the strength to tear ourselves away from thinking and talking about hell, devils and all that. It is unnecessary and is positively harmful to boot. And we must resist the temptation to give credence to the resurgent stories of the fundamentalists on those issues." [72]

Apocalypticism, mentioned earlier, is a thread woven through both Jewish and Christian scriptures. Jesus was an apocalyptic believer, stressing the Kingdom of God was imminent, though it wasn't realized in his lifetime. New Testament scholar Bart Ehrman writes, "Out of the ashes of failed apocalyptic expectation there arose the Christian doctrine of heaven and hell." [73]

The Apostles' Creed references hell, but only after Jesus was crucified, died, and was buried, when "he descended into hell." Why did he visit hell? (It evidently *does* have an exit.) In contrast, *The Nicene Creed* doesn't even mention hell.

I recall a nun spending much time instilling in us the eternal tortures of hell. There would be no end to its horror chambers. The imagery she used is still with me, though fortunately I have been able to tear myself away from her original terrifying tale. Her teaching certainly was effective—more than sixty years later I still remember it. This nun was otherwise a conscientious teacher, but the Roman tradition was keen in inculcating everlasting fear—and good, simple, but unquestioning women like her obediently instructed us with scary ghost stories.

The RCC boasts repeatedly of its majestic sense of tradition, but it has no deeper tradition than impounding fear into naive, susceptible believers. Its intent has long been to scare humankind into doing good and avoiding evil, since sin came into the world through fictional first parents, Adam and Eve. The pedagogy of fear was skillfully and persistently employed, implying that humans could not be motivated by love to avoid evil, that evil was ultimately stronger than love. Though Jesus' mission statement was to liberate people, the RCC ignored it. Instead it imprisoned people, warning them to beware of the "Prince of this World."

Still, the gospels offer eleven references in which Jesus refers to hell, and even torture, "with its unquenchable fire." In other instances, he says there will be eternal punishment in the afterlife. (Mt 25 and Lk 16) How do we reconcile this with Jesus' teaching on liberation and love? As noted, Jesus never wrote anything. Others formed the gospels and put words in his mouth. Certainly parts of the gospels can be consumed as new wine, but a lot of old wine is mixed in. Strains other than Judaism may have seeped into the potion, diluting what might have been the original words of Jesus. Zoroastrian eschatology and demonology circulated in Palestine, and with them the descriptive worldview of a battle between good and evil. Jesus' new wine distinguishes itself from tradition. To understand the power and dynamic of the new commandment Jesus gave, we need to strain the juice from the pulp, and as Westley says, to "find the strength to tear ourselves away from thinking and talking about hell, devils and all that." [74]

To love, especially to love one's enemy, is new wine. This has not exactly flourished in the history of a fear-driven humanity. Revenge, torture, and murder continue to plague us, and all we have to turn to is a pedagogy of fear. To have faith is to imagine a new way of responding, rejecting motivation by fear. The new wine of perfect love is an inducement to tear away from the old, to move beyond uncontrolled, primitive urges. "Now that I am an adult, I put away childish things." (1 Cor 13:11)

In Exodus, Yahweh sends an avenging angel in his name to the Egyptians. "But if you truly obey his voice and do all that I say, then I will be an enemy to your enemies and an adversary to your adversaries." (Ex 23:22) This is one of many texts that serve old wine. The new wine of loving the enemy is a radical break and a refreshing relief. It is humanly possible for people to change their behavior toward those who have hurt them. Does an almighty God have less capacity for change?

People often generalize that the Christian scriptures are all about love, conveniently forgetting embarrassing episodes of violence, as found in the Jewish and Muslim scriptures. In the gospels, violence is not blatant and overt, but it is clearly yet subtly present. Hector Avalos, author of *Fighting Words: The Origins of Religious Violence*, contends the Christian scriptures' attitude toward violence is "deferred." In the end, God will get you! In reviewing the moving parable of Matthew 25, where concern for "the least ones" is the basis for judgment as a disciple, Avalos holds the judgment described is nothing but an act of revenge. When the sheep and goats are separated, a vindictive wrath is heaped upon the goats. [75] "Depart from me, you who are cursed, into the eternal fire prepared for the devil and his angels." (Mt 25:61)

Matthew 25 underscores the judgment of discipleship is based on how we care for the least among us, the vulnerable. But tacking on a condemnation to hell for all who fail to comply assumes they cannot be motivated to join in solidarity with "the least ones" except for fear of damnation. Some people, however, *are* motivated toward solidarity through love of the other. In 1 Corinthians 13, Paul notes, "If I give all I have to the poor, but do not have love, it profits me nothing." So, Paul might argue, if a person feeds the hungry from fear of being separated at the end as a goat from the sheep and thrown into the everlasting fire prepared by the Devil and his angels—not from love of the hungry people—it does the person no good. Only love is the pure and lasting motivator. If there is no new wine in Jesus, then we must look to other sources to tame our inhumanity.

Despite all our reservations, many of us secretly sanction the existence of a hell. We humans have an innate desire for fairness. If it is not experienced in the here and now, then hell is the last hope for justice. But when we disdain this world and consider the life to come as the only important one, we have less inclination to pursue justice here, even allowing injustice to flourish. The Kingdom's beatitude to hunger and thirst for righteousness (Mt 5:16) is meant for the *here and now*, not some future world.

It is those who value this world who have been instrumental in doing what is right, standing up for justice, creating a body of laws now international in scope. Historically, people didn't see beyond their own tribe, beyond their own country. Now we live in a universal society, a global village. What happens in one locale affects the whole world. In 1945 the International Court of Justice, under UN auspices, came into being to settle disputes considered motives for war. In 2002 the International Criminal Court emerged to try the perpetrators of war crimes, genocide, crimes against humanity, allowing victims to see justice done. These secular institutions reflect the Kingdom's thirst for righteousness, here and now.

The movement for human rights, securing equal treatment and freedom for all persons, has become virtually universal in scope. Minorities, victimized and suppressed throughout history, have in many nations gained the legal equality previously denied them. Laws in many countries are being rewritten to expand on liberty, equality, civil rights. Individuals are being held accountable to laws safeguarding the common good. Such progressive movements indicate that people can be motivated to act for the good without coercion, force, or fear. Justice is the minimum demand of love. Brakes are continually being applied on revenge, torture, and murder, the pressure supplied by people who love this world. Many are less interested in "a pound of flesh" than justice, see nothing gained by the death of a sinner.

The RCC not only failed to notice such hunger and thirst for justice, but it also redirected its members not to take this life seriously, to focus on an imagined one to come. And it not only failed to implement the Beatitudes, but it also was too often the cause and perpetrator of the injustices they decry. If we were focused on righteousness here on earth, we would have less interest in a hell where we could consign others eternally. Laws regulate our external behaviors, but again, the new wine of Jesus challenges us to look to our internal attitudes, our motivations and desires: "Whoever looks with lust upon a woman has already committed adultery in his heart." (Mt 5:28) Martin Luther King, Jr. realized the limitations even of good and just laws: "It may be true that the law cannot make a man love me, but it can stop him from lynching me, and I think that's pretty important." [76] Would that the RCC emphasized the internal law written in the heart, and supported society in controlling external behavior.

Perhaps no one has more eloquently put to rest the notion of heaven and hell than Ron Williamson, who was tortured by his fellow citizens and unjustly executed. As John Grisham notes in his nonfiction book, *The Innocent Man,* Williamson wrote at the end, "I hope I go to neither heaven nor hell. I wish that at the time of my death that I could go to sleep and never wake up and never have a bad dream. Eternal rest, like you've seen on some tombstones, that's what I hope for. Because I don't want to go through judgment. I don't want anybody judging me again. I asked myself what was the reason for my birth when I was on death row, if I was going to go through all that, what was even the reason for my birth? I almost cursed my mother and did—it was so bad—for putting me on this earth. If I had it all to do over again, I wouldn't be born." [77]

This is but the cry of Job: "Let the day perish in which I was born .... why did I not die at birth, come forth from the womb and expire ... O why was I not buried like a stillborn child, like an infant that never sees the light?" (Job 3:16)

PURGATORY
"As soon as a coin in the coffer rings, a soul from purgatory springs." – Johann Tetzel

Supposedly, the sacraments are channels of grace, and supposedly, Catholics strive to always be in the state of grace (well, especially at the time of death). But grace doesn't suffice, doesn't automatically guarantee a fast track to heaven—another theological *Catch-22*. Evidently, even the state of grace is a state of imperfection.

Therefore, a further purification is required. Enter purgatory, which interestingly, is a *process*, not a *place* (unlike the other afterlife options), claims the RCC. Evidently, no one instructed Faustina about this: "I saw my Guardian Angel, who ordered me to follow him. In a moment *I was in a misty place* full of fire in which there was a great crowd of suffering souls. They were praying fervently, but to no avail, for themselves; only we can come to their aid. The flames, which were burning them, did not touch me at all. My Guardian Angel did not leave me for an instant." (Emphasis added) [78]

So when/how does this purifying process take place, and why are members implored to pray for the "poor souls" forced to go through it? The theology of fear successfully keeps us on cosmic tether hooks. Holy Mother the Church wants to hang onto that control it has over us, even in death—even *after* death. Like a nagging mother, it won't let go—can't stop bringing up every little fault (or suggesting helpful solutions). True, dying with a little leftover venial sin on our soul won't dispatch us to hell forever, as will mortal sin, but it might keep us from going directly to heaven. To enter the pearly gates, we have to be thoroughly purified, uncontaminated by any earthly detritus. One teeny venial sin, like a speck of sand, could well screw things up and bump us from the express lane to heaven. No matter how hard we try to love or do good, Holy Mother's theology of fear keeps us in a constant state of spiritual angst.

Purgatory, not the place but the process, is a required service providing the necessary purification treatment for even one venial sin. It is a state of temporal punishment, though complete with blazing fires and horrifying dungeons. The good news is that a soul about to undergo this institutionalized procedure, with its roaring infernos and bloodcurdling screams, will be comforted by the notion that it's only a *temporary* hot patch (I'm surmising) before heaven. How long it will take, only God knows. There are no parole meetings to plead for early release. Whenever God decides he is good and satisfied, the cleansed and scoured soul will be redeemed.

The formulation of purgatory wasn't announced until the early medieval period, between 1100 and 1300. (At least some believers were spared the anxiety.) In this vale of tears, a purging process was invented and members were instructed to pray ceaselessly for "the poor souls in purgatory." That anxious prayer is still robust today, a constant refrain in the rosary.

It is an interesting sociological observation that when people write their loved ones' obituaries, they *always* consign them to heaven—never to purgatory (or hell!). Purgatory may be important in the eyes of hierarchs, but not in the popular imagination of believers. The RCC's overwhelmingly belief in purgatory is just another extension of its theology of fear. Its unwillingness to liberate people from their fears of the afterlife demonstrates its determination to control souls even beyond the here and now.

Protestants generally reject the idea of purgatory, and non-Christian religious tribes only allude to some vague notion of a purification process. But the RCC pontificates at great length on this temporal process, ultimately reinforcing its permanence in our minds. How and when can one escape this Catholic-based purgatory? How *temporal* is temporal? What venial sins are so deadly that they deserve a taste of hell's flames and tortures? Who knows? The dead are kept in suspended animation—and so are the living. Purgatory creates angst in the living. People realize their deceased loved ones or friends, while decent human beings, were not without their flaws and peccadilloes, and thus prime candidates for a hot stint. To envision the dead as enduring purifying torture can only unnerve the living, if they take this to heart.

The RCC doesn't distribute free "get-out-of-jail" cards. Instead, it burdens the living with the added religious responsibilities—atop so many others—to intervene and bring relief. And, incredibly, the obliging believers will never be certain their actions were successful. They must remain in the trenches, ceaselessly praying for the dead, offering masses, earning indulgences. Admittedly, praying for one's deceased relatives is an ancient tradition, as in the Chinese ritual of praying to the ancestors. But for Catholics, the reason is to reduce their sentence, to petition the celestial parole board—or so we are instructed. The RCC capitalizes on purgatory as a means of yoking the living to the dead in a vise of fear—not just fondly remembering them, but desperately begging for their discharge.

Are some prayers more conducive to releasing the dead, terminating their temporal sentence? Having masses said is promoted as the more salutary, efficacious form of petition. But masses come with a price. The faithful have to shell out a monetary contribution or other offering. For those with low incomes, this is a financial imposition that, faced with the theology of fear, they are compelled to endure.

As it turned out, purgatory became a real moneymaker by the Middle Ages. Roman clergy managed to successfully live off the dead. Stipends paid for masses to be said for the departed were a means of income. "Mass priests" said back-to-back masses each day in exchange for monetary offerings. This was their sole responsibility— breadwinners for the community. To bring in more cash, masses were designated as "high" (singing included) or "low" (purely recited). Of course, the high mass cost more, but it was advertised as more speedy and efficient in ejecting the poor souls. This easily evolved into a mathematical formula, a financial game.

A contemporary twist to that game allowed believers a higher volume of masses said at a lower rate. Several times a week in my Baltimore parish, a mass was said for a couple who had died years before my arrival, "August and Augusta Bopp," which came at $2 a pop. A two-for-one. They had wisely requested regular $2 low masses, ensuring continual prayers after their deaths in case they ended up being "processed" in purgatory without anyone left to pray for them. By leaving money in their will for continuous masses, they managed to cover all the bases, hoping the hired prayers of some future priest would spring them from imposed agony.

"Perpetual Mass Cards" became big moneymakers in the USA. This scheme added the name of the deceased to an existing list, to be remembered under a general rubric like "for all our faithful departed" or some other vaguely worded cover. Purchasing one Perpetual Mass Card guaranteed the deceased would join the club and be remembered collectively (unlike Mr. and Mrs. Bopp's $2 mass stipend, which bought the exclusive grace of a particular mass). Masses for the dead were a kind of death insurance, promising "get-out-of-purgatory" cards on some future date. Until Vatican II, daily masses were generally requiem masses to facilitate the purgatory industry. This strange and arcane practice (or quackery) of awarding indulgences, exclusively promoted by the RCC, is complex and difficult to comprehend. Better to expend brain power on the problem of evil than the rubbish of indulgence. Wasting time on this idiocy ought to be a mortal sin.

And yet another paradox exists. An indulgence is remission of "punishment due" for sins that have *already* been forgiven (supposedly). Another ecclesiastical *Catch-22*. While still alive, the pilgrim had confessed, done penance, been absolved. The sins had been forgiven. The soul had been wiped clean. But hold on. After death, it suddenly needs more cleaning. And luckily, indulgences can reduce the afterlife's cleaning process. Sins are hardly "forgiven" then, if a surtax is attached in the form of temporal punishment due.

I don't think even Jesus himself, divinely intelligent and having a high human IQ, could have fathomed this convoluted, twisted logic. It makes great sense, though, in the context of a theology of fear that is resistant to liberation, even from purgatory. "If you can't convince them, confuse them!"

Lest anyone think this is a medieval theological sideshow, note that during the relatively recent reign of Pope Paul VI (1963-1978), indulgences were kept alive with some modern updating. He introduced the expression *partial indulgence*, indicating the person who benefitted from the pious action is granted "in addition to the remission of temporal punishment acquired by the action itself, an equal remission of punishment through the intervention of the Church." That clarifies it!

St. Peter's Basilica in the Vatican is a magnificent obscenity, a monumental symbol of the RCC's use of indulgences as fundraisers through its theology of fear. The costly undertaking of building St. Peter's required a steady stream of funds. Selling indulgences to the simple faithful perturbed over the status of their dearly departed tapped into their fears and became a cash cow for the building fund.

Martin Luther railed against this papal simoniacal abuse. He attributed the campaign slogan, "As soon as a coin in the coffer rings, a soul from purgatory springs" (Thesis 28), to the Dominican indulgence huckster, Johann Tetzel. Luther, in one of his celebrated ninety-five theses, charged the pope should pick up the tab for St. Peter's by dipping into his personal wealth. Luther's attack should have made him fodder for a bonfire, but fortunately he had political protectors. The ultimate cost of St. Peter's contributed greatly to the Protestant Reformation. We are still paying the price.

The Hindu concept of reincarnation—returning to life in another form to be purified for a higher level of existence—is a more welcome situation. It beats a blazing purgatory where one is dependent upon the actions of others back on earth, humans who are busy, distracted, or forgetful. As least if we are recycled we can be our own agents, like Bill Murray in *Groundhog Day*, to get it right of our own accord.

If the RCC wanted to reduce the fear factors plaguing its twisted theology, it would be a sign of a conversion, a change of heart, to shut down the purgatory production lines. With the power of the pen along with the power of the keys, popes can do as they please. Perhaps a Vatican decree will be forthcoming, terminating the license for purgatory's continuing operation. It happened before. Limbo was put out of business by Benedict XVI, effective April 20, 2007. He needs to continue the roll that he started with limbo.

LIMBO
***"Being on tour is like being in limbo.
It's like going from nowhere to nowhere." – Bob Dylan***

One of Benedict XVI's stunning feats was to shut down limbo. For centuries until that moment, it was a real place envisioned and sanctioned by the Church—and vividly imagined and feared by family members the minute a child was born.

Like purgatory, limbo was created during the early medieval period. For centuries, parents feared for the fate of their non-baptized offspring. Finally, Anselm of Canterbury (1033-1109 CE) devised the "twilight theology" of limbo—a place where non-baptized infants hung outside the border of heaven, free from the tortures of hell, but deprived of ever seeing God.

Limbo existed until Benedict XVI issued his forty-one-page declaration repudiating it. Unfortunately, this didn't positively identify the whereabouts of all those souls consigned to limbo over the centuries. It was only a hope—not a certainty—that they would now see God's face. Though the RCC claims infallibility, it wouldn't declare infallibly that these infants were saved and give anxious parents some peace. A lingering dread remains in those who failed to have their infants baptized before their untimely deaths. This anxiety especially affects simple, sincere persons—"the little ones."

A 2007 *Slate* piece analyzes this quandary: "If limbo never existed in the first place, you might assume that these souls passed straight through St. Peter's gates. But the carefully worded document from the Vatican's International Theological Commission stops short of certainty in this regard, arguing only that there are 'serious theological and liturgical grounds for hope,' rather than 'sure knowledge.'" And though the Vatican has effectively done an about-face, "it won't directly state that limbo never existed. Instead, it said that official church dogma never included the concept and that limbo remains 'a possible theological hypothesis.' Why the hemming and hawing? An outright reversal would go against hundreds of years of theological interpretation." [79]

So in its vaguely worded statement detaching itself from limbo, the RCC continued to use the fear factor to control gullible people. If it truly were an agent of liberation, it wouldn't keep members in limbo. Benedict's declaration effectively said there are serious theological and liturgical grounds for maintaining fear. And he has done little to calm that fear since then, even among educated Catholics.

In a 2011 edition of *St. Anthony Messenger*, a pitiable and thoroughly unnecessary letter is addressed by Fr. Pat McCloskey via his column, *Ask a Franciscan*. He headlines the letter, "A Question That Keeps Recurring." This in itself reveals the anxiety remaining when an institution fails to unequivocally communicate otherwise. The distraught writer has an agonizing question: "Although I've been a Catholic all my life, in my twilight years I am encountering several changes that I do not understand. For example, what happened to all those babies who died before being baptized, who died when the Church was teaching about limbo? I had a family member who had a nervous breakdown because a child died before being baptized. Was her worrying all for naught?" [80]

Fr. McCloskey seeks to console the writer: "I have addressed this question several times over the years, but it remains an unresolved issue for many Catholics. How else can we explain why the same question is asked so frequently?" He doesn't question the failure of the institution to unequivocally teach otherwise, doesn't challenge its pedagogy of fear. He concludes by offering a useless bromide: "That family member and the child whose death prompted the worrying were always in God's loving care." [81] Evidently the letter writer didn't sense the certainty of "God's loving care" when the family member had a nervous breakdown.

The RCC distances itself from real life when it imposes teachings and doctrines that severely impair simple, sincere believers. It is quick to pin sins on members' behavior but excuses its *own* behavior when it inflicts suffering on innocent people. Jesus attacked religious leaders for teaching as doctrine mere human precepts. Too many rules the RCC imposes are fabrications, a sinister means of infiltrating minds and hearts. "Whoever causes one of these little ones who believe to stumble, it would be better for him if, with a heavy millstone hung around his neck, he had been cast into the sea." (Mk 9:42)

Sadly, the RCC hangs heavy millstones on the necks of believers already burdened with the horrific misery life can inflict. Those who manufacture more suffering in a world already convulsing with suffering act in an unconscionable manner. The millstones are around the wrong necks.

HEAVEN
"Everyone wants to go to heaven but no one wants to die to get there." – Anonymous

When I was growing up, wakes were social events for adults. It was customary for my Irish immigrant parents to sit in our small kitchen after work for their "happy hour." My mother would sip tea and my father would slowly work on a quart of beer. They would pour over the obituaries ("the Irish sporting pages") in the Chicago *Daily News* to see if they knew anyone, however obliquely. If they spied someone, they had their nightlife. It remains my perception they would attend wakes at least twice a week. After paying respects, the men adjourned to the closest tavern for a drink while the women headed to the corner coffee shop for tea.

As a result of this fond memory, I always read obituaries, in any paper, in any city I find myself. They provide a lot of social data, and they offer a daily meditation upon death—one's imminent passing is only a posting away. At one time, obituaries for the common man read like templates and gave only the facts, as if to say, "Life is short, and inconsequential."

Today, the trend is toward more elaborate narratives, providing colorful commentary beyond the basics. Some people write their own in advance, paying extra for a longer version. They may be dealing with a terminal illness, hitting a "certain age," or just dutifully taking care of business. Or they may simply want to ensure they won't pass unnoticed, their accomplishments forgotten, and so issue a statement that their life counted.

Again, I am struck by the volume of death notices that promote loved ones immediately to heaven. There is often no reference to a religion during life or at death. Nonetheless, heaven is the assigned destination, as if it were not an exclusively religious domain. Often the obits affirm the deceased will be united with loved ones who died, and the living look forward to an eventual heavenly reunion.

The Population Reference Bureau reports the most perennial question it receives asks how many people ever lived. It offers a semi-scientific estimate of almost 108 billion since the dawn of the human race. [82] Obituary writing is a relatively new phenomenon. Those remembered, famous and infamous, are proverbially a drop in the bucket.

Growing up, we were taught that in heaven we would experience the Beatific Vision—seeing God "face-to-face." Young and clueless, we gullibly accepted the idea, but it did little to excite us. It was hard to get a handle on so abstract a concept. Seeing God face-to-face? I imagined everyone sitting in an amphitheater viewing this huge image of a godhead, like a museum piece sans torso, or an oversized Easter Island statue.

Later I would learn that God cannot be anthropomorphized since God is a spirit and spirits don't have human bodies so God can't have a face upon which to gaze for all eternity. "Face-to-face" would become a metaphor for an imagined meeting with the divine, whatever that might be. There is no natural human inclination to contemplate something so vague that lasts for all eternity. Heaven can wait.

Images of heaven are as varied as our human imaginations. We are essentially clueless, as no one has returned to provide a tourist impression (except for dubious Catholic visionaries). Many more depictions of hell are out there. This underscores that fear, more than love, is the preferred motivator.

Again, we turn to Faustina, the recently certified extraterrestrial guide: "November 27, 1936. Today I was in heaven, in spirit, and I saw its unconceivable beauties and the happiness that awaits us after death. I saw how all creatures give ceaseless praise and glory to God … The sight of this great majesty of God, which I came to understand more profoundly and which is worshipped by the heavenly spirits according to their degree of grace and the hierarchies into which they are divided, did not cause my soul to be stricken with terror or fear; no, no, not at all!" [83]

She is much less descriptive of heaven than hell—was there only in spirit, after all—though she was finally free of fear. But alas, even in heaven there is no equality. Spirits are separated by degrees of grace, divided hierarchies—at least according to St. Faustina.

The most popular image of heaven involves a family reunion. This is consoling for some, but it can be tricky. What if certain family members didn't especially like each other? Now they're stuck in the heavenly family circle for all eternity. Might seem more like hell.

Family relationships can be messy, but now they're everlasting. What happens with multiple spouses? Which becomes paired in heaven? Or are all past wives still part of a man's claim? That was the question Sadducees put to Jesus about a woman with multiple husbands, and he rejoined by saying in the resurrection there is neither marriage nor will anyone be given in marriage. Does this mean marriages will be nullified? Couples won't be reunited? Some don't *want* to be trapped with spouses, anyway. They did their time on earth and would find an everlasting reunion a bit much, a punishing sentence even for heaven.

And what will the body be like? Catholics and others believe in a resurrected body. But which body will be the eternal one? If a guy in his younger days had abs that knocked 'em out but in time had a belly to equal the Buddha, which would be his resurrected form? Will the blind see, will the deaf hear, will those who lost erectility arise? Will cellulite and wrinkles be blissfully absent?

Will everyone be part of one big happy tailgate party? Or will they be disappointed, finding some questionable souls there while missing worthy ones who didn't make the cut? Will their grief over those assigned elsewhere affect their feelings for all eternity?

The Latter-Day Saints are strongly family-oriented and look forward to the family reunion in heaven, but it may be complicated, given polygamy was once their norm (and is still practiced). And Mormonism condemns homosexuality. Will the absence of gay members make the survivors sad, or provide double joy? Mormons have a most explicit vision of heaven. It is not an equal-opportunity environment—it involves various degrees of glory. Will this cause jealousy and envy? Mormons, though, are flexible in attempting to get as many people as possible into heaven. They conduct rituals for non-Mormons, baptizing them posthumously. This raised the ire of Jews who discovered them baptizing deceased Jews.

The Islamic vision of heaven probably won some converts, especially after males learned seventy-seven virgins awaited them in a martyr's victory celebration. Some men will die for one woman, but the promise of seventy-seven virgins adds a certain urgency. In the Koran, Mohammed creates a *paradise* (the preferred term) that offers the best of the earth in eternal abundance. That beats seeing God face-to-face. The Islamic view is attractive and quite detailed, allowing a foretaste of what's to come. Anything wanted or needed will be available—unlike on earth, where we have to separate our wants and needs or end up bankrupt. The heart will be free of ill feelings, minus pain and suffering. For the desert people who first heard Mohammed, the vision of a verdant paradise—overflowing with water and fruit trees and rivers of the finest wines in endless abundance—caught the imagination. Islam frowns on alcohol, so the finest wines are free from it to prevent intoxication. Wine that's free from alcohol? Sound like grape juice. That could be a downer.

Jews, on the other hand, would not be adverse to intoxication in heaven. In the Messianic period, there would be wine in abundance. Real wine, not grape juice. The Jews had no problem with the fruit of the vine, never having been afflicted with a temperance movement like that advanced by Seventh-Day Adventists and early Methodists. To their credit, while not entirely dismissing an afterlife, Jews focus instead on improving this life on earth. This is not to deny that Jews make life hell for Palestinians, just as they claim Palestinians make life hell for them. This enduring conflict indicates hell does exist, for we have unresolved torture and violence without end, right here. But Jews spend little time speculating on the afterlife. "For the future is inscrutable, and the accepted sources of knowledge, whether experience, or reason, or revelation, offer no clear guidance about what is to come. The only certainty is that each man must die— beyond that we can only guess." (Wikipedia) The less said, the better.

Hinduism offers a detailed view of the afterlife. It involves six heavenly planes, with 330 million gods dwelling on the second level. One verse in its ancient scripture says, "That supreme abode of Mine is not illumined by the sun or moon, nor by fire or electricity. Those who reach it never return to this material world." (Bhagavad Gita, As It Is, 15:6) The Lord's devotees reside eternally in loving relationship with the Lord—in the dark.

Religious groups have notions of an afterlife, but so do individuals. Farrell had his character Studs Lonigan thinking about his deceased high school buddy, Paulie, and considering him better off in hell than heaven. In heaven, it seemed to Studs, everyone had to be on their best behavior, and Paulie would eventually crack under that strain. [84]

Non-believers, rejecting a notion of the afterlife, argue the earth is to be taken seriously and is not simply a way-station. If this life is all there is, then humans need to work to create paradise here rather than pine away for a future one.

Some atheists point out that belief in a reward after death is poor motivation for moral behavior while alive. Neuroscientist and secularist Sam Harris stresses this: "It is rather more noble to help people purely out of concern for their suffering than it is to help them because you think the Creator of the Universe wants you to do it, or will reward you for doing it, or will punish you for not doing it. [The] problem with this linkage between religion and morality is that it gives people bad reasons to help other human beings when good reasons are available." [85]

Others feel that an irrational belief in heavenly rewards may actually motivate believers to do horrible things while on earth. Scientist and author Richard Dawkins sums up this view: "Promise a young man that death is not the end and he will willingly cause disaster...There are would-be murderers all around the world who want to kill you and me and themselves because they are motivated by what they think is the highest ideal [...] the suicide bomber believes that in killing for his god he will be fast tracked to special martyrs' heaven." [86] Incidentally, his foundation's website states its mission as supporting "scientific education, critical thinking, and evidence-based understanding of the natural world in the quest to overcome religious fundamentalism, superstition, intolerance, and suffering." Quite distinct from the RCC's mission. [87]

Pioneering anarchist and feminist Emma Goldman said, "Consciously or unconsciously, most theists see in gods and devils, heaven and hell; reward and punishment, a whip to lash the people into obedience, meekness and contentment." [88] Her comment hits close to home as the RCC whips members into fearful submission with its pedagogy of fear, promoting the contradictory idea that Jesus saved everyone, *but* everyone has to work out their salvation in fear and trembling.

Ultimately, everyone is stuck trying to save themselves, Jesus' rescue work notwithstanding.

The promise of heaven can certainly be a motivator. Growing up, insurance salesmen would visit neighborhood homes each week to collect premiums. Customers made sure they had the money handy, as they didn't want to miss a payment and risk being left out in the cold in a time of need. Years ago, the primary reason for attending Sunday mass was "insurance" against your worst nightmare. It was like paying a premium—*just in case*—to avoid being left out of heaven if death should suddenly arrive. Missing mass would be a mortal sin, perhaps the most notable transgression that hung over Catholics.

For younger Catholics today, the weekly churchgoing requirement under threat of mortal sin just doesn't register, because Vatican II downplayed the mortal consequences of missing mass (though this remains "on the books"). Simple, sincere people will bear this burden scrupulously, though. And with the advent of more conservative priests, the insistence on attending mass under pain of mortal sin returned.

If heaven is the abode of god or the gods, what kind of god(s) do we want to spend eternity with? What if our image is Yahweh, a Jekyll and Hyde, compassionate one moment and terrorizing the next? Would we seriously like to hang out with a mercurial monster who can raise an ugly rant when easily provoked? If our concept of God is one who will arbitrarily punish or retaliate, is this a heaven worth longing for?

Jesus is depicted as subscribing to the God of Abraham, Isaac, and Jacob in the same context as regarding the woman with multiple husbands. This God of "Abraham & Company" is Yahweh, who throughout the Jewish scriptures repeatedly is portrayed as punishing, petulant, and vindictive. Or, was some storyteller having Jesus serve old wine?

The concepts of various gods that circulate on earth, heading up a myriad of religious traditions, are unanimous in their lack of unanimity as to their unequivocal god-like nature. The gods described by these sects contain every variation of every human emotion and activity. Are we to expect something different in heaven?

If heaven represents the ultimate reward—blissful union with God— then it seems believers could hardly wait to get there. But in reality few are in a big rush, instead working to delay the journey as long as possible, even when life is fraught with hardship.

Richard Dawkins shares a story about Cardinal Hume and the Abbot of Ampleforth. "When Cardinal Basil Hume told him that he was dying, the abbot was delighted for him: 'Congratulations! That's brilliant news. I wish I was coming with you.'" [89] Atheist Dawkins applauds the abbot for being truly consistent with his Christian beliefs.

St. Paul at least recognized the dilemma. "For to me, to live is Christ and to die is gain. But if I am to live on in the flesh, this will mean fruitful labor for me; and I do not know which to choose. But I am hard-pressed from both directions, having the desire to depart and be with Christ, for that is very much better; yet to remain on in the flesh is more necessary for your sake. Convinced of this, I know that I will remain and continue with you all for your progress and joy in the faith, so that your proud confidence in me may abound in Christ Jesus through my coming to you again." (Php 1:21)

So heaven can wait for Paul, too?

If heaven exists, I would expect only pleasant surprises. Anything less than that, then it would be better if heaven were a void, a vacuum, where only eternal rest reigns and there is no memory, just endless peace and quiet. Like a wonderful night's sleep. No dreams, no nightmares.

CHAPTER FIVE

LAW TRUMPS KINGDOM:
LOSING THE MESSAGE AMONG ALL THE RULES

"Rules are not necessarily sacred, principles are."
– Franklin D. Roosevelt

Jesus may have been divine, but he made human mistakes.

He erred in believing the Kingdom of God would be realized in his lifetime. If he was human but also God, as defined by the Council of Nicea (325 CE), did God err, too? Or was it just his defective humanity, as is ours?

At first, Jesus thought some of his disciples "will not taste death" before the Kingdom would come. (Mk 9:1) As discussed, he believed the end of all things would come before this generation passed away. (Mk 13:30)

This didn't happen. There was expectation that Jesus' proclamation of the Kingdom would lead, in Harvey Cox's words, to a "regime change." For he said his Kingdom was "not of this world." (Jo 18:36) Then he was crucified.

That version of the Kingdom was not realized in his lifetime, or in almost 2,000 years following it.

119

"You can kill the dreamer, but not the dream," commented Rev. Samuel Kyles, shortly after witnessing Dr. King's assassination in 1968.

The time since Jesus has hardly been an epoch of universal peace, as implied in the Jewish prophets' and Israel's longing for a Messiah. Many reject Jesus today because no substantive difference has been seen in the world since his birth.

What, then, is to be salvaged out of the Jesus story?

A BLUEPRINT: THE KINGDOM OF GOD DOWNGRADED
"The doctrine of the Kingdom, which was the main teaching of Jesus, is certainly one of the most revolutionary doctrines that ever stirred and changed human thought." – H.G. Wells

Analogously, the tradition of democracy to which we trace our current American form arose in the fifth century BCE.

It has had a long and twisted history. At times, the sprout seems to have withered. Then it would emerge with new growth. It has finally seen the light of day, firmly rooted in some places. Though in others it is yanked from the ground or doused with weed killer.

At its birth in Greece, a radical form of democracy was practiced— everyone who could vote participated, and those who didn't were considered idiots. Democracy as defined by the American government is less pure (and much greater in size). We have a representative democracy—we vote for someone to vote for us. This leads to easier manipulation of a massive population, and creates a situation in which those candidates and elected officials can be (and continually are) bought off by moneyed special interest groups.

American democracy remains a work in progress. So does the Kingdom of God.

While Jesus proclaimed the Kingdom as central to his ministry, the RCC suppressed this proclamation, shoving it aside and emphasizing the Seven Sacraments as the main priority. The Kingdom's liberating message was torpedoed from within.

In explaining the Kingdom, Jesus told the parable of the farmer who went out to sow. Seed fell on different types of soil, mostly resistant. But in rich soil, it produced an abundant harvest.

Perhaps we are at a stage in history more open, more receptive, to receiving the seed of the Kingdom. And many willing to hear of the visions and values of the Kingdom are not necessarily Catholics. Some seeds have slowly pushed forth new shoots in surprising ground.

"Seek first the Kingdom of God and everything will be added unto you" (Mt 6:34) is the gospel imperative. The Kingdom is a prophetic vision for humanity, shaped by "the signs of the times," based on the *praxis* of love, challenging us to create paradise right here, right now. But as Westley points out, the Kingdom of God is not foremost in the consciousness of Catholics.

The repetitive rituals of the sacraments need to take a back seat to the Kingdom's invigorating *praxis* of love and liberation.

Fuellenbach has this to say: "The Kingdom could be seen as a hidden yet effective moral ferment within the body politic. It has a social momentum whose *kairos* will come when the circumstances are right for the movement of the Holy Spirit. To identify this 'revolution' for justice, peace, and human rights as the Kingdom at work in the concrete situations of human history means to read the signs of the time from the commitment of faith." [90]

A new "Trinity" now thrives in the institutional RCC, formed by its three priorities: the Seven Sacraments, Canon Law, and Natural Law. The Kingdom of God doesn't even make the list, isn't even on the radar. To resurrect it as the top priority would entail a true "*metanoia*" (conversion) of the entire organization. The RCC is not shy about calling people to conversion, yet strangely, it resists being converted itself. Even the "New Evangelization" the Vatican is promoting does not focus on the Kingdom.

The Ten Commandments gave the Israelites a tribal identity, but were among 613 commandments observant Jews were to follow. This Torah Law made them distinct from other tribes. In time, the

RCC would impose the Seven Sacraments to make its members a distinctive religious tribe, and to micromanage their lives.

Seeking first the Kingdom of God was not the priority—it was too relative, too open-ended, too flexible, too easily influenced by the times. But the sacraments were easy—they were cut-and-dry absolutes.

CANON LAW: A METHOD OF MICROMANAGEMENT
"If you have ten thousand regulations you destroy all respect for the law." – Winston Churchill

Again, as Loisy reminds us, Jesus came with Good News and the Church gave us Canon Law. Jesus tried to simplify all the commandments of Torah Law, reducing it to the command to love. In his Kingdom teaching, he offers a challenging love that the human spirit is capable of realizing. St. Philip Neri (1515-1595), who organized a new religious order in the Rome the Counter-Reformation, declined to write an elaborate, detailed rule for daily living. Rather he wished members be bonded to one another by charity alone.

The RCC didn't go for that. Its laws, not love, would bond members slavishly.

St. Augustine, the first and foremost moralist of the RCC, perhaps in a loose moment, proclaimed, "Love, and do what you will. If you keep silence, do it out of love. If you cry out, do it out of love. If you refrain from punishing, do it out of love." [91] His words reflect the new wine the liberating love Jesus advanced. To act out of love is to be fearless, vulnerable. Or as Carl Jung articulated it, "Where love rules, there is no will to power; and where power predominates, there love is lacking. The one is the shadow of the other." [92]

Jesus constantly clashed with enforcers of the Torah Law, which micromanaged people's lives. Jesus wasn't opposed to law *per se*, but stressed that law exists to serve the well-being of the person.

The person—not any law, not even sacred Torah Law—was absolute.

Law is a means of power and control when it doesn't serve people. Jesus endeavored to woo people (particularly men) away from power, to embrace service over authority and control. In time, the RCC was seduced to embrace power by Constantine, and did it wholeheartedly—it remains among the power elites of the world. Canon Law would make members subservient, and it was men who controlled its creation and enforcement.

The difference between power and service can be visualized in posture and body language. Those who wield power are positioned, whereas the powerless have to come begging, often on bended knee. But those who serve seek out the other and take the initiative in intervening. That is the ongoing image of Jesus in the scriptures. He is continually on the road, looking to intervene in solidarity and healing. Those in the Roman hierarchy are positioned in their offices. Petitioners may try seeking them out but often fail to be granted an audience. The powerless get little access, whereas anyone with a tinge of power is ushered to the head of the line.

Bernard Häring, a moral theologian, sought to refocus the teaching of Jesus by emphasizing love as the priority in human morality. His groundbreaking work, *The Law of Christ*, was published on the eve of the II Vatican Council. Cullen Murphy cites this in his own book, noting that Häring identified *moral theology* not as a negative catalog of sins but a positive articulation of the revelation of love that is the essence of God. Häring, then, would concur with Paul, "Love is the fulfillment of the law." (Rom 13:10)

This seems like an oxymoron—love and law are opposites, right? But Paul offers a new meaning for law—it is not an abstract, mental, rational formula but an act of the will. Häring redirects the understanding of moral theology into a context for understanding law in Jesus as rooted in his new wine of love. The "law of Christ" has love as the starting and ending point, the alpha and the omega. Paul concluded, "For the one who loves another has fulfilled the law." (Rom 13:8). Law is linked to loving others, not following formulas.

Murphy stresses Häring's breakthrough moral theology was not viewed as refreshing and reflective of the Kingdom of God by many. Häring was held as suspect by the Vatican. He was summoned before the Congregation for the Doctrine of the Faith (under Ratzinger) without charges or accusers identified. He compared it to what he endured at the hands of Nazis. "During the Second World War," Häring writes in a memoir, "I stood before a military court four times. Twice it was a case of life and death. At that time I felt honored because I was accused by the enemies of God." But to stand accused by the Church he had served all his life? "I would rather stand once again before a court of Hitler." [93]

While Häring gave primacy to love, Augustine was conflicted, unable to surrender to the risk, to the impulse and motivation of love as a liberating act of the will. He was a man ultimately obsessed with order and unity, as was the Empire. He taught the dangerous doctrine that error has no rights. For him, coercion was justified. In the parable of guests invited to a banquet who failed to send their regrets, the master ultimately sent servants to "compel them to come."

Augustine combed the scriptures, found this one instance, and made an absolute of it—rejecting his own admonition, "If you refrain from punishing, do it out of love." If anything, Augustine proved that "man is an animal consistent only in his inconsistencies!" He favored coercing, forcing, and compelling rather than allowing, encouraging, and freeing. And the Roman Church gladly institutionalized his interpretation.

The RCC embraced Augustine's emphasis on coercion again and again. It returned to the imposition of laws in the tradition of Torah Law with the development of Canon Law. While Jesus angrily shot down useless laws and commandments, the RCC willfully increased them.

Laws and rules still *do* dominate clerical thinking, as confirmed in new research by the Center for the Study of Church Management at the Villanova School of Business. Its director, Charles Zech, collaborating with Jesuit business professor Fr. William Byron, found that overemphasis on rules and regulations turns off Catholics and is one reason they leave the Church. The *National Catholic Reporter* states this unusual study involved no scientific random sampling, but interviews of almost 300 ex-Catholic volunteers who felt strongly enough to participate. Data indicated that Church officials responding to confused or angry Catholics too often fail to engage in "constructive dialogue" but rely on "a simple reiteration of Church rules or policies."

In the article, Byron cites this comment from a disaffiliated Catholic: "Ask a question of any priest and you get a rule; you don't get a 'Let's sit down and talk about it' response." [94] Again, most priests are enforcers, not investigators.

Augustine was the architect of the so-called "just war theory," which gave the RCC cover for supporting war. No loving the enemy, turning the other cheek, walking the extra mile here. And certainly no advocacy for pacifism.

Originally, followers of "The Way" (of Jesus) managed to thrive without Canon Law. They were "one in heart and spirit" ("*cor unum et anima unum*"). (AA 4:32) Though the scriptures record extensive disagreements among them, it appears they were able to work them out without recourse to any law, without lethal persecution of one another, but with openness to the Spirit among them. And when law *did* reemerge, Christianity became seriously fragmented. Unity is the work of the Spirit, not law. When law suppressed the Spirit, the enforcement of law sought to maintain conformity. St. Paul spends a significant amount of time wrangling with the law and efforts to separate himself from the law that permeated his life.

Despite Paul's suspicion of the law, it would become dominant when the RCC devised its own brand of law—Canon Law, a sterile body of regulations void of the Spirit and of human compassion that micromanages its members. Though it took centuries, it currently numbers 1,752 canons, a far cry from the 613 commandments in Torah Law.

The Emperor Constantine, not a pope, inaugurated the first universal church council. Order was extremely important for the cohesion of the Empire, and bringing the Christian communities in line would benefit the Empire. Gradually, religious laws were enacted to govern behavior and belief, and the RCC developed its counterpart to Torah Law.

This new Christian tribe came to be defined by conformity to a rigid bureaucracy, not creativity of an unbridled spirit. Interestingly, as the oldest religion on earth, Hinduism survives without rigid conformity (unlike Judaism or Christianity). To an outsider, Hinduism probably seems kaleidoscopic; every twist spins 360-degree differences. Yet it survives without a bureaucracy, without a hierarchy, without a code of law.

The RCC, through Canon Law, makes the person subservient, once again. Jesus made the person absolute when he argued the Sabbath is made for man, not man for the Sabbath. (Mk 2:27)

Canon Law would rule every aspect of Church membership. Its prominence would overshadow the gospels. Rare is the prelate—pope, cardinal, bishop—with a degree in scripture today. The vast majority of clerics are sent to obtain a degree in Canon Law, not scripture, underscoring the RCC's top priority.

When I studied theology, Canon Law clearly outranked all other theological subjects. A seminary rector who taught the course would kiss the Canon Law book and remind us that if we followed the canons faithfully, our salvation would be insured—just as Jews kissed the fringes of their prayer shawls, a daily reminder to be faithful to each of their 613 commandments.

I recall a pastor to whom I was assigned sometimes getting up from the dinner table to retrieve his Canon Law book, to flip through and find a canon bolstering his argument. He never got up to retrieve the Bible to make a point. He was so obsessed with Canon Law we joked that instead of scripture readings at funerals, he would recite favorite canons of the deceased (as if lay persons knew or cared much about Canon Law, despite the fact that it ruled their lives).

Nowhere in the entire Code of Canon Law is there any discussion or reference to compassion. Nor is the ethic of love even a minor contributing factor. Biblical references are rare (as if the gospels might actually have some relevance in the lives of followers). The kicker is the absence of *Jesus* as a point of reference. This elaborately detailed document manages to exist entirely independent of his humble influence.

Since 9/11, we've become more aware of Islam's complex system of regulations, Sharia Law. Several state legislatures have recently passed laws banning its implementation (though one might argue it prohibits something that would never have happened anyway). In 2010, Oklahoma's referendum to ban Sharia Law passed with flying colors. Yet as long as the RCC has been in the USA, Canon Law has been fully operative, and no state legislature worries about *that* influence. Roman bishops here look *first* to following Canon Law, *then* to the law of the land. In the clerical sexual-abuse scandal, bishops have totally ignored U.S. law. But there hasn't been any legislative referendum to ban Canon Law, not even in Oklahoma!

For Paul, Torah Law was ultimately a means to an end—a tutor, not a master. A profound conversion for an observant Jew like Paul! The law of love, the way of the Spirit, was now to take precedence over manmade law. But over time the community of Jesus became defined more by law than love. Its leaders imposed and enforced upon members arbitrary rules, which eventually evolved from helpful guides to be consulted into hardcore masters to be obeyed.

Members were forced to seek dispensations and exemptions from these arbitrary laws, which became absolute when the RCC began "teaching as doctrine the precepts of men." (Mt 15:9) Rather than seeking the minimum number of laws to guide the community, the RCC maximized the number to cover every possible and conceivable means to curtail its freedom.

Recently in Minneapolis, MN, a group called the Catholic Coalition for Church Reform planned a synod of baptized members. When the local archbishop, John Nienstedt, was invited to join, he slammed the door in their face. He wrote a letter stating that Canon Law said only a *bishop* could convoke a synod, and he would not give his permission to the coalition, labeling it "an affront to the hierarchical ordering of the church ... and a threat to her unity." [95] If he were truly a shepherd-servant, he would have been first to ask how he might assist. Rather, he viewed the participants—his fellow members of the Body of Christ—as a threat.

With reports of sexual abuse by priests, lay people and the general public were made aware of Canon Law, as bishops ran for cover to excuse their coddling of predators, checking first to see that no canon was violated in the rush to judgment of an accused cleric. Yet there was no urgency to intervene on behalf of the victims. Children are largely nonpersons in Canon Law, only referenced as generic receivers of sacraments.

The scandalous founder of the Legion of Christ, Marcial Maciel, who lived a double if not *triple* life, was charged with multiple sexual-abuse crimes but avoided any Canon Law indictment. Three of his victims, prominent educators, released *The Will Not to Know* on the eve of the pope's March 2012 visit to Mexico, accusing him and his top aide of tampering with Canon Law to protect Maciel (and himself). The *National Catholic Reporter* says "the book's most striking accusation" is made by José Barba, a retired professor with a Harvard doctorate: "In 2001 Cardinal Ratzinger and his chief canon lawyer, Archbishop Tarcisio Bertone, modified the statute of limitations in Church law regarding sex with minors 'retroactively in favor of the Legionary founder, and injuring the human rights and legitimate interests of us, his victims.'" [96]

These are devastating charges against John Paul II, Ratzinger, and Bertone, implying justice suborned. Canon Law is the work of clerics, and it just happens to favor them, particularly at the highest level. The pope is the supreme arbiter of Canon Law and largely has a *carte blanche* capacity to do as he wishes with it. There are no checks and balances. The international scandal that has stained Benedict's papacy stems from an archaic justice system that gives popes, cardinals, and bishops *de facto* immunity from prosecution.

The laity, though, is expected to tow the line. The hierarchy feels it has to micromanage every aspect of human life, lest things get out of control. As Thoreau reminded us, "That government is best which governs least." The law of love is not imposed on others. It governs least. It nurtures a dialogue.

The Republican Party today clamors for less government regulation. The Libertarian movement espouses the autonomy of the individual, the freedom to decide what is best for oneself. The Vatican is resistant to both ideas as it continues to treat members like children—like children *in the 1950s*, for "father knows best" (while mother rarely gets to voice her opinion).

The Kingdom of God is the unleashing of the Spirit as a guide for us humans, who could use a breath of fresh air. "The wind blows where it wishes and you hear the sound of it, but do not know where it comes from and where it is going; so is everyone who is born of the Spirit." (Jo 3:8) Canon Law would view this as the whirlwind of chaos.

The Church prefers a hermetically sealed room where all natural forces are controlled. The window Pope John XXIII cracked open has been slammed shut.

NATURAL LAW: A NEW EMPHASIS ON SEXUALITY
"Sex is a part of nature. I go along with nature." – Marilyn Monroe

The Kingdom of God is also subjected to Natural Law. Both Canon Law and Natural Law should be processed through the gospels, particularly its teaching of compassionate love. But the order is reversed—the *gospels* are processed through them.

In the seminary, Natural Law was rarely mentioned, only in passing. In recent times, the Vatican has emphasized its preeminence, consistently and insistently, particularly in reference to sexual issues: abortion, contraception, and homosexuality—the new "Sex Trinity."

The importance that the RCC now ascribes to Natural Law is overreaching, trumping all biblical concepts and moral teachings. It would have helped if Jesus, as divine and equal with God, had clearly revealed Natural Law as foundational to his teaching. *Omniscience*— the ability to know—is attributed to God. It has become contentious in these latter days, and his failure to anticipate this leads a person to question Jesus' sense of omniscience.

While origins of Natural Law predate Jesus, to Greek philosophers, its absence in the Jesus story might indicate his ignorance of it, or his low priority for it, compared to "Mosaic Law," all-pervasive in Jewish tribal life. In the RCC's *Catechism*, Natural Law is given by God and is present in the heart of every person. This is an assumption—not everyone would agree. And even if they did, not everyone would interpret Natural Law the same way. In Hinduism, *karma* is considered natural to all. Romans would certainly reject *that* idea.

From a faith perspective, *everything* is given by God. Faith is not something evident in Natural Law but something "supernatural." It doesn't follow that Natural Law has priority over the gospels, is revered as a unique revelation, and is preeminent to the point where a Christian is to filter all daily activity through its prism.

To speak of Natural Law is confusing. Depending on who's talking, it's viewed as "moral theory," considered "legal theory," or confused with "scientific theory." Natural Law is not synonymous with the laws of nature that science seeks to define—it looks to reason to explain and understand, but not necessarily to provide empirical evidence, and it would not factor in something considered "divinely revealed."

The RCC interprets Natural Law as it wishes, treating it as a Procrustean Bed and forcing favored positions to conform to it. It declares homosexuality is *"contra naturam"* (against nature), even though nature abounds with homosexual manifestations.

Petter Boeckman, academic advisor for the "Against Nature's Order?" exhibition, explains: "One fundamental premise in social debates has been that homosexuality is unnatural. This premise is wrong. Homosexuality is both common and highly essential in the lives of a number of species." Boeckman then proceeds to identify 1,500 animal species that practice homosexuality. [97]

Benedict XVI as Cardinal Ratzinger, backtracking, interpreting Natural Law to fit his already-made conclusion, claimed homosexuality is intrinsically an objective disorder. "Although the particular inclination of the homosexual person is not a sin, it is a more or less strong tendency ordered to an intrinsic moral evil, and thus the inclination itself must be seen as an objective disorder." [98]

On the one hand, he says homosexual inclination is not a sin, but on the other hand, he says it has a strong inclination to a moral evil. Uh, what? He has no scientific or psychological basis for this assertion, and figures it should just be naturally evident to all.

Might this be a strange subspecies of Natural Law, like Ratzingarian Natural Law?

The gospels, though, reveal faith, imagination, resourcefulness—the non-rational capacity to perceive new possibilities for humanity in reading "the signs of the times." In the parable of the sower, it says people have ears but do not hear, and eyes but do not see, lest they hear with their ears and see with their eyes, and understand with their hearts and be converted. There is more to the body's organs than physically hearing and seeing. There is the capacity to understand with the heart, a non-rational experience.

Helen Keller, unable to hear or see, wrote, "The best and most beautiful things in the world cannot be seen or even touched, but just felt in the heart." [99] She taught humanity how to understand with the heart.

If everything is to be filtered through Natural Law, what, then, is the point of faith as imagination? Unconditional love and compassion are not natural. They make sense only in the context of faith, and the capacity to understand with "the ear of the heart," said Enda Kenny, the Irish Prime Minister, quoting St. Benedict when denouncing the Vatican's mishandling of clerical sexual abuse.

In interpreting Natural Law as moral order, the RCC claims it is so self-evident and universal that everyone should get it. Yet universally, people do not consider Natural Law when making moral decisions. The RCC is silent on what is central to the Jesus story—love and compassion. It doesn't even give them honorable mention.

Ironically, a favorite expression of Natural Law depicts certain human acts as "*contra naturam*" (against nature). But love and compassion themselves are "*contra naturam*." The Jesus story demonstrates that humans can rise above their innate limitations.

Sympathetic to the spirit of Jesus, Alexander Pope said, "To err is human, to forgive divine." The capacity to forgive others who have committed egregious acts manifests a state of mind (or heart) well beyond reason and logic, beyond whatever comes naturally.

Morality eventually became linked to Canon Law. But Natural Law became the source of moral wisdom, more than the gospels. The language of commandments, laws, and obligations ignored the soul of Christian tradition—the inclusive love revealed by Jesus. The Church's emphasis on Natural Law and Canon Law replaced the law of Christ, the law of love.

While the RCC complicates and burdens individuals with zillions of laws, it deviates from the simplicity of the Jesus story. "A new commandment I give you, love one another." (Jo 13:34) People had loved previously, but what is "new" in this commandment is an *inclusive* love—love thy neighbor, identifying the neighbor as beyond one's own tribe, the stranger, the sinner. "Owe nothing to anyone except to love one another; for he who loves his neighbor has fulfilled the law." (Rom 13:8)

To ground its moral view, the RCC looks outside its own revelation—the scriptures—to Natural Law. To enforce its interpretation of morality, it looks beyond the scriptures once again—to Canon Law. In doing so, it ignores the new wine.

Regular people have neither the time nor energy nor intellectual stamina to pursue the complexities of Natural Law and Canon Law. But these unnecessary burdens remain on their shoulders.

Yet the ethic of love as a moral guide is something the most sophisticated and the most simple can easily and equally grasp—do to the other as you would have the other do to you. How complicated is *that*? This is the respect and acknowledgement—the moral regard—we all desire.

Why not inspire members with this universal guide, instead of losing them in a maze of regulation?

The RCC failed to serve the new wine of love as the primary law of Christ when it subverted the gospels to Canon Law and Natural Law. By giving law priority over the gospels, the RCC doesn't free persons but subjects them. If it promoted the ethic of love and compassion, unequivocally and unambiguously, the Church would be an agent of spirituality, not an enforcer of law.

LET MY PEOPLE GO: A MANTRA FOR THE AGES
"Freedom is never voluntarily given by the oppressor; it must be demanded by the oppressed." – Martin Luther King, Jr.

When Moses and Aaron said to Pharaoh, "Let my people go," it became a cry of freedom calling out from the ancient world. It reverberates today with the same human yearning.

Historically, attempts to smother the cry for freedom have been perpetrated by tyrants, dictators, warlords, authoritarian and totalitarian regimes—and religious institutions. Throwing off the yoke of oppression is an ongoing struggle. Even in democracies, the majority subjects the minority to its rule. Liberation is the supreme, unfinished human aspiration.

This universal longing for freedom is acknowledged in the Kingdom teaching, in seeking the truth that releases us.

Many Catholics do not find their religious identity in the Jesus story. They depend on popes, bishops, and pastors to tell them what they should believe. Devoted and well-meaning individuals do not realize how indoctrinated they are because the religious teaching began in early childhood, before they had a sense of an independent self. They may be sadly unaware of the cognitive dissonance operating in their lives.

"The church I was raised in values unquestioning obedience over critical thinking," writer Carrie Sheffield notes. "This caused trauma and cognitive dissonance when I questioned church doctrine and official history." [100] Sounds like Sheffield was raised a Catholic. In fact she was raised a Mormon. In response, a reader replies, "The writer's experience with the patriarchal church, led by an infallible old man, is incredibly similar to Catholicism: The lack of concern with the humans impacted by rigid policies, the resistance to critical thinking or questioning, the willingness to ostracize and destroy dissenters, it all sounds amazingly familiar."

While the Mormon Church may shun and ostracize members, it never subjected them to torture.

The RCC gives more priority to the latter-day imposition of Canon and Natural Law than the "law" depicted in the scriptures. Yet the scriptures are foundational to the tradition. It is there that the Kingdom's impulse for human liberation *jumps off the page.*

The scriptures are foundational to the tradition, more than the latter-day imposition of Canon and Natural Law.

Even the RCC would never deny the scriptures are "the revealed word of God." Canon and Natural Law should not be treated as such. Though in practice, in reality, in the everyday lives of Catholics, they are.

CHAPTER SIX

THE SACRAMENTS:
PAVING A PATH TO PERDITION

"God is always coming to you in the Sacrament of the Present Moment. Meet and receive Him there with gratitude in that sacrament." – Evelyn Underhill

Jesus would be surprised to see what's happened with his Kingdom.

His central proclamation has been suppressed, replaced by the Seven Sacraments. They were developed into the major theological construct of the RCC over the centuries, evolving into an enforced spirituality with no obvious and direct link to Jesus' proclamation.

Most Catholics are well acquainted with the Seven Sacraments, but the idea of the Kingdom of God as central to their spirituality is foreign to them.

The sacraments are supposed to represent an encounter with Christ. Largely, though (other than the Eucharist), they have become personal rites of passage, nothing profoundly new or prophetic, just a means of identifying individuals as members of this particular religious tribe.

Often, as someone noted, these individuals receive the sacraments more as "Social Sacramentarians."

Supposedly the sacraments exist to dispense "grace." Yet failure to properly observe them leads to innumerable opportunities to commit mortal sins, ultimately sending members to hell.

Most Catholics assume the sacraments were somehow present from day one. They weren't. They are not immediately evident in the gospels. Only after centuries of trolling texts did the RCC construct a formal (albeit wobbly) structure for the official, distinct, and separate Seven Sacraments: Baptism, Penance, Eucharist, Confirmation, Marriage, Anointing of the Sick, and Priestly Ordination.

(The Orthodox represent the only other Christian tribe concurring in number, but they differ in dispensing them. Some Christian sects have no sacraments. Others, like Anabaptists, practice "foot-washing" as a sacrament.)

Participation is in severe decline. Sacraments are becoming less relevant in members' lives and are not particularly attractive to non-members. Many members no longer feel compelled to receive them. Consequently, the entire sacramental system is collapsing.

But this is good news. The dismantling of the sacraments as the accepted priority of Catholic life might enable a rediscovery of the Kingdom of God as a truly challenging spirituality, with the potential to renew the face of the earth. It might enable a rediscovery of the Beatitudes for those who do not live on bread alone, who hunger for something more to nourish and enrich the human spirit.

Yet the RCC continues to use these Seven Sacraments as a means of control, and views itself as the gatekeeper. Receiving sacraments is less a spontaneous spiritual experience than a reflection of Canon Law—sacraments have to be validated, authorized, licitly confected. The RCC therefore appoints itself to validate who (and who will not) have access. Jesus sought to circumvent the Jewish debt and purity codes, which determined who was righteous before God. The dwelling place of God was not the Temple, but the person. He made grace *easily* accessible. And he made himself *supremely* accessible. "For where two or three come together in my name, there am I with them." (Mt 18:20)

A review of the sacraments reveals how the RCC uses them to shape and mold people's lives, often causing terror in tender souls who only want to faithfully comply. Rather than discovering an opportunity to encounter the liberating spirit of Jesus, the Christ, such dedicated followers might find themselves on the road to perdition.

BAPTISM: THE GATE TO DAMNATION
"I am the slave of my baptism. Parents, you have caused my misfortune, and you have caused your own." – Arthur Rimbaud

In Judaism, circumcision initiated males into the Jewish tribal religion. While genital circumcision of women was practiced elsewhere (and still is, usually in a coerced and disfiguring way), among Jews only males were put to the knife, to be marked forever. Christians rejected circumcision and looked to a different ritual to initiate tribal membership—the baptism of new converts, male and female.

"One thing that is clear is that baptism marked a dividing line between the old and the new," writes Joseph Martos, "between waiting for the messiah and finding him, between living with guilt and living with forgiveness, between being in a community of law and being in a community of love." [101] In practice, the RCC hardly presented itself as a community of love. Followers were constantly under the gun, worried about ending up in hell if the sacraments were not valid.

Initially, baptism of adults was the norm. Baptism slowly evolved from a ritual of initiation to a required act that removed any sin an individual had committed. Some speculated it would be better to hold off on baptism till one's deathbed—then there would be little chance of lapsing back into sin, and a strong chance of riding the express lane to heaven.

The Emperor Constantine supposedly put off baptism until his deathbed (in 337 CE), probably to minimize punishment for his nefarious acts. He was a murderer, having killed his son, Crispus, and wife, Fausta. Being a warlord, he was well aware of his capacity to eliminate anyone standing in his way or merely appearing suspect.

137

Today, the Orthodox Church reveres him as a saint. Though his bloody sins were as red as scarlet, the last-minute baptism apparently painted him as white as snow.

In the same century, Augustine strongly linked baptism to "original sin," the murky state into which every person is born, automatically tainted because of Adam and Eve. Only Catholic baptism would erase it, placing the baptized in a state of grace.

The British monk Pelagius rejected Augustine's perspective and held that babies were born into "original grace." But the RCC embraced Augustine's fearful position, condemning Pelagius as a heretic.

In his youth, Augustine was a Manichaean. This theology promoted a dualistic view of good and evil being fought out in the soul of the individual—between God's proxy (man) and God's enemy (Satan). Human flesh was seen as defective, as it contained both good and evil. The Pelagians contended that Augustine's position on original sin was affected by his association with Manichaeism. And the RCC, again, affirmed Augustine.

If baptism washed away the universal guilt of original sin, it was easy to deduce that those who died with this sin on their souls would be lost for all eternity. Once this teaching of Augustine kicked in, parents rushed to have their newborns baptized—given high infant mortality—to save them from "where their worms die not."

It was not until centuries later that "limbo" was invented by Anselm of Canterbury (1033-1109), a pleasant enough place where babies went if they died before baptism, though they would never see God there.

Demand for "infant baptism" escalated. It became so momentous an issue that force and violence were employed to reserve baptism *only* for infants. In sixteenth-century Europe, adult baptism was a capital offense. "It threatened the marriage of civil and religious authority that had developed over the centuries ... it also granted automatic citizenship, which gave civil authorities the power to tax and conscript. Adult baptism challenged the existing status quo, threatening authority in church/state relations." [102]

Today, the RCC strongly promotes infant baptism. The ritual itself has been watered down, but forced baptism ensures a potential pool of future members. Without the ongoing baptism of babies into the Roman Catholic and Orthodox religions, new membership would consist of only the rare adult who decides to join the club.

Many other Christian tribes *rejected* infant baptism early on. Most Protestant sects rely not on baptizing babies, but on evangelizing adults—something the Roman clergy loathe since it takes actual effort. Adults are less inclined to glibly and uncritically accept something told to them. They are not easily convinced by an argument from a distant authority. They may not accept answers to questions that are not asked.

Instead, the RCC targets babies. Helpless newborns with no free will of their own are unknowingly made official members of this powerful institution, then forced to bear the lifetime burden of compulsory obligations to which they gave no consent!

Canon Law insists that an infant be baptized within weeks of birth. (Canon Law 867, paragraph 1) Even against the will of parents, a dying infant must be baptized. (Canon Law 868, paragraph 2) These canons reinforce a God of fear who punishes his children, not a God of unlimited liberation who unendingly cares for all his creatures, "for not a sparrow falls to the ground apart from your Father." (Mt 10:20)

Some baptized Romans are now asking to be "de-baptized." In a recent civil suit in France, a man requested that the record of his baptism be erased from the parish registry. [103] Catholic theology teaches that an indelible mark is placed on the soul at baptism. Then how can one erase it? Once baptized, one is held liable to observe the teachings and practices of the RCC. Even if one is not practicing, one is *still* accruing mortal sins.

And the RCC preserves the number of living baptized Catholics, regardless, in order to call itself the largest Christian denomination in the world. In 2009, the total reached 1,181,000,000. [104] If the inactive were subtracted from that sum, the RCC might well lose its cherished numerical superiority.

Catholics have been indoctrinated in the urgent necessity of intervening to baptize an ill or dying child when no priest is available. In the mid-1800s, Anna Morisi, a fourteen-year-old servant girl working in a Jewish household in Bologna, Italy, reportedly baptized a questionably ill six-year-old, Edgardo Mortara. Unfortunately, the family lived in the Papal States, so the RCC in its absolute power abruptly wrenched the child away. He ended up under the care of Pope Pius IX himself, who wouldn't return the boy unless the parents converted from Judaism. They refused. There was no court of appeals. The pope was the ultimate authority in the Papal States. And he was hardly inclined to rule against himself.

Only recently, the RCC has acknowledged that the rights of parents take precedence. It still theorizes that members (and apparently non-members) are incapable of doing what is not "of the mind of the Church." A priest can't walk into a bakery and consecrate all the loaves, because this is not "of the mind of the Church." Yet it wouldn't apply its "mind" when a nearly illiterate girl baptized a Jewish child. Again, it is consistent only in its inconsistencies. It perpetuates the charade that the *"Magisterium"* (Teaching Office) has consistently taught and practiced its timeless teachings. (Though "The Magisterium" in Kildare, Ireland is a pub—that's something to drink about!)

The Church admits a person blessed with water and the Trinitarian formula is validly baptized. But if Catholic parents (or guardians) have their children baptized in a non-Catholic religion, they are punished with a censure or other "just" penalty.

In his revolutionary proclamation of the Kingdom, Jesus appealed to adults to embrace a new vision for humanity. The baptism of infants had nothing to do with it—children were incapable of making this decision freely. In fact, there is no biblical record of his baptizing infants.

In the movie, *My Big Fat Greek Wedding*, a young man wants to marry a woman of Greek Orthodox background. For the sake of her tribal family, he compromises and agrees to be baptized, though the Orthodox Church usually baptizes infants. And he is treated like an infant—he wears a diaper-like wrap as a bejeweled and robed priest pours the water and says the Trinitarian formula. Then the prospective groom emerges from the baptismal font and announces, "I'm Greek!" Scriptwriter Nia Vardalos certainly grasped baptism as a rite of passage, an entrance into a culture or a tribe, much more than an individual faith experience or conversion.

Forced baptism of infants perpetuates a widespread ignorance of what actually has been done in the name of these unsuspecting individuals. Many people grow up without understanding their commitment instilled at baptism. In recent times an aggressive group has emerged within the RCC—the Neocatechumenal Way, or "Preparation for Baptism"—identifying itself as an "instrument" available to parishes for bringing back those who have abandoned the Church. In its emphasis on adults, it inadvertently acknowledges infant baptism has had a lukewarm effect. But it has developed into a cult-like organization that indoctrinates adults into rigid conformity, a Roman version of being "born again." A German parishioner in her sixties was urged by her pastor to join the group. "'The pattern was always the same in many meetings,' she says. 'You stood up front and said: I was a bad person, and it was only through the Neocatechumenate that I was led to the path of improvement.' When she had questions, they were quickly dismissed." [105] Yet another Vatican-sanctioned version of mind control in the name of religion.

Controlling the education of the young has always been a great way to develop and strengthen a religious tribe. In many locations the RCC had total control over local schooling, essentially allowing for rampant indoctrination. In 1884, the Third Plenary Council of Baltimore exhorted that every parish have a parochial school. Bishops had the freedom to impose mortal sin according to their whims, as in Cincinnati, Ohio, where it was linked to school admission: "Confessors are hereby forbidden to give absolution to parents, who without permission of the Archbishop send their children to non-Catholic schools, unless such parents promise either to send them to the Catholic school, at the time to be fixed by the Confessor, or, at least agree, within two weeks from the day of confession, to refer the case to the Archbishop, and abide by his decision. If they refuse to do either one or the other, the Confessor cannot give them absolution, and should he attempt to do so, such absolution would be null and void." [106]

Imagine the unnecessary stress put on parents of a century ago, who, for a variety of reasons, sent their children to public school. That a bishop could cavalierly slap a mortal sin on them staggers the imagination. True to its theology of fear, the RCC discovered more opportunities to separate people from God than unite them. Pronouncing as a mortal offense such an insignificant issue as school attendance is hardly the act of a community of love.

Many countries subsidized the RCC's schools. Entire orders of men and women were formed for this task, forfeiting their lives to indoctrinate children. In Catholic Ireland the government allowed the RCC extensive control over its schools, offering few independent educational opportunities for non-Catholics: "Roisin Hyde was five when she was hastily baptized a few days before she started primary school. Hyde's parents were agnostic but because non-Catholics in Ireland had few other places to learn how to read and write, the family latched onto the only option they knew. Thirty-five years on and Hyde, an architect in Dublin, is struggling over where to educate her own two-year-old son. It's a dilemma faced by parents the world over. But in Ireland where the Catholic Church runs more than nine in ten primary schools and half of all high schools, it's a question that too often has just one answer. 'I would say that a lot of my friends, the only time they have been inside a church is to get their kids christened so they could go to the local school,' Hyde said. 'I just feel so hypocritical doing it, going along for one day and then not attending.'" [107]

Baptism is reduced to a meaningless formality when it becomes a perfunctory requirement to enroll a child in a state-supported school. Priests in this environment know such rituals are shams. How could they not be bored out of their gourd presiding over these charades, all the while promoting the hypocrisy? Do they struggle with cognitive dissonance?

The carefully orchestrated education of the young is essential to maintaining membership. St. Ignatius of Loyola perhaps best understood instructing the child as a means of owning the member. "Give me the child for seven years, and I will give you the man." Even the atheist Vladimir Lenin realized the importance of capturing the mind and heart of the young: "Give me four years to teach the children and the seed I have sown will never be uprooted."

But others cautioned about indoctrination's consequences. Søren Kierkegaard, noted earlier, warned that a wrongful perspective acquired in childhood does not go away but remains to skewer adult belief (perhaps indicating it is not so easy to put away childish things). And Buddhist monk Thich Nhat Hanh strongly opposed pushing beliefs on others, regardless of reasons or circumstances. "Do not force others, including children, by any means whatsoever, to adopt your views, whether by authority, threat, money, propaganda, or even education."

Children learn morality from parents, not from schools. At best, schools (and churches) reinforce parental morality, but they cannot take its place. In *The Road from Coorain,* Jill Ker Conway describes her childhood on an isolated sheep farm in New South Wales, Australia. No places of worship existed for her Catholic father or Protestant mother. No formal religious education was imposed on children. Only the example of her parents guided her young life: "I was puzzled about the whole question of religion myself, since both parents seemed highly moral people to me." [108]

Adults are moved by actions, not words. And so are children—they learn not by pious lecture, but by real-life example. And keenly sense the difference. To paraphrase Ralph Waldo Emerson, "Your example speaks so loudly, I can't hear what you're saying." When Jesus talked of the Kingdom he meant practice, not doctrine. We don't need more words, we have plenty of words. We need actions.

But just as Augustine cited the parable of the invited guests and seized on the word *compel* as grounds for the use of force, some interpret Jesus' words, "Suffer the little children come to me," as an instruction to baptize babies and begin the indoctrination process.

Though Benedict shut down limbo, he did little to reduce unnecessary anxiety about the youngest of souls. Why is the Vatican reluctant to declare infallibly that non-baptized infants do indeed see God, eliminating one more fear?

But fear remains alive and well today. Just as circumcision of males makes them irrevocably, with an indelible cut, part of the Jewish tribe, so baptism of infants makes them irrevocably, with an indelible mark, part of the Catholic tribe.

There is no reason for babies to be forcefully baptized. To do so is a form of abuse. Baptism should be restricted to adults, a rite of initiation in embracing the vision of the Kingdom. Clergy would have to hustle to gain fully consenting candidates rather than relying on a pool of unsuspecting babies.

Infant baptism is grounded in fear. If the RCC is to embrace the liberating Good News, it needs to end infant baptism altogether. The result will be a more mature Body of Christ.

PENANCE: A SACRAMENT IN INTENSIVE CARE
"I'd stand in line for Confession with old people and little kids, and as the line moved up, I knew when I got into the box that I would lie! Again!" – Mercedes McCambridge

The Sacrament of Penance (or Confession, or Reconciliation) is on the endangered-species list. If something doesn't change, it may soon be extinct.

It wasn't always that way. Hearing confessions used to be a time-consuming obligation for a priest, especially on Saturdays—"bath night!" The RCC's enforcement of this sacrament was spectacular—building confessional booths, manning them with priests, herding the masses in to confess, and frequently. So many sins, so little time! Catholic guilt strove to outdo Jewish guilt. Mandatory confession was an effective venue to ratchet it up.

But today, penance is surely dying without a concerted movement to kill it. And the stragglers who still wander in shouldn't be encouraged to return. The RCC itself has nearly succeeded in demolishing it. By trivializing matters that should never have seen the darkness of the confessional, it reduced a sense of morality rather than heighten it.

In essence, if *everything* can be a sin, then *nothing* is a sin.

The RCC has been ineffective in enabling members to identify, weigh, and differentiate the many levels of human imperfection—from common psychological issues, to difficult ethical dilemmas, to true moral failures. Many who dragged themselves to confession on Saturdays needed counseling more than chastisement. But the confessional booth was not a place for counseling, and clergy were not trained as counselors.

As Americans became more formally educated, culturally sophisticated, and politically aware, they liberated themselves from much of what the RCC deemed sinful. Fr. Andrew Greeley took issue with Pope Paul VI for reversing the progressive direction set by Vatican II, believing his birth control encyclical didn't win unquestioned obedience but only made members wake up and grow up. William Donohue, president of the Catholic League for Religious and Civil Rights, notes that Greeley said the encyclical "shattered the euphoria that had flourished after Vatican II" and "sent the Church into a sudden and dramatic decline." [109]

And when the damning consequences for eating meat on Friday were lifted, many began to question the whole house of moral cards. The amount of ink Catholics have spent on the issue of eating meat on Friday is enough to fill the Black Sea. As Benedict XVI wiped out limbo with his pen, Paul VI okayed eating meat on Friday—almost. It's *still* possible to commit mortal sins on Ash Wednesday and Good Friday if one flagrantly consumes animal flesh and fails to confess this moral evil.

When Paul VI announced this change, many wondered what would happen to those currently in hell for eating meat. Was it retroactive? Comedian George Carlin joked that it wasn't a sin anymore to eat meat on Friday, but he bet there were "still some guys in hell doing time on the meat rap," imitating one poor guy confiding to another that it was a baloney sandwich that did him in.

The ubiquitous visualization of Jesus on the cross—the familiar image duplicated by the millions around the world—is a constant reminder that he died for our sins, we were led to believe. Paul underscores this, reminding us, "All have sinned and fell short of the glory of God, but they have been made right with God freely by his grace, through the redemption that is in Christ Jesus." (Rom 3:23) We refer to Jesus as "savior." But the theology of fear doesn't give him credit for the job. The RCC insists we need to work out our own salvation, and to keep at it, "in fear and trembling." Ultimately—and repeatedly—we have to save ourselves. The atoning sacrificial death of Jesus doesn't give complete coverage. The Sacrament of Penance is like supplemental health insurance—Medicare doesn't cover all, so we have to pay part of the bill.

Fewer people confess nowadays, and those who do tend to be the oldest and youngest, both fiercely indoctrinated. The few sins older people still confess include missing mass, sexual indulgence, impatience—and for children, always disobedience. In Romans 1, Paul is beside himself describing the wickedness of humanity, how it stirs up God's wrath. He goes overboard listing individuals deserving of death, among them children disobedient to their parents. Fortunately, I was ignorant of this all those years hearing children's confessions, or I would have had to consign the death penalty to thousands of kids. Paul's attitude here reveals baggage he wasn't able to shake. If he could be so vindictive toward children, what else in his theology should be questioned?

Today, the RCC's singular moral issue is abortion. Since the children of our mythical parents began to copulate, abortion has been part of human history. In the Greco-Roman world of Jesus and Paul, abortion and infanticide were part of the fabric of society. Yet both are silent in this regard. If Paul could put disobedient children on his hit list, surely he would include abortionists. But he didn't.

The RCC twisted the Good News by focusing on individual sins that don't even get close to meeting the standard of moral evil, shaming people for inconsequential acts, adding burdens rather than lifting spirits. The theology of fear keeps them forever wallowing in guilt, never quite sure of escaping hell. Confession offers an ideal venue for the scrupulous. "Catholic guilt" weighs heavily.

I recall a wickedly humid August afternoon in a Southern town. An elderly parishioner called and inquired if she could come to confession early, as she had no ride. The poor soul struggled to walk in the torrid weather and climb the church steps, only to confess inconsequential human peccadilloes like being impatient or missing daily prayers. There was absolutely no reason for her to confess, but the burden had been placed on her spiritual shoulders in childhood. And now, marshaling her energy, she made the journey when the heat equaled a waiting room in hell. Nonsense, but nevertheless real agony that perturbed her soul, and many like her. The theology of fear once again triumphed, even at the sunset of life.

Until 1910, children were held back from confession and communion until at least age twelve. Then Pius X allowed them to receive both at seven, the "age of reason." After all, at this earlier age indoctrination could take place in earnest, while a few years later an acquired moral conscience or personal awareness might interfere. The pope was hailed for allowing younger children communion, but there was a trick—they had to confess five years earlier, and to God knows what!

Today the RCC demands children confess before receiving First Communion. The negative is accentuated over the positive. At their young age, they are incapable of mortal sin. Why force them to confess, except to weave a pattern of guilt and control at an early age? God forbid they might think Jesus in the Eucharist is an unconditional gift.

What was commonly promoted as adult-sized sin in the last century largely involved personal areas, particularly sexual issues, and of course missed mass. While it was a mortal sin to miss mass, it was not a mortal sin to ignore a person in need, or (at least in my neighborhood) to harbor racial animosity and act in a prejudiced way. Liberation Theology would consider complicity in the institutional sin of racism, but there was no enabling of critical thinking in our Irish ghetto.

Growing up during a period of heightened racial tension provided an education of its own. The Southside of Chicago was hugely Catholic in the 1960s. When Martin Luther King, Jr. led an integration march through Marquette Park, he reportedly faced "thousands of jeering, taunting whites" carrying signs and throwing bottles and rocks. He later said, "I have to do this—to expose myself—to bring this hate into the open." Veteran though he was, he expressed shock at the depth of racism he encountered: "I have seen many demonstrations in the South, but I have never seen anything so hostile and so hateful as I've seen here today." [110] Despite the anger spilling into the streets, Church leaders totally ignored the racial climate that had been simmering and rising to a boil, to eventually burst in the heat, as the play set in Chicago said, like a raisin in the sun.

In a strange twist that only the RCC could set up, the confessional itself became an occasion of sin for the confessors, as mentioned earlier. In the 1960s when I began to hear confessions, many teenage boys confessed to masturbation. (I don't recall young women doing so.) There were ways that the priest could see who came into the confessional. Later, in light of the clerical sexual-abuse scandal, it became clear to me how a priest could have become a sexual predator toward youngsters after hearing their confessions. And even if a priest told his bishop he couldn't hear confessions because he found himself sexually tempted, the bishop would hardly honor his request.

If it weren't for the Sixth Commandment, the waiting lines for confession would have been much shorter. The Church succeeded brilliantly in making Catholics feel guilty about normal sexual acts, but failed miserably in educating them about the wrongness of bearing false witness, supporting violence in acts of war and capital punishment, advocating economic inequity, or upholding discrimination—issues greatly affecting the common good of society. The emphasis on individual sins rather than social ills made the typical Catholic feel that evil was only a personal issue.

Fortunately, it is rare today for teenagers to confess masturbation, except in conservative Catholic communities. Yet it remains listed in the *Catholic Catechism* as a mortal sin that separates a soul from God. Maybe younger people aren't 'fessing up, but "ignorance of the law is no excuse."

When I was a novice in a Catholic society, the year was spent in isolation from the world. No access to phone, radio, television, newspapers, magazines, or visitors, except on rare occasions at the discretion of the novice master. We were twenty-some males, ranging in age from late teens to early forties. Each evening before bedtime, the novice master would give a little meditation. Of the 366 talks, I remember only one—the story of an Italian seminarian who had masturbated during the night, died in his sleep, and because he didn't get to confession, got a one-way ticket to hell. There was no opportunity to question the novice master about this tale. Besides, the RCC had us thoroughly indoctrinated, gullibly believing whatever we were told. We didn't even know what to ask.

I never forgot this bedtime story, wondering for years why he told such a tale. He was a sincere man, above reproach, without guile. Thirty years passed before it dawned on me. We each had a weekly private meeting with him, a time he encouraged us to use for confession. Perhaps many confessed that they had masturbated. The tale he told of hellfire and damnation might make us think twice about doing it. He was sincerely trying to save us from eternal suffering for this fleeting act of pleasure. (Technically, Canon Law said he shouldn't have heard our confessions. But it all depended on who was enforcing Canon Law.)

Once an older man supported by crutches, living alone with little human contact, confessed to masturbating as his only "sin." I felt terribly for him, particularly when he shared his grim life in a remote town with few people and scarce attractions. The sexual act was one of his only pleasures. But it didn't last nearly as long as his guilt.

When I would attempt to downplay the seriousness of masturbation, the penitent would often react disconcertedly and defensively, arguing that "I've always been taught it's a mortal sin." Unfortunately, the environment of the confession box is hardly conducive to instruction and discussion, and something long considered a mortal sin would take more than a few words of explanation. And anyway, who was I to pontificate? I was only a lowly priest, not the pope.

Parvity is a word you'll not find in a dictionary. If there is an exclusively Roman Catholic word, this may be it. The phrase *parvity of matter* refers to gradations of severity regarding moral failings. Dropping nuclear weapons on Hiroshima-Nagasaki is much more serious, has greater parvity of matter, than hitting someone with a cream pie (as happened in Belgium to Archbishop Andre Leonard when he denounced sex-abuse victims seeking financial compensation). While it will acknowledge parvity of matter in other areas (e.g., use of violence), the RCC does not admit or allow parvity of matter regarding *any* sexual acts. An individual indulging in self-pleasure through masturbation or any minor sexual titillation sins just as mortally as one who rapes a child.

Its obsession with sex reflects the virus of Manichaeism, which it never tried to eliminate but instead adopted and enforced. Manichaeism distrusts the body—best to flee it, as it is the cause of sin. The RCC has long maintained that virginity (male and female) is a higher state in life than marriage. Jonathan Kirsch claims the book of Revelations views sex as something dirty and defiling under all circumstances, indicating that the only "pure" human beings are virgins. [111]

Not surprisingly, the "Fathers" of the Church (there obviously being no "Mothers") were contemptuous of women, who were "the devil's gateway, the root of all evil," as the Christian writer Tertullian (160-225 CE) called them. "Fierce is the dragon and cunning the asp but women have the malice of both; the world of her body is nothing less than phlegm, blood, bile, rheum and the flow of digested food; why was woman created at all?" [112] He was evidently ignorant of the scriptures, which never mention women as "the root of all evil." That was "the love of money." (1 Tim 6:10)

Regardless, the RCC still pours that same old wine and has never refuted the Fathers' misogyny, a perpetual theme in Catholic tradition. They saw Eve as the original culprit; her feminine wiles caused Adam to sin. Perhaps we can forgive men of centuries past due to archaic cultural values and social beliefs. But whenever contemporary men assert such arrogant assumptions, they only underscore the widespread suppression and oppression of women in the community and negate their universal equality, despite Jesus' and Paul's teaching.

Previously, I shared from the memoir of Mario Valentini his being informed, while preparing for First Communion, that there was *something more dangerous and powerful than Lucifer*. The priest kept the class of little boys hanging for a week before revealing this *something*:

"'I'll tell you what is worse than Lucifer ... La carne,' he says. My mind is scrambling. La carne? Meat? ... What sort of meat? Lamb, beef ... 'The flesh! ... The temptation of women!' I can't believe what my uncle is saying. Is he saying that those lovely things we look at in magazines, the legs, the tight dresses that show bosoms and curves, all the things that make us go red, laugh, feel excited, and that we enjoy more than anything else, these things are *worse than Lucifer*? For the first time he doesn't look so important, so clever, so scary, so *right*. This time he's *not* right, and I know it inside. I *won't* believe it." [113]

Valentini at a very young age experienced a beautiful epiphany regarding Natural Law. How could women—"those lovely things we look at"—be viewed as *worse than the Devil*? What came natural to him was not natural to the priest.

And again, why should discussion of Lucifer and "the flesh" dominate First Communion preparation? Wouldn't it have been more appropriate for the priest to explain how the bread of the Eucharist was the real flesh of Jesus? Guess not—too theologically challenging.

Genesis proclaims Yahweh looked at everything he made and saw it was "very good," but the RCC proclaims everything he made is "very bad," particularly in its push for acute guilt about sexual activity. How many fortunate people outside the RCC are without guilt regarding sexual matters? They have a better chance of being saved—from sexual neurosis.

John Paul II's major opus, *The Theology of the Body*, attempts to cover over the Manichaean bed upon which, nonetheless, its theology rests. It proposes absolutely no change of attitude toward contraception, family planning, masturbation, or human sexuality. The only thing new is the book cover.

Celibates are hardly the best teachers of human sexuality. In my thirteen years of indoctrination, sexuality was ignored except when referring to sexual sins. Celibates didn't even teach about *celibacy!* For an institution basing its teaching on Natural Law, it will not admit that the idea of celibacy is unnatural. All creation cries out for coupling, connection. Though the (mostly lay) Papal Commission on

Birth Control strongly advocated for birth control, Paul VI rejected its studied effort. The old wine, the fear of the body and all its natural functions, filled the glasses once again.

But look at the membership's response. Today, 98 percent of sexually active Catholic women use a form of contraception banned by the Vatican. [114] Of course, they are all in mortal sin, but they no longer run to confession. It seems that personal conscience suffices. The RCC's rigid, absolute position on sexual activity prevents its clerics from being competent counselors in the most personal aspect of human existence. It rejects "the signs of the times" as relativism. As the RCC tried to control Galileo's command of physics, so it tries to control today's science of biology. It always knows better.

Scandinavian countries are incredibly free of the sexual tyranny of the RCC. They have trail-blazed toward a healthy understanding and practice of human sexuality, while reducing sexual transmitted diseases, teenage pregnancies, and abortions. They offer an aggressive sex education program for all citizens, beginning at an early age. Meanwhile, the RCC fights ferociously against any public sex education programs—at least, in the countries where it still has some clout.

Technically, Catholics have to confess only mortal sins, not venial, whether they know it or not. But as late as 1994, John Paul II said venial sin "must never be underestimated, as though it were automatically something that can be ignored or regarded as 'a sin of little importance.'" This encourages scrupulous members to continually analyze their thoughts and behaviors, find minor indiscretions, and feel guilty.

When a prelate makes the font of mercy more easily accessible, as in group absolution, the pope pounces faster than on any priestly pedophile. Bishop William Morris of Toowoomba, Australia allowed group absolution, essentially breaking down barriers for the saving work of Jesus. The pope removed him from office, indicating that members cannot just show up for a public penance ceremony—they must take on sacramental action, and being in the presence of a priest doesn't suffice, only confessing personally to a priest does.

Having the *intention* to seek forgiveness doesn't suffice? So, God no longer does the forgiving?

Catholics now represent the population most alienated from God due to the multiple mortal sins they feel they constantly commit. Meanwhile, popes and bishops try to entice Catholics back to confession. Ironically, though cheerleaders for this sacrament, they do not schedule themselves to hear weekly confessions. Evidently, they have more important things to do.

The focus on personal sin identifies the individual as the problem. It keeps ordinary people in bondage due to their private, and quite human, failings. They are made to feel guilty, as if they alone are responsible for the shortcomings of life.

Unlike old-time hell-bent preachers, many modern "mega-church" evangelists rarely even mention sin. Today's televangelists preach consumerism and pop psychology, essentially saying, "God wants you to be happy and wealthy! You just need to stop your negative thinking!" (Like the old theology, "You just need to pray harder!") It's a new form of guilt to put on simple, sincere people. If they aren't wildly happy and materially well off, it's because of their negativity. "God wants you to be rich! You just need to be more positive!" The guilt prevails, only in new clothes.

Liberation Theology examines institutional and structural devices by which the individual is judged, accused, and controlled. It points out that "the little ones" are taught to view themselves as the problem. Constantly placing the onus on them to shape up—*or else!*—is not welcoming liberation, but twisted bondage. Created and maintained by the theology of fear.

In *The Moral Underground*, Lisa Dodson discusses the personal work ethic of the poor and refers to sociologist Jacob Hacker, who considers the refusal to recognize structural failure as the triumph of what he calls the Personal Responsibility Crusade: "Keeping all attention on individual behavior—at least when it comes to poor people—is a common conservative tactic to deflect recognition of a failing economy and government. In the past, the talk was about paupers, vagrants, and hobos rather than joblessness. Over the last decade, we heard a lot about deadbeat dads and welfare moms but not about poverty wages at a time when corporate wealth spiked. I was fascinated to see how 'welfare moms' are doing exactly what was supposed to exonerate them—they are employed." [115]

Catholicism and televised Christianity do have one thing in common—both make sin personal. Both fail to scrutinize the social impact of power that affects individual lives—mere pawns of governments, corporations, schools, ethnic and religious tribes. Today, the average person may try to be positive, but working at a minimum-wage job has few exits. They're not unlike the Dutch boy putting his finger in the dike. No amount of confessing or positive thinking will magically produce success when the tide is rising and the wall is about to burst.

Liberation Theology de-emphasizes personal sin. It investigates social sin and its impact on the individual, analyzing the effects of larger forces. It holds that salvation, spiritual success, will not come by individual efforts alone, but by solidarity with one another.

THE EUCHARIST: VEHICLE FOR HOLY GRACE OR GRAVE SIN?
"It is up to the communicant to decide whether they are in a state of grace and worthy to receive the Eucharist. Each one of us makes that decision." – Roger Mahony

"I've had some threaten not to give Communion to me, even though they don't know my position, just because I'm a Democrat. I've had cardinals refuse to shake my hand because I'm a Democrat." – Bart Stupak

Of the Ten Commandments of the Jews, the Third was to keep holy the Sabbath. But if a Jew failed, no mortal sin was slapped on the soul. In the Eucharist of the Christians, there is a special encounter with Jesus. But if Catholics miss mass on the Sabbath or Holy Days of Obligation, they're zapped with a mortal sin, sent on a fast track to hell.

Originally, the Eucharist celebration was a simple gathering to share the Jesus story (usually orally, even after it was committed to manuscripts since they were hard to come by) and a meal where bread and wine were passed around in remembrance of him, the innocent one. When early followers of "The Way" were thrown out of synagogues, they gathered in homes. Informality was the natural result.

Under Constantine, the Eucharist ritual became a state function. He provided government subsidies to build basilicas—large, adorned buildings in which the Catholic liturgy became a divine spectacle. The Eucharistic gathering became a clerical performance, with lay persons reduced to spectators.

Brian Moynahan describes one such gathering: "The ordinary wooden table once used for the Lord's Supper became a fixed altar on a raised platform at the front of the apse. The only light came through the doors and from windows pierced in the 'clear story,' or clerestory, the walls of the nave above the columns. Darkness heightened the sense of mystery; it was softened by candles and garlands of flowers, and the sweet odor of incense, pagan devices now adopted by the Church. The apse and altar were placed at the western end so that the rays of the rising sun fell on the bishop as he faced eastward toward the congregation; from pagan habit, worshipers often bowed to the sun before entering the basilica." [116]

The Eucharist is an encounter with the living Jesus, and failure to show up is a mortal sin. The believer who misses without a valid excuse, and doesn't confess, gets a ticket to hell. If there is one sin the Church has inculcated into the consciousness of its members, it is the obligation to attend weekly mass or be subject to eternal damnation.

As a tornado hit Springfield, MA in June 2011, a young man was crushed to death when a tree collapsed on his car. The pain of the sudden loss was acutely experienced by his mother: "She [the young man's sister] said her father is trying to be strong, but her mother is suffering, in part because Sergey was the only one of her children who did not go to church, and she fears he may not have gone to heaven. 'It's killing her,' Irina Livchin said. 'It's heartbreaking.'" [117] Simple, sincere people have been indoctrinated that the consequence of missing church is eternal damnation. Would that they were taught that exploiting people, discriminating against people, would send them to hell.

155

In hearing confessions for about forty-five years, I found that other than sexual indulgence, missed mass was the most commonly confessed sin, drummed into people as a serious offense. When questioning the circumstances as to why they missed, many would say they were sick. And if reminded that sickness excused them, many would counter they "felt better" to confess anyway. For many, they attended not in joyful anticipation of encountering the Risen Christ but in fear of eternal damnation.

For centuries, those present did not receive the Eucharist, as the Church set the bar so high that many felt unworthy to receive, reinforcing Paul's warning not to take it unworthily. It would become a reward only for those who were in the perfect state of grace, not a means of attaining wholeness. A different interpretation of Paul's words would remind us that this is the gift of a gracious giver and not the result of our own righteousness.

Much quibbling ensued as to what legalistically constituted "hearing mass." In Ireland, standing around outside the church building and smoking while still able to "hear" the mass let many males off the hook. Others undoubtedly "heard mass," physically present but emotionally and spiritually unconnected. Social conformity was powerful in small communities, and everyone knew who the no-shows were. A friend said of church attendance in his Irish town, "The true believer may be the one who *didn't* show up."

The RCC maintains there is no salvation outside the RCC. If you're outside, you're out of luck. But even if you're *inside*, you're not truly saved anyway!

Members have endless opportunities for being lost, while non-members are going about their business, less concerned about racking up misdeeds that will separate them from God.

For fundamentalists and evangelical Christians, salvation depends on being "born again." It's a one-shot, either-or deal. But for Romans, salvation is full of traps.

Members who are divorced or active homosexuals are counseled they are not worthy to take communion. Rather than nourishment for all those on the human pilgrimage, the Eucharist is reserved for the perfect, the righteous (as defined by the RCC), yet another element used as a means of control rather than shared as a sign of hope, a free gift from a God who loves unconditionally.

Membership is a field so fraught with landmines that easily trigger mortal sins, it would be less stressful for the human heart to simply ignore it. Maybe in some organizations "membership has its privileges," but in the RCC "membership has its punishments," especially for failing to show up for its weekly ritual.

In recent years, the Eucharist has become a political football. Right-wing hierarchs refuse communion to American politicians— primarily Democrats who are pro-choice. Republican politicians who are pro-capital punishment get a pass.

This self-righteous pontificating leads one to question the efficacy of even taking communion, when those who do receive may fail to demonstrate a minimum amount of charity and justice. Why receive, if it only leads to feeling superior and judging others?

Tragically, the political use of the Eucharist is not new, though perhaps less violent than in the past. John Philip Jenkins writes of various Christian factions that held different interpretations of the nature of Jesus and forcefully used the Eucharist to coerce submission to their position: "Other bishops were even more savage, acting in ways that foreshadowed the pogroms and heresy hunts of the High Middle Ages. In the great eastern city of Amida, the new bishop, Abraham, burned and crucified those who defied him, using his soldiers to force communion bread into the mouths of the reluctant. One priest who resisted even these efforts was remembered ever after under the heroic name of Cyrus the Spitter— although Cyrus himself was burned alive afterward." [118]

Since the Eucharist has evolved into a political weapon, a withheld privilege, and a symbol of disunity, it would be better to refrain from taking it altogether.

Why not settle for a "spiritual communion" instead? Who knows which is more efficacious?

CONFIRMATION: A SACRAMENT IN SEARCH OF ITSELF
"Home and farm duties seemed much more important than seeing the bishop ... when confirmation might consist in nothing more than holding a child up to receive the bishop's anointing as he passed by on horseback." – Joseph Martos

Confirmation is perhaps the most unnecessary and irrelevant sacrament. It need not be a separate sacrament, since it is the outpouring of the Holy Spirit, which supposedly happens at baptism. Joseph Martos writes, "The rite which is now called confirmation has meant different things in different periods of history, and theologians today are hard put to say which is *the* meaning of the sacrament." [119]

The Orthodox freely offer a three-for-one when an infant is baptized—the Sacraments of Confirmation and Eucharist are packaged along with the Sacrament of Baptism. The Romans parcel the rewards out individually.

However, confirmation may be the safest sacrament for the clergy, one in which a priest would *not* fall into mortal sin—unless that "priest" is a "bishop." Bishops subsume the right to confirm, except for rare instances when they delegate a lowly priest to handle confirmation, usually at their own convenience.

It's expected that the confirming bishop receive a handsome stipend for his laborious efforts. Strictly speaking, this is not an act of "simony," the selling of holy offices for material gain (which rankled Dante enough to imagine popes in hell). This is a "stole fee." That's different. Simony was to be separated from stipends or stole fees, but in reality, it's a very fine line. In all practicality, stipends and stole fees are subtle forms of simony, because money changes hands for the spiritual gift.

This is not a new phenomenon.

"By and large, the Protestant reformers looked at what went on at confirmation and decided that it was neither Christian nor scriptural," writes Martos. "To some it looked like another Roman ruse designed to glorify bishops and fill their pockets. To others it seemed to deny that the Holy Spirit was given at baptism." [120]

A *sacrament* is defined by the RCC as an outward sign, instituted by Christ, to give grace. Considering what confirmation has become, one could make a case for finding a new sacrament.

Among Anabaptist Christians, foot-washing is considered a sacrament. At least there is clear evidence of Jesus washing feet at the Last Supper. A lengthy *Washington Post* article documented its increased popularity, citing applications that brought people together regardless of race, status, or income, and in a variety of situations—wedding ceremonies, political settings such as Germany's lower house, public reconciling between Hutus and Tutsis after the Rwanda civil war. And soup kitchens. In 2005 a Richmond, VA soup kitchen instituted a foot-washing ceremony for the homeless before its Friday meal. Polly Chamberlain felt "a huge disconnect between the volunteers and the homeless people they served. 'How can we really care about them when we don't even know them?' So she and others started washing the feet of the city's poorest every Friday before lunch, as a way to break the ice. The goal was to bond with their patrons in a profound way, show them someone cared, and by doing so, recapture the spirit of Jesus," the article said. "Many of the homeless said they were wary of the foot-washers at first but have grown attached. 'At first it was weird,' said Dawn Wright, 32. 'Because you have corns and bunions, you know, you don't want nobody to be handling your feet.' Pregnant and homeless since November, Wright had drifted with her 7-year-old daughter from shelter to shelter. One constant in her life has been the Friday talks over foot-washing with the volunteers. She said she doesn't know the Bible story it comes from or the theology and long history that come with it. But she knows one thing for sure: 'When they put my feet into that hot water—whew!' she sighed. 'It sure feels like heaven.'" [121]

Imagine what the RCC would be like today if its clergymen had been practicing foot-washing for centuries instead of performing ritualized confirmations. Perhaps Catholics would see service as the antidote Jesus advocated to curb power, and understand that men especially are called to serve also, not to dominate only.

Maybe foot-washing was discarded by the hierarchy precisely because those in power didn't want to be humbled, to be continually reminded of Jesus' instruction to serve. Maybe they just ignored it and waited for it to go away. It would be too uncomfortable if it remained as a constant reminder. "Now you know this truth: how happy you will be if you put it into practice." (Jo 13:17) It sounds a bit sanguine to think those who cling to power would be only too happy to put foot-washing into practice.

A reader responding to a posting on this wrote, "I will never forget the last line of a homily Cardinal Dearden delivered at a Holy Thursday Chrism Mass at Blessed Sacrament Cathedral in Detroit many years ago. 'It is difficult to look down on someone when you are washing their feet.' I think we all need to get down off our clerical pedestals and become 'foot washers.'" [122]

The RCC would do well to eliminate the Sacrament of Confirmation and replace it with the Sacrament of Foot-Washing. The process itself and the fellowship it generates would have more relevance and meaning for members, and it would be practiced by willing adults, not forced on children.

MATRIMONY: A SINFUL BED
"Marriage is a wonderful institution, but who wants to live in an institution?" – Groucho Marx

What is marriage? Conflicting definitions abound nowadays.

The heated debate over the defense of marriage in the USA, seeking a political amendment that says marriage is between one man and one woman, overlooks its sordid history. "The origins of marriage are as obscure as the origins of the human race itself ... And whether marriage began with promiscuity or fidelity, monogamy or polygamy, matriarchy or patriarchy is a historical question that likewise may never be answered." [123] In progressive societies, laws are more flexible regarding what constitutes a legal marriage.

The Sacrament of Marriage offers more opportunities for committing mortal sins than perhaps all the other sacraments combined. As sexual activity is a great dynamic in marriage, the occasion of sin is ever-present. Then again, this sacrament is denied to homosexual members. A blessing in disguise—they will technically commit fewer mortal sins, since their union is not blessed by the RCC.

The RCC would like us to think that from the very beginning, when "God created man in his own image, male and female he created them," (Gen 1:27) marriage as an institution existed, and marriage was "always" between a man and a woman. It conveniently avoids mentioning that polygamy was an early arrangement, already practiced as early as Genesis 4. Perhaps the failure of one man and one woman to be compatible convinced others to check out alternatives. It wasn't until the twelfth century that the RCC came up with a ritual to bless the union of two people, and it wasn't until the Council of Trent (1545-1643 CE) that a standardized marriage ceremony was finally enacted.

Today the gay rights movement is generating a reexamination of marriage itself. We can no longer assume it is as it "always" was. It isn't. Yet the Romans (and Mormons and other conservative religious groups) pour an enormous amount of money into efforts to thwart the recognition of gay marriage by governments.

U.S. law views marriage not as a sacramental covenant, but a legal contract. This doesn't stop the RCC from imposing its view of marriage on *all* American citizens (and essentially all world citizens). It asserts that God's original intent is—and always has been, and always will be—marriage between a man and a woman. It doesn't explain why Yahweh was tolerant of polygamy from the beginning. Still holding onto the Constantine mindset, it wants states to impose its interpretation on all—regardless of their religious affiliations or lack thereof, regardless of their rights. It is unconscionable that the hierarchy diverts massive funds—which could be used to make life easier for "the least ones"—to impose its rigid interpretation of marriage upon civil, democratic societies.

The Kingdom's message is one of invitation, not imposition. But we're talking here about the RCC, the Church of Imposition.

Hierarchs love to point out that Jesus' presence at the wedding in Cana revealed God's divine plan for marriage. But John's gospel is primarily a book of signs, pointing to the Kingdom of God. His description of Jesus adding to the wedding's supply of wine is most memorable—six stone water jars, each holding twenty to thirty gallons, means well over a hundred gallons of new wine were now

THE THEOLOGY OF FEAR

available, after everyone had already drunk the old wine (and had probably gotten drunk). This new infusion of wine might only make everyone wasted. But it was high-quality wine. The steward said to Jesus, "Everyone brings out the choice wine first … but you have saved the best till now." (Jo 2:10) The text says this was his first miracle, his first *sign*. This abundance of new wine is a *sign* of the Kingdom of God, that the best is yet to come when the Kingdom is fully realized. It is not about the Sacrament of Marriage.

Increasingly, contemporary Catholics are not making their public commitment before a priest, in a church, with a mass. They are choosing their own venue, replacing the clerical witness, doing without the mass.

Marrying "outside the Church" has always been a point of contention. Historically, prohibiting members from marrying non-members has caused much pointless anxiety, separation, and sorrow. Until recent times, ceremonies for these so-called "mixed marriages" were not even allowed in a church, but only at some other location on church property, without fanfare, reinforcing disapproval of such a union. And today, the RCC demands members request a dispensation before entering into such relationships.

In fact, many dispensations need to be obtained before various types of marriages will be recognized as valid and licit. Marriage between a Catholic and a non-baptized person cannot be celebrated at a mass, while one between a Catholic and a person validly baptized in another Christian denomination requires permission for a mass. Of course, the non-Catholic is not permitted to receive communion at the nuptial mass. Marriage symbolizes union, but the Church manages to make its ceremony divisive, preventing the non-Catholic spouse from participating. And it still designates such a union as a mixed marriage, an attempt to punish the Catholic for loving the outsider, even if the "outsider" has been baptized in another Christian denomination. Again, the Church achieves its goal of making members feel abandoned and shamed.

Ne Temere, the 1907 decree of Pius X, demonstrated the stringent control the RCC wielded over the personal lives of its members. It decreed that non-Catholics had to sign papers indicating they would raise any offspring in the RCC. Today, the Catholic parties must still promise to do all in their power to raise children in the Church.

My mother's father came from a mixed marriage. At that time, all the male children of the union were to be Catholic, as his father was Catholic, and all the female children were to be Protestant, as his mother was Protestant. This rule was subsequently suppressed. And good that it was—chaos would have reigned if the RCC had extended this idea universally. It would have lost all control.

If Catholics wish to marry outside a church building, they need a dispensation from the canon that specifically requires a "sacred" location, otherwise the marriage will be invalid. Also, a priest would not be allowed to witness it, and if he did, he would face censure. Even though theology says the two people getting married act as ministers of the sacrament, the canon says they can't officiate at their own wedding wherever they wish! Canon Law trumps Catholic theology once again, as well as any potentially compassionate interpretation of it.

The *Boston Globe* recently reported on a dying man wishing to be married in the hospital. Evidently an observant member despite his declining health, he forwarded a request for a dispensation, which he received from Rev. Richard Erickson, the vicar general of the Boston Archdiocese: "Erickson recalls being asked to give special permission for a terminally ill man to be wed on his deathbed because he deeply wanted to marry before he died, 'My answer was an instant yes,' he said." [124] Thankfully, Erickson granted permission immediately. But why does a person have to jump through such bureaucratic hoops to begin with, especially a dying person? No compassion for the dying— law trumps spirit.

Interestingly, the powerful and the privileged are more likely to get prompt dispensations than run-of-the-mill Catholics. When John Kennedy, Jr. and Carolyn Bessette, both Catholics, wanted to be married in a non-denominational chapel, they needed a special dispensation from Canon Law. The powerful Kennedy connection came through. The marriage ceremony was hastily arranged and the local bishop promptly granted the dispensation.

I once petitioned my bishop to grant a dispensation for a couple who wanted me to witness their marriage in a lovely park by a river. The request was denied, and they had the ceremony without me. I would have been censured for performing it without the proper dispensation.

A Catholic has to be free of mortal sin to receive the Sacrament of Marriage worthily. If one is in mortal sin at the time of the marriage ceremony, one is hit with yet *another* mortal sin. Usually the night before, at the wedding rehearsal, the priest finds himself in the confessional. He wouldn't want the poor couple to start their married life bound for hell instead of a honeymoon.

Canon Law says Catholics who get married ("attempt marriage") outside the RCC without proper dispensations are *not* considered married (though the state would disagree). Should they divorce, they can later get married in the Church without going through the arduous annulment process, because as far as the RCC is concerned, they were just fornicating in the previous relationship (though that in itself meant multiple mortal sins, of course). As always, a denial of the spirit (the intent of the couple) is superseded by a focus on legalism (the power of Canon Law).

In most American dioceses, couples planning to marry must attend a Cana Conference where, among other things, "Natural Family Planning"—the *only* birth control method approved by the RCC—is foisted upon them. There is no open-ended discussion about family planning, contraception, or the joys of married sex.

Some bishops insist couples who live together must separate before receiving the sacrament. "It is good for a man not to marry ... But if they cannot control themselves, they should marry, for it is better to marry than to burn with passion." (1 Cor 7:9) Again, the couple's intention to commit to one another becomes secondary to some legalistic interpretation. Marriage is already present in the intent; a public ceremony only acknowledges the private prior consent between the two.

In religious orders, novitiates generally take "simple vows" for three years before taking "solemn vows." Living under simple vows for some time enables both the individual and the community to determine if they are compatible. If so, both proceed to celebrate solemn vows. Similarly, living together for some time before contracting the Sacrament of Marriage is a very reasonable way to determine whether to proceed with solemnizing the union. Of course, if they live together "as brother and sister," the RCC has no problem with it. But if they indulge in sex, the RCC has an issue.

Humanae Vitae (Human Life) represented a very unpopular decision by Pope Paul VI. His commission (seventy-two mostly lay members from five continents) deliberated for some time, and in 1966 strongly recommended that he lift the RCC's ban on artificial birth control. He refused, and in fact reinforced it with vigor, and with this document. For him, it is always intrinsically wrong to prevent a birth through contraception, which he defined in Section 14, entitled Unlawful Birth Control Methods, as "every action which, either in anticipation of the conjugal act or in its accomplishment, or in the development of its natural consequences, proposes, whether as an end or as a means, to render procreation impossible." This includes sterilization, condoms and other barrier methods, spermicides, *coitus interruptus* (withdrawal method), the Pill, and all other methods. [125]

The RCC's resistance to contraception is relentless. In the dustup over President Obama's Affordable Care Act, under which all institutions and organizations are to allow contraception coverage, U.S. bishops mounted an attack, hoping to exempt this provision. They clamored that religious liberty was being undermined by forcing Catholic institutions to provide coverage. This issue demonstrates their defiance against contraception use altogether. The religious liberty angle simply cloaks this in a loftier ideal.

Calling something "intrinsically wrong" is code for labeling it "mortal sin." So each time Catholics use birth control, even within a fully sanctioned and Church-approved marriage, they commit mortal sin. If they have sex several times a week, they commit several mortal sins. And the old question comes up—if one mortal sin totally separates a person from God, how much more separation can multiple sins cause? Some "liberal" defenders of the Church's position would contend that the two people are simply in a state of mortal sin, totally separated from God, despite the number of times the act takes place. *That* relieves a lot of anxiety.

The papal decree deems *any action* that will "render procreation impossible" as intrinsically evil. But wait. People using the sanctioned Natural Family Planning have the *intention* of preventing procreation, including those practicing the pope's "rhythm method." Sin is an *intentional* act. It is hypocritical to absolve them of any wrongdoing, since they have the exact same *intent* as others who are sentenced to hell because they happen to choose a different form of birth control.

Furthermore, the Vatican contends "artificial" birth control is mortally sinful—but Natural Family Planning follows Natural Law and therefore is not artificial. This is disingenuous at best. Theologically, intent, not method (the ends, not the means), constitutes mortal sin.

Many Catholics grew up unaware of the RCC's cognitive dissonance, but they're catching on. As one gentleman put it, in responding to a Yahoo! blog discussing Natural Family Planning, "By the way, I tried it the pope's way and ended up with four kids in five years. So I decided to get cut and now I shoot blanks!" Of course, a vasectomy is just *another* mortal sin.

But it's back to the same riddles. *Maybe* it would be less offensive to God because it counts as only one mortal sin, while regularly using a condom would rack up countless mortal sins. So, along those lines of reasoning, *maybe* it would be meritorious to have the vasectomy. And if that logic makes sense, then *maybe* the Church should be encouraging vasectomies to prevent millions of mortal offenses against God!

In defining the nature of marriage—and the intimate lives of all those who enter into it—the RCC has effectively guaranteed a steady stream of new little members and a continuation of its control. After all, the vast majority are born into it. Few adults join because they're somehow convinced of its claims (usually, it's to be religiously compatible with a spouse). For the same reason, many Catholics defect to other churches, synagogues, mosques, or temples—or no religious affiliation.

Once members navigate all the obstacles to enter the Sacrament of Marriage, it is extremely difficult to exit. Until present times, dispensations to terminate marriages were granted only in extreme situations. Of course, the powerful and privileged could readily obtain them. Dispensations are granted more frequently for upper-crust Catholics than garden-variety Catholics. No one ever accused the RCC of applying Canon Law fairly and equally.

The most celebrated request for a dispensation to end a marriage was Henry VIII of England, hoping to divorce his wife, Catherine of Aragon, widow of Henry's brother. Henry had received from corrupt Pope Leo X (1513-1521) the title "Defender of the Faith" for his book, *Defence* [sic] *of the Seven Sacraments*, wherein he defended the sacramental nature of marriage and affirmed the supremacy of the pope. After his roving eye locked on Anne Boleyn, he wanted a dispensation from his twenty-four-year marriage. Under normal circumstances, as a powerful king and protector of the papacy, it would have been a done deal. But Catherine of Aragon's uncle, Charles V of Spain, was ruler of the Holy Roman Empire, a larger political domain than Henry's England. By denying Henry the dispensation, the Roman Church lost England. It was not a religious but a political consideration that influenced Pope Clement VII's (1523-1534) anguished decision.

Historically, ordinary members had great difficulty obtaining a dispensation to end a marriage. The only recourse was to petition the Vatican, where the request could languish for years. To allow for the ultimate happiness of a couple in a far-off country, to lift the burden of two ordinary people who found themselves in an intolerable situation, was hardly the compassionate concern of a distant pope and his curia. Until recently, the Vatican reserved all rights to grant dispensations.

In some countries, men of means, in lieu of a dispensation, resolved this by taking on mistresses to satisfy their pleasurable pursuit of sex. Each act of sex with a mistress would constitute at least two mortal sins—adultery for the married man, and fornication for the unmarried woman. (And don't forget birth control.) A brief sexual dalliance would consign two people to hell for all eternity, yet another case in which the punishment doesn't fit the crime.

Divorce has been particularly condemned by the RCC. "Divorce is a grave offense of the natural law," states the *Catechism*. "Divorce does injury to the covenant of salvation, of which sacramental marriage is the sign." [126] Church leaders show little compassion toward those suffering a hellish marriage. What do they care? It's no sweat on their part to repeat the pious platitude, "You have to carry your cross." This is a horrible misapplication of Jesus' admonition to "take up your cross." Individual priests may quietly counsel some to divorce, but they don't publicly encourage it lest the Church divorce *them*.

Countless women throughout history have been locked in abusive relationships but unable to divorce, particularly in societies where the RCC dominated. Men had free rein to be abusive, and women had few resources to survive. Those who divorced were shunned by the community. Those who divorced *and* remarried outside the Church were denied communion and remained excommunicated, unless they got a Church-sanctioned annulment or vowed to live together as brother and sister.

The RCC claims it is compassionate when it provides the internal forum. In his 1981 "Familiaris Consortio, On the Role of the Christian Family in the Modern World," Pope John Paul II says, "Reconciliation in the sacrament of Penance which would open the way to the Eucharist [internal forum solution], can only be granted to those who, repenting of having broken the sign of the Covenant and of fidelity to Christ, are sincerely ready to undertake a way of life that is no longer in contradiction to the indissolubility of marriage. This means, in practice, that when, for serious reasons, such as for example the children's upbringing, a man and a woman cannot satisfy the obligation to separate, they take on themselves the duty to live in complete continence, that is, by abstinence from the acts proper to married couples." [127] This is hardly a realistic or healthy solution for two people who once shared the pleasures of sex— suddenly being expected to settle for a platonic relationship, while setting themselves up for continual temptation. In fact, the whole arrangement contradicts RCC theology, which contends that if you find yourself in an occasion of sin, you must remove yourself from it.

The Church's magic solution is the "annulment"—its form of divorce (though it is quick to assert that *annulment* and *divorce* are not synonymous). When it grants an annulment, it contends there never *was* a marriage in the first place, even if a couple was married many years, had children and grandchildren. The original union was not entered validly.

As more Catholics clamored to end their marriages and have new ones blessed by the Church, annulments suddenly mushroomed, particularly in the USA. While only about 6 percent of Catholics reside here, 60 percent of its annulments are granted here. It has been described charitably as a sham, humiliating and demeaning to many who enter the process, often forced to participate because a spouse wants out of one marriage and official sanction for a new one. James Carroll said, "Annulment is now a form of divorce in every way but name, and the Church (hierarchy) refusal to acknowledge this is deeply corrupting. Moreover, the Catholic annulment procedures hurt children, are cruel to former spouses, force applicants to misrepresent the past, mock well-meaning priests, and drive many thousands out of the Church. It is a disaster." [128]

Unhappily married Catholics aren't allowed to trust their own judgment, to acknowledge that their marriage is dead and remaining in it will harm all concerned. If they were mature enough, they would follow their conscience rather than go through the legalistic games of the annulment process. The Church holds—rightly—that one must follow and be true to one's conscience. But then it creates yet another Catholic *Catch-22*. Members must have an "informed conscience," but the only authority to "inform" the conscience is the RCC.

Children certainly are a primary concern in the breakup of a union. But staying together for the children isn't necessarily in their best interests. If the RCC were primarily focused on healing persons, as was Jesus, it wouldn't send its clergy to study Canon Law as therapeutic counseling for those who need to heal. The Orthodox are more compassionate, realizing human error and allowing for up to three divorces.

The inability to act on one's own conscience is indicative of immaturity, the need for approval or authorization of an institution to feel at peace with every personal decision. So members seek annulments because they need an authority to salve their conscience. Yet authority can be dead wrong, as demonstrated repeatedly throughout history. Fortunately, fewer members are clinging to dependence on the institution as they become educated and live in pluralistic, democratic societies.

Our conscience is our soul. The most ancient of wisdom was enunciated in Shakespeare's universal truism, "To thine own self be true." To deny one's conscience is to deny oneself.

Some clergymen do understand this. Recall the toast Cardinal Newman once gave after a dinner: "If I am obliged to bring religion into after-dinner toasts (which indeed does not seem quite the thing), I shall drink ... to conscience first, and to the Pope afterwards." 129

Even Joseph Ratzinger acknowledged this in his 1968 commentary on the II Vatican Council, admitting that "over the pope ... there still stands one's own conscience, which must be obeyed before all else, if necessary, even against the requirement of ecclesiastical authority."

He probably wishes he wasn't on record for *that* one, now having to eat his words. Maybe it was a one-time statement exclaimed in his exuberance over the new wine served at Vatican II. But it should be carved in stone in St. Peter's Square. How many Catholic preachers and teachers persistently keep *this* principle before their members?

The RCC is quick to assert Jesus was the champion of the indissolubility of marriage, quoting that man cannot separate what God has joined. It's more complicated than that. As Ched Myers points out, "there was no recognition of the reciprocal rights for women in Jewish law of his time." The context of the times was patriarchy. The deck was stacked against women. "The problem, as E. Schüssler Fiorenza sees it, is that the legal issue was totally male-centered and presupposed patriarchal marriage as a given." [130] The new wine here is Jesus' assertion that within the social relationship of marriage, both people are to be treated as equals. But the RCC refuses to read "the signs of the times." For Benedict XVI, this is relativism. He staunchly rejects "the signs of the times," and therefore the admonition of Jesus. Heretical, he?

Canon Law asserts the Church must defend the "bond of marriage" and actually assigns a person as the "defender of the bond" (*"defensor matrimonii"*). It makes an abstract concept into something that must be championed, protected, and preserved—no matter what. To make this "bond" an absolute, and to subject the person to it, denies the new wine of Jesus in which the person is always absolute and the Law—*all* laws—always relative, meant only to serve the well-being of the person.

The "bond of marriage" is an abstract construct, treated as superior to an actual person. In similar fashion, the U.S. corporation is now treated as a person, and in reality becomes superior to any person, because of its financial clout.

The RCC believes "the grace of this Sacrament perfects the love of husband and wife, binds them together in fidelity and helps them welcome and care for children." [131] Well, this grace must not be very efficacious, since the Catholic divorce rate in America is no better than that of most other religions.

Surprisingly, a 2000 study by independent researchers found that born-again Christians, particularly Baptists, had a higher divorce rate than atheists and agnostics, who reject any notion of grace being implanted in the relationship when they vow to marry. Ron Barrier, spokesperson for American Atheists, stressed that religious claims of superior morality were invalidated by this study's data: "Atheists reject, and rightly so, the primitive patriarchal attitudes so prevalent in many religions with respect to marriage." [132]

Marriage is not easy *with* grace, but how do people handle it *without* grace? A poet identified the paradox: "By virtue, some men fall, and by vice, some men rise!" Atheists sound like Pelagians, suggesting that people can do good without grace. The atheist position on marriage is reflective of Jesus' intervention in the issue when he sided with the woman as an equal in the marriage, rejecting the old wine of patriarchal dominance. It was an incredibly progressive stance to take at the time.

And so yet another sacrament in my review here seems to generate more anguish and heartbreak than grace and spirituality. An objective person considering the Sacrament of Marriage, with all of its traps and pitfalls, might well decide it's not worth it. It just adds another ongoing occasion of sin, a loaded environment that can only cause God pain. Better not to take the sacrament at all.

ANOINTING OF THE SICK: A PLACEBO?
"It's no longer a question of staying healthy.
It's a question of finding a sickness you like." – Jackie Mason

The Sacrament of Anointing of the Sick is widely misunderstood. Some of the confusion stems from its ongoing evolution. Since Vatican II, it underwent some major changes. For centuries it was called Extreme Unction, though that's rarely heard anymore. Pre-Vatican II, it was associated with the Sacrament of the Last Rites, confected for a dying person—hearing confession, anointing with oil, giving communion.

A "happy death"—the chance to have the Last Rites confected by a priest—would be the greatest blessing of all (outside of being baptized on one's deathbed). This provided immense relief for an anguished family, knowing their loved one would escape the fiery pit of hell, particularly if the person had neglected Catholic obligations.

At times like this, members wanted a priest more than anyone else, even a doctor, because the Last Rites were balm against the terror of hell, in which they had been thoroughly indoctrinated.

Catholics have long associated the Sacrament of Anointing the Sick with the Last Rites (which occurs when death is expected). It was not exactly reassuring. To call a priest in to confect the anointing of the sick often startled the sick, panicking them. It must mean the end. Was the illness fatal? Did family members know something they didn't know?

"To the hour of death, the priest may bring comfort or torment; to this day, Catholics who have ceased to believe are seen to turn back then, as if held by an inner chain." [133]

Considering the anxiety implanted in their earliest days, even some fallen-away Catholics would not refuse the Last Rites at the time of death. The old wine of fear always kicked in, and the reason is clearly stated in the Letter to the Hebrews: "It is a terrible thing to fall into the hands of the living God." (Heb 10:31) As Jacques Dupuis notes in *The Christian Faith*, "In accordance with God's universal ordinance the souls of those who die in actual mortal sin descend immediately after death to hell where they are tormented by eternal punishment." [134]

The infamous Fr. Marcial Maciel, whom John Paul II acknowledged as an "efficacious guide for youth," refused this sacrament on his deathbed. When a priest tried to anoint him, he grew belligerent, yelling, "I said no!" According to reporters, he "did not believe in God's pardon." [135] If anyone might have benefitted from the sacrament, he would have.

Over time, the role of the priest evolved to the point where he would be "on duty" around the clock much like a firefighter ready to put out a fire (in this case, the fire of hell), to confect the anointing.

Why? Because Catholics could never be sure they were in the state of grace. The RCC had scattered the seeds of anxiety, and they had successfully taken root. Joan of Arc's inquisitor questioned her: "Do you know yourself to be in God's grace?" If Joan answered *yes* she would commit heresy, as the Church taught no one could be certain of being in God's grace. She deftly passed through the horns of the dilemma: "If I am not in God's grace, may God put me there; if I am, may God keep me there." Her right answer didn't save her, though.

The fear of dying is humanity's dread (except for the wretched of the earth, for them dying is a blessing, a reprieve from the harsh sentence life has dealt them through no fault of their own). The anxiety over dying is particularly compounded for Christians and Muslims, since an afterlife of eternal torture looms as a real possibility. But it is especially onerous for Catholics, because the theology of fear has identified countless occasions of sin that will get them there. It has succeeded in telling the greatest *horror story* ever told.

Some will retort it was Jesus who initially told the horror story, citing passages attributed to him in Luke 16 and Matthew 25, and particularly Mark 9, when guilty parties are condemned to a terrifying place "where their worm dies not, and the fire is not quenched." (Mk 9:48) His message here contains no liberation, no reassurance, and no fresh interpretation of the hellfire of scriptures. Revenge and punishment are old wine. And while unconditional love, even of the enemy, is a refreshing prospect for imperfect humanity, this needs to be true of God as well.

If the Jesus story simply reaffirms what a terrible thing it is to fall into the hands of the living God, where the hell is the new wine, the good news? Hell is old news, old wine.

The Sacrament of the Anointing of the Sick is embraced because there is already so much suffering here, anticipating more in an afterlife is beyond the comprehension of the human psyche. Since Vatican II, reception of this sacrament has been encouraged even when *not* on a deathbed.

Humans instinctively want to minimize suffering. Some may turn to this sacrament, but it seems inadequate, as those frantic for relief flock to shrines and holy sites, sanctioned by the Church, where reportedly "miraculous" cures have taken place. The most famous of course is Lourdes, with about 5 million annual visitors. Lourdes is only one of many. One list shows ninety-seven saints, each assigned to a specific illness or ailment—St. Vitalis for venereal diseases, St. Fiacre for fistulas, and on and on. It amounts to a veritable Hindu-like pantheon of mini-gods. Many have shrines, and some are big money-makers. As with the sacraments, paying for prayers for the sick only emphasizes how easily the vulnerable are fleeced. It adds an unnecessary burden to those already desperate, and arguably superstitious.

While the RCC officially denounces "superstition," it passively condones operations that are essentially religious con games. The desperately sick go to great lengths for relief, forfeiting whatever they have for a cure. If Church leaders were sincere, they would counsel the sick to stay home and pray where they are. Better their money was offered for medical research. Some will argue that petitioning saints acts as a placebo, and placebos do have positive effects. Okay. But why demand a fee? Why not freebies for the ill?

Unfortunately, there is no shortage of charlatans who will seize any opportunity to add to the woes of the ill by promising false hope—at a price. Televangelists in particular make money selling "blessed cloths" and "sacred oils" to people yearning for relief from suffering and pain. It's a market for the unscrupulous, and many wolves in sheep's clothing come to fleece the flock when they are down. These unprincipled hirelings have taken a cue from the RCC's success in maintaining a miracle industry.

A key description of Jesus is that of a healer. While people sought him out, he also took the lead and intervened on behalf of the suffering. John Dominic Crossan says, "I'm completely convinced that Jesus was a major healer. I don't think anybody would talk about Jesus if all he did was talk." [136] Jesus was depicted as a miracle worker, and that certainly remains an attraction for desperate folks.

We tend to project from the present to the past through our own personal lens. While Jesus is a healer, as Crossan holds, what he did is not necessarily what we would describe as a healing, that is, a miraculous recovery or removal from a life-threatening illness or disease. "Jesus and all healers of that period could only perceive illnesses and not diseases … Notice in each healing instance the almost total disregard of symptoms (something very essential to disease). Instead there is constant concern for meaning … Jesus' activity is best described as healing, not curing. He provides social meaning for the life problems resulting from the sickness." [137]

In the time of Jesus, illness was associated with impurity or sin, which excluded a person from full status in the community. When Jesus healed, he restored an excluded person to the community. This was a disruptive activity, rendering him a threat to "civic order." [138] Disease understandably terrified people who had little understanding of it and no remedy for it. Quarantine was a knee-jerk reaction, one that we continue today when a new threat such as AIDS appeared. For Jesus, a person was healed not in isolation but within the community. Fear, however, will cause people to reject even their own, lest they too become contaminated.

The mistaken notion that Jesus went around favoring some people with a cure has led, in these latter days, to the belief that invoking Jesus (or a Roman saint) will single out a person for a special physical cure. Kind of a spiritual lottery game. This plays well to the gullible and sincere, "the little ones."

For a person to get the green light to be canonized, two miracles are required. God then must act in a capricious way to single out some and not others, causing an added burden of rejection for those who don't get the ultimate blessing.

This two-miracle standard for sainthood is a latter-day control mechanism of the RCC. It encourages people to "pray hard" for a miracle. But how hard is hard enough?

If a common thread waves through the human race, it is the suffering endured from the earliest records to the present. When authors in antiquity recorded the life they experienced, it was an endless list of personal and societal disasters—violent weather, drought, famine, pestilence, venomous snakes, rabid dogs, scorpions, lack of sanitation and shelter, constant warfare, disease (typhus, influenza, measles, leprosy, syphilis), as well as epidemics and plagues for which there were no cures.

"Drug craft was arguably the Classical world's greatest resource," writes D.C.A. Hillman in *The Chemical Muse.* "It should not be surprising that our ancestors resorted to chemical recreation. Nor should we be afraid to admit that some of the most distinguished members of the ancient world used recreational drugs. After all, these people lived in a time that demanded much more of the psyche as well as the body; and pharmaceutical bliss was nothing more or less than a gift, a chance to relieve the heavy burden imposed by the dreadful living conditions of Classical civilization. As Aldous Huxley said most eloquently: 'That humanity at large will ever be able to dispense with Artificial Paradises seems very unlikely. Most men and women lead lives at the worst so painful, at the best so monotonous, poor and limited, that the urge to escape, the longing to transcend themselves if only for a few moments, is and has always been one of the principal appetites of the soul.'" [139]

He went on to list "art and religion" as well as "chemical intoxicants" as "modifiers of consciousness." [140] Never enough freebies for the sick.

"The longing to transcend themselves" has been a universal quest for humans, especially when ill. People instinctively reach for relief— including drugs and religion. In fact, Karl Marx linked the two. Unfortunately, both come with a price tag.

THE PRIESTHOOD: O GOD! WHAT A LIFE!
"Hell is paved with priests' skulls." – St. John Chrysostom

"One cannot escape the harsh fact that as a ministerial profession, the priesthood has very serious problems. They are not new. They did not develop yesterday or last year." – Andrew Greeley

Priests are essentially dispensers of grace. Their ability to confect, to make sacraments happen, allows this. "Through Holy Orders, men receive a share in the priesthood of Christ, and receive the power to confect the sacraments, especially the Eucharist, Reconciliation, Anointing of the Sick and Confirmation." [141]

Like marriage, the priesthood can be its own occasion of sin. If a priest commits a mortal sin, then confects a sacrament, he commits "sacrilege," which of course is another mortal sin. If he proceeds, un-confessed, to confect more sacraments, he amasses multiple mortal sins. Of course, he was already separated from God. One did the trick.

But there's a loophole. Canon Law 916 fortuitously grants him a temporary reprieve to confect sacraments without incurring more mortal sins if he resolves to confess as soon as possible. Of course, some priests might not get around to confessing for some time (such as missionaries hundreds of miles from other priests). The Letter of

James counsels, "Confess your sins to one another," but lay people can't give absolution, so why bother disclosing anything to *them*?

Since the priest confects the sacraments *"in persona Christi,"* he acts as a medium, channeling Jesus. He may pronounce a verbal formula, employ the necessary materials, and make the required gestures, but it is Jesus who actually performs the transformation of the sacrament. The priest merely pronounces precise words over an object—and, voilà, Roman magic happens.

Church theology invented a disingenuous device, which essentially makes the person of the priest irrelevant, *"ex opere operato"* ("from the work worked"). Whoever came up with this clever theological scheme foresaw that many sticky situations could potentially block the flow of grace. Perhaps it was initiated to cover for bad popes and priests.

Not to worry. As long as the priest says the correct words (form) and employs the required elements (matter)—presto! A sacrament is confected!

The priest has no personal or professional input as long as he sticks to the official confecting directions. He may be agnostic or atheist— he may be immoral, intoxicated, or insane—just not illiterate. This reflects Evelyn Waugh's witty observation: "There is a species of person called a 'Modern Churchman' who draws the full salary of a beneficed clergyman and need not commit himself to any religious belief."

This bare-minimum requirement is unfortunate. Throughout history, notorious popes and clergymen confected sacraments despite an unsavory character—it didn't matter. Perhaps if it did, these men might have reconsidered their personal lives. Today, priests are expected to act as robots—just read the instructions, with no interpretations or additions, and remain compliant to the directions of hierarchs.

I spent *thirteen years* preparing for ordination, when *seven days* would have sufficed. Each day of the week, an instructor could easily cover the confecting of one sacrament. In a week, the official curriculum ("Sacraments 101") would conclude. Basically, the only requirement is reading ability. There is to be no ad-libbing, no deviating from the script. The priest is reduced to a hollow man.

Words speak louder than *actions* in the Vatican's oversight of its priests. It is eternally vigilant in making sure the right words are recited during its rituals. Since Advent 2011, it has forced an archaic, cumbersome translation of the mass on the masses. All part of the stealth measure to subvert Vatican II.

One priest in the diocese of Bellevue, IL rearranged the words in an effort to make them more understandable. The local bishop accepted his retirement, at a time marked by a desperate shortage of priests. This same bishop, Edward Braxton, dragged his feet in paying for the pain caused by a pedophile pastor in his diocese. The jury awarded $5 million, and twice Braxton petitioned the Illinois Supreme Court to overturn it. Twice he failed, and ultimately had to pay an additional $1.3 million. A man regarded as a sensitive pastor was muscled out because of a few *words*, yet the Vatican did nothing to a bishop because of his harmful *actions*, for he is one of their trusted own.

Every day, a priest is obliged to recite the breviary, the collection of psalms and prayers that monks chant in choir. This is partly to give him something to do during the day. It takes a half-hour or more, depending on how rapidly he can read and pray. But the duty comes with an eternal price. Failure to pray it daily is—you guessed it—a mortal sin. Each day it's neglected—another mortal sin. Again, there are more interesting ways of going to hell than skipping repetitive psalms.

Priests have been known to read the breviary while drinking, smoking, or watching TV. They are well aware that prayer is supposed to open the mind and heart to God, but that isn't the point. The point is to avoid being slapped with a mortal sin.

Following the letter of the law, not the spirit, is what counts.

Today's institution is more reflective of the priesthood of the Roman Empire than of the gospels. Consider the issue of "female priests."

The RCC claims Jesus didn't ordain women as priests, so today there can be no women priests. End of story. But Jesus didn't ordain *men* as priests. He sought disciples for the Kingdom of God, male and female. Historically, and largely still, women have been the service providers, men have exercised the power. Jesus sought men to embrace service as the antidote to male power.

In fact, Jesus never used the word *priest* in referring to his disciples, and neither did Paul. It gradually crept into acceptance and came to identify an elite group of males who had power over believers, enforcing the rules and obligations of the RCC, doling out the consequences to those who failed to obey. Priests were the moral cops on the ground, enforcing the theology of fear, like today's religious police in Muslim countries of the Middle East.

Furthermore, priests lived with the onerous burden of having to uphold programs that were immoral, often failing to grasp the evil they committed in the pursuit of enforcement: "In July 1597, in a field outside Brussels, forty-five-year-old Anna Utenhove was, with the consent of Albert (archduke) and Archbishop Hovius, buried alive." [142] Who was Anna Utenhove and what warranted her grisly death? She was a simple servant woman who was victimized by a priest acting as a moral constable on patrol. A local pastor, Francis Eland, observed that since she had neither confessed nor communed, she must be a heretic. There is no record that the pastor or his archbishop had any qualms of conscience about burying this woman alive. Public executions of heretics were routine activities during the RCC's reign of terror. People believed out of fear—fear of an imminent, torturous death here and of everlasting pain in the next life. While the Church today touts itself as pro-life, much of its history has been anti-life. And its clerics have been expected to participate.

Regrettably, the priesthood is fraught with mortal dangers. As noted earlier, the obligation to hear confession can lead to sin, as priests are forced to listen to details of sexual transgressions.

A *New Yorker* magazine cartoon depicts a dowdy, rotund, elderly woman commenting to an equally dowdy, rotund elderly priest outside the confessional: "I bet your confessions are more interesting than mine!"

A priest, supposedly a channel of grace, easily falls from grace himself. He is under the gun to enforce a version of morality possibly in conflict with his conscience. He may mature to where he no longer believes many of the tenets of the RCC and passively resists enforcing them, or does so most reluctantly. But it is a rare priest who will act out or speak out against them, as this brings swift and immediate reprimand. (The exception is clerical child abusers, however, who will be treated to the intricate loopholes of Canon Law.)

The number of men who have left the priesthood since Vatican II is estimated at more than 150,000. [143] The reasons are manifold. Many left to love and marry rather than continue to "stay and play." The Church is unforgiving if a priest decides to live authentically in an open, loving relationship. Instead, it countenances a "don't ask, don't tell" policy. But not all left simply to marry a woman (some were gay). Some left because they rejected the institution, were dissatisfied with the life, or wanted to pursue other careers. Perhaps the greater number left because they no longer believed in the RCC's interpretation of its own dogma and the subsequent effect on human morality. To remain would mean living with a constant conflict of conscience, with ongoing cognitive dissonance.

In the days when there were plenty of priests, there were few prayers for priest vocations. With the severe decline, heaven has been bombarded with prayers for priests, as seen in liturgical documents and texts. The response has been dismal. This questions the efficacy of prayer.

A pious prayer for priests by Père Lacordaire describes a priest as living in the world without desiring its pleasures, a member of every family yet belonging to none, sharing all suffering, penetrating all secrets, healing all wounds, connecting God with men, all the while having a heart of bronze for chastity. He ends it by exclaiming, "O God, what a life!" This prayer was framed and hung on the wall leading to the cafeteria at my high school seminary. Often a classmate emphasized the last line by negatively accenting it and comically moaning, "O God, what a life!"

That classmate didn't continue on the path to priesthood. Apparently he was prescient in realizing it as an unnatural life designed by the

THE THEOLOGY OF FEAR

RCC to lure young idealistic males into embracing something ultimately hazardous to their spiritual health and detrimental to their souls.

It is a healthy sign when young men reject the celibate priesthood. This abnormal way of life is an unnecessary burden to men, and to the community. The end of clericalism due to the clerical sexual-abuse scandal is a strange blessing, an answer to prayer in an unexpected way. An elite clerical culture undermines the new wine of the Kingdom's teaching of equality. It is a privileged caste system in the RCC, more reflective of the priesthood of the Roman Empire.

The sacraments are narrow legalistic requirements demanding no personal contribution from the one confecting, no "heavy lifting." So why the need to maintain an ecclesiastical welfare system for a privileged class?

A month after I was ordained in 1966, the pastor gave me a check. I asked what it was for and he replied, "Your salary." I said, "You get *paid* for this?" I assumed all one got was room and board. There had been no discussion in the seminary about financial compensation or benefits, nor had we inquired. At age twenty-seven, I was naive on many levels.

Many religious groups function just fine without subsidizing those who act on behalf of the community, who largely volunteer their services. This open model reflects the Kingdom.

All disciples of the Kingdom are supposedly equal. But the priesthood remains a huge obstacle to true equality within the RCC. A priest is viewed as special, "another Christ." Priests immediately become "holier" at ordination (which invalidates baptism) and automatically remain "holier" indefinitely just because of their office. People venerate priests, seeing them as superior, kissing their hands, and of course genuflecting to the pope, the holiest priest of all, *the* Holy Father.

Lord Acton's most well-known quote, absolute power corrupting absolutely, overshadows a comment later in the same passage: "There is no worse heresy than the fact that the office sanctifies the

182

holder of it." According to Sean O'Conaill, "Acton was clearly indicting both Catholic clericalism and the monarchical principle—the notion that either kings or clerics are sanctified—made holy—by the offices they hold." [144]

Either baptism sanctifies all equally, or it doesn't.

"ALL REPETITION IS ANTI-SPIRITUAL"
"Endless repetition, in and out of season, has spoiled for us the freshness, the naiveté, the simple romantic charm of the Gospels."
– Oscar Wilde

As I've demonstrated, the RCC deemphasized Jesus' proclamation of the Kingdom and emphasized the Seven Sacraments as its primary focus. When a priest is selected and elevated to become a bishop, he generally stops confecting at least four sacraments—baptism, confession, anointing of the sick, and matrimony. Save for media photo opps or celebrity situations, confecting these sacraments is the grunt work of lowly clergy. The hierarchy can't be bothered.

When the deaconate was restored, it was a great opportunity for priests to shed some sacramental duties, particularly baptizing infants and witnessing marriages. If they could, they would gladly let deacons take on more of the sacramental workload.

A cleric recently accused of adult sexual and financial misconduct, Fr. John Corapi, is the RCC's version of a televangelist. He reportedly made this comment as he separated himself from priestly activities: "'Nothing much will change,' he says, explaining that he really had little to do with the sacraments, anyway—saying mass, hearing confession, anointing the sick." [145]

Truth be told, most priests would welcome delegating their duties.

Confecting the sacraments means reading through the rituals. It doesn't take long for the sheen to wear off—repeatedly baptizing screaming and squirming infants, being tortured by children's halting confessions, reciting liturgy after liturgy—and to become bored by the repetition, tired of the dry ritual that prohibits innovation or improvisation.

Oscar Wilde rightly noted that "all repetition is anti-spiritual." The replicating drone of stylized liturgical text easily dries a priest up.

When I was younger, I questioned why so many older priests seemed bored when confecting the sacraments. Now I know. In the movie *Harold and Maude*, based on the book, an older priest about to begin yet another funeral mass for an anonymous soul pauses to exhale, letting out a noticeably glum sigh before reluctantly cracking open the ritual book. He is as lifeless as the corpse!

Burying the dead eventually became an essential part of the priest's job description. Unfortunately, the priest has become the auxiliary undertaker. This entails a significant portion of time.

The parish in which I grew up was approximately one square mile. The pastor constantly boasted from the pulpit that he was "pastor of the largest parish in the largest archdiocese of the world!" Who were we to question him? On Sundays the parish offered thirteen masses, using an upper and lower church. There were 2,200 students in the parochial school, more than 1,000 girls in the high school, more than seventy sisters in the convent, and six full-time priests in the rectory. Funerals were a daily occurrence, often two or three per day, six days a week.

The focus on performing funeral masses that remains today undermines Jesus' challenge. "Let the dead bury their own dead; but as for you, go and proclaim everywhere the Kingdom of God." (Lk 9:60) The prophetic proclamation of the Kingdom was suppressed when the Seven Sacraments became the top priority of the RCC. "The harvest is plentiful but the laborers are few." (Lk 10:2)

The Kingdom seeks prophetic servants, but this will come with a personal price, jeopardizing one's salary. Currently, men serve less often as prophetic proclaimers of the Kingdom, more frequently as auxiliary undertakers. John Paul II viewed the priest as a "functionary." He was more in sync with the latter than the former.

CHAPTER SEVEN

THE COST OF DISCIPLESHIP: SAVING SOULS VERSUS SECURING STRUCTURES

"I was brought up as a Catholic and went to church every week and took the sacraments. It never really touched the core of my being." – Sting

Jesus is big business. Anyone can take a copy of the New Testament (as there are no copyright laws), gather a few people together, and begin collecting money from them as they hear the Good News.

Why has Christianity become so expensive, when faith is a free gift? Why are so many willing to pay for this free gift, and pay handsomely, often at personal sacrifice? Why are so many clergy willing to fleece the flock for their personal well-being?

THE GOOD NEWS AS A BRANDED PRODUCT
"The corruption of the American soul is consumerism."
– Ben Nicholson

Only in America do churches become family dynasties. They keep everything in the family because the good news is there's big money in preaching the Good News. Only in America, religious entrepreneurship thrives. Millions are willing to shell out billions.

The most famous of family ministry dynasties is the Billy Graham Evangelistic Association. It serves as a template for other Christian organizations that want to mimic his success. Spouses, children, and family-friendly folks are board members. The ministry is passed on from generation to generation like any family-owned business, except this one is about selling God, an extremely profitable commodity in America.

Then there's Joyce Meyer, Creflo Dollar, Paula White, Jimmy Swaggart, Kenneth Copeland, Joel Osteen, Benny Hinn, etc.—all ministers who successfully launched multi-million dollar ministries by stacking the board with relatives and keeping things in the family.

One dynasty that shattered and splintered, though, was run by Robert Schuller, famous for his Crystal Cathedral. His son and daughter became embroiled over control of the operation. His dynasty is dying, and Schuller, who preached positive thinking, is sinking into a sea of unmanageable negative debt. But bankruptcy is salvation. The diocese of Orange, CA recently purchased the iconic mega-church (and setting for Schuller's evangelical TV broadcast) for $57.5 million. Despite having paid out millions for clerical sexual-abuse cases, it was still able to buy this glass menagerie, and spend millions more retrofitting it for Catholic worship. There *is* room in the inn, when you buy the inn.

Senator Charles Grassley (R-IA) launched a 2009 investigation of six televangelists, questioning alleged abuse of their nonprofit status in purchasing luxury homes and airplanes while racking up questionable credit card expenses. Religious nonprofits fought back. In 2009, there was no charge of a "war on religion" as currently seen over the Obama administration's contraceptive coverage. Grassley's investigation of three years was inconclusive, as his panel had difficulty obtaining complete financial records.

Christianity seems to be singular and peculiar in selling its "Good News" for profit, or at least for a comfortable living and extravagant lifestyle. Jesus has been a bountiful blessing for an elite cadre of preachers preaching a gospel of wealth. They have become wealthy at the expensive of "the faithful" (more accurately, "the gullible"). They don't expound on Jesus' admonition to go and sell what you have and give it to the poor. There is no parallel in any world religion. This seems an exclusively Christian phenomenon. You'd be hard pressed to find any imams, rabbis, or Buddhist monks who sell their brand of religion and promote themselves as celebrities.

In the Jewish tradition, there needed to be ten men present in the Temple for a legitimate prayer service. Women didn't count. But men who weren't Jewish would be considered if necessary. Jesus sought to economize access to God by claiming that two or three persons sufficed, without indicating male or female, and there was no need for a Temple. The idea was simply to worship in spirit and truth.

The commanding physical presence of the RCC might have inspired televangelists and mega-church pastors, realizing they too could build a kingdom. It was Constantine who began state subsidies to the RCC and undertook a massive building plan.

This model remains intact. Catholics today contribute enormous sums for buildings, maintenance, clerical staffs, and staffs for the clerics. Fundraising has become an unofficial "sacrament" practiced in every church, everywhere, all the time—in Jesus' name. Amen! Proclaiming the Kingdom has been replaced with creating a personal kingdom.

It wasn't always that way.

Somehow before Constantine the RCC thrived as a subversive sect within the Roman Empire without possessing any prominent buildings, or subsidizing any clergy. *Somehow* simple gatherings thrived when two, three, or more met to share the Jesus story and attempted to practice it. *Somehow* disciples became more numerous. *Somehow* a group effect was sensed among the population. "See how these Christians love one another," or so Tertullian reported what others were saying about his fellow disciples.

What priest, minister, or evangelist today would be willing to proclaim the Good News (via mass media, online media, in person) without any material compensation? How many would be willing to support themselves so they can bring the Jesus story to others?

The cost of discipleship is high. It's expensive to maintain buildings used for a few hours in a week, pay salaries and offer benefits for clergy and staff, provide "services." Too much is invested to take the risk of being prophetic and losing it all.

But isn't that part of the Jesus story? "Whoever wishes to come after me must deny oneself ... whoever loses his life for my sake ..." Isn't that the personal cost of discipleship?

RELIGIONLESS CHRISTIANITY AND THE COST OF COMPLIANCE
"Christianity had two faces which bewildered me—two pictures which didn't fit." – Lionel Blue

One can safely say Germany in the 1930s was overwhelmingly a Christian nation, split between Protestants (first) and Catholics (second) in church membership. Jews numbered approximately 500,000 in a population of 62 million. One might think they were more numerous, considering Hitler's relentless rant to rid Germany of Jews. After Cardinal Pacelli's Vatican Concordat with the Third Reich, the Catholics fell in line, and the Protestants signed their own accords with Hitler.

One can then safely conclude that 61 million German Christians (subtracting Jews and brave non-believers of the dominant churches) essentially enabled Hitler's Reich to function like a well-oiled machine. Christian resistance was numerically insignificant compared to Christian compliance. Without ecumenical support, Hitler could never have built his complex state bureaucracy, peopling factories, military units, and concentration camps.

Compliance was brutally demanded, all for the sake of the system. *"Alles ist in ordnung."* ("Everything is in order.") One can imagine clerics reminding Christians to "obey your leaders and submit to their authority." (Heb 13:17) It was a perfect storm, in Hitler's favor.

A prominent Protestant theologian at the time, Paul Althaus, known for his aversion to extremes and highly respected by his colleagues and the public, was described as having "no character defects ... he [exhibited] ... a warm and human personality. He was the perfect gentleman, friend and teacher." [146] As Hitler rose to power, Althaus saw no extremism in him, proclaiming, "Our ... churches have greeted the turning point of 1933 as a gift and miracle of God." [147]

Another Protestant theologian in Nazi Germany, Dietrich Bonhoeffer, reacted to the easy compliance of Christians and was instrumental in creating an alternative church (the "Confessional Church") to the state-supported Lutheran Church, which largely acquiesced to Nazi rule, conforming rather than "stirring up the people."

Bonhoeffer spoke truth to Nazi power. He ultimately came under surveillance by authorities. He was conflicted about the use of violence to remove Hitler and at one point seemed to embrace pacifism. In the end, though, he planned with others to assassinate Hitler, and was hanged days before Germany was liberated.

The cost of discipleship defined Bonhoeffer's life. (His classic, *The Cost of Discipleship,* published in 1937 as Hitler's regime ravaged Europe, describes a Christianity built around the Sermon on the Mount.) He was willing to put himself on the line rather than submit to Nazi rule, as many pastors unfortunately did. Bonhoeffer inadvertently witnessed against the cultural Christianity that the papacy epitomized.

Resistance to culture and state is imperative when their values clash with Kingdom values. Bonhoeffer coined the term *religionless Christianity*, pointing to a mere cultural phenomenon, and to Christians indulging in "cheap grace" instead of the real thing, "costly grace." The main distinction between the two involved the failure to "take up the cross." Or as radio commentator Garrison Keillor cleverly put it, to "give up your good Christian life and follow Jesus."

Of all the history I've read and studied, most involved the Third Reich. As a prerequisite for a B.A. degree (which I didn't receive) in college seminary, we had to choose a field of study and write a paper. All but two of us selected a philosophy topic. Someone chose English literature and I chose History. The title of my paper was, "The Resistance of the Catholic Church to National Socialism in the III Reich." The year was 1961 and a trickle of studies examining that nightmare epoch was just beginning to appear.

Prior to writing the paper I had contacted Dr. Gordon Zahn of the sociology department at Loyola University, Chicago. He was among the first Catholic authors to investigate the Church's relations with the Third Reich, and had written extensively on Catholic support of Hitler's wars. He cautioned against writing on this topic since, as a seminarian, it would lead to a troubling conclusion that would bring me into conflict with seminary authorities. He was right about the conclusion but wrong about the conflict, as the authorities apparently never bothered to read it.

I had to imagine living in Nazi Germany. How would I have reacted to the terror Hitler unleashed during his vicious reign? The bravery of the few who resisted compared to the passivity of the total population continues to captivate me. Resisters came from a wide range of backgrounds and used various means to oppose the regime. One couple clandestinely displayed postcards in public places all over Berlin denouncing Hitler, and totally upending the Gestapo, though eventually caught, tortured, and executed. German author Hans Fallada told their story in his 1947 book, *Every Man Dies Alone*.

I would like to think I would have resisted in some way, no matter how small. I can't go back in time, but the question remains today. How compliant or resistant am I to a culture or state whose values I feel are in opposition to Kingdom values? Will I remain silent and private, or go public and speak out?

If I want to maintain a comfortable lifestyle, I am not going to "take up the cross."

THE RED, WHITE, AND BLUE VERSION OF CHRISTIANITY
"Christianity has not conquered nationalism; the opposite has been the case. Nationalism has made Christianity its footstool."
– Arthur Keith

Germany is just one example. America is a Christian country, at least according to a legion of believers who relentlessly reiterate this as fact, fueling the "culture wars" stoked by politicians mainly of the political right. The issues behind the culture wars often relate to sexuality and so-called "family values." True equality and equity, Kingdom values, are not favored by the majority of Christians.

If America is truly a Christian country, then Christianity failed the litmus test of the Kingdom of God in two dominant areas: equality of all persons, and equitable sharing by all of the common good.

Despite their numerical dominance over non-Christian groups here, throughout the nation's history, most Christians failed to influence American society to make any substantial changes. On the contrary, Christians gave substantial cultural support to the darkest days of our history in these two critical areas. Christianity historically failed to be prophetic and is now rather a prop, a pillar of support for the status quo. Martin Luther King, Jr. is a model for Christians in challenging that "this nation will rise up and live out the true meaning of its creed." He was vilified by many Christians here with a relentless screed that demonized him. King was keenly aware of the cognitive dissonance between the ideal and the reality. He chose the painful prophetic route. "Would that all God's people were prophets." (Num 11:29)

Christian churches have acted as powerful instruments of racism against native people and people of color. Christians supported the institution of slavery, save for a handful of brave dissenters, almost too few to count. Christian churches, especially in the South, condoned slavery, resisted post-Civil War Reconstruction, and later championed segregation and opposed the civil rights movement.

On Saturday evenings, Christians burned crosses under the cover of dark nights and white sheets, fostering a reign of terror, eerily Hitlerian. And on Sunday mornings, the men of darkness preached and sang hymns of light and love. Was there no inkling of cognitive dissonance? They may have publicly praised Jesus, but Jim Crow was their savior.

With the advent of the civil rights movement, Christians employed new means of maintaining a divisive society—racially segregated Christian academies as well as White Citizens' Councils, whose membership included clergy as well as prominent lay persons.

Today, racism is not politically correct. It's gone underground. It rears its ugly head through code words—*law and order*, or *war on drugs*. The disproportionate victims of this "new racism" are black, often poor, living in ghettos. Black Americans remain targeted and profiled—"Driving While Black" and more recently "Walking While Black," as in the 2012 case of murdered Florida teenager Trayvon Martin. Not unique, only ubiquitously otherwise ignored.

In this Christian nation, the economic disparity widens. The Kingdom teaching of the common good, sharing "so that no would be in need," (AA 4:34) is attacked as socialism by the power elite, and Christians largely join a supportive chorus that thunders "Amen!" When one has a surplus, one is to help another in need, and if that person someday has a surplus, he or she is to reciprocate. (2 Cor 8:14) This attitude is an anathema in a society whose gospel is rugged individualism, whose Christians are compliant rather than complaining of the collapse of the common good.

James Madison, slaveholder, Founding Father, and fourth president, sought this in the proposed Constitution: "They (landholders) ought to be protected, so constituted as to protect the minority of the opulent against the majority." [148] His wish has effectively become ingrained in American democracy, which faithfully observes the *new* Golden Rule: "He who has the gold makes the rule!" The economically powerful have the means (wealth) to maintain the end (more wealth) for the already opulent.

American Christians are in opposition to the Kingdom in repeatedly failing to be prophetic against the status quo, the few over the many. Instead they embrace a "gospel of wealth." They will hardly confront the company they wish to be part of one day. American Christianity is largely cultural, supporting rather than confronting the status quo. True as ever, Jesus came to "afflict the comfortable and comfort the afflicted."

Anyone who embraces Kingdom teaching, in any society, will ultimately cause division. But in solidarity with others who espouse Kingdom values, the possibility exists to offer an alternative for the common good of that society. Certainly in repressive totalitarian regimes it is more challenging to resist. America aspires to be an open democratic society, yet many of its Christians are reluctant to challenge inequality and inequity, here in this land of the free.

192

WHERE IS THE PROPHETIC COMMUNITY?
"We are prophetic interrogators. Why are so many people hungry? Why are so many people and families in our shelters? Why do we have one of six of our children poor, and one of three of these are children of color? 'Why?' is the prophetic question."
– Jim Wallis

Discipleship comes with a price. The "cost of discipleship" in the Jesus story is "taking up the cross" to challenge the status quo, speak truth to power, stir up the people, and resist oppressors that rule the masses. Discipleship means being part of a prophetic community. "So we have the prophetic word made more sure, to which you do well to pay attention as to a lamp shining in a dark place, until the day dawns and the morning star arises in your hearts." (2 Pe 1:19) A message of vigilance till the Kingdom comes on earth.

But most contemporary Catholics do not think of themselves as part of a "prophetic community." Those in the newly founded pro-life movement may claim the Church is prophetic in defending the life of the unborn. But if it is perceived as less compassionate toward the needy and vulnerable *already* born, it certainly will not convince others to intervene on behalf of those *not yet* born.

As constituted, the pro-life movement chooses to highlight one solitary situation, but fails to be prophetic about countless moral issues that will overwhelm humanity for the next fifty years. As listed by the late Nobel laureate in chemistry, Richard Smalley, these include energy, water, food, environment, poverty, terrorism, war, disease, education, democracy, and population.

This narcissistic institution focuses inward, inordinately on select issues. It has grown into a bloated bureaucracy, maintaining control over members, centralizing and solidifying power. Currently, the Curia is under siege over leaked documents. Curial infighting is causing an international scene as factions seek to consolidate power for the next conclave.

The poor are the primary focus in the Jesus story, but not in the present-day Catholic Church. Under John Paul II and Benedict XVI, the "preferential option for the poor" was suppressed. A story is told

THE THEOLOGY OF FEAR

of St. Lawrence, perhaps apocryphal: "The Prefect of Rome, a greedy pagan, thought the Church had a great fortune hidden away. So he ordered Lawrence to bring the Church's treasure to him. The Saint said he would, in three days. Then he went through the city and gathered together all the poor and sick people supported by the Church. When he showed them to the Prefect, he said: 'This is the Church's treasure!'" (Wikipedia) Nice story, but in reality the RCC's true "treasure" is its vast art collection.

The phrase *preferential option for the poor* is credited to the "Father of Liberation Theology," Fr. Gustavo Gutierrez, who wrote *A Theology of Liberation: History, Politics, and Salvation.* The idea is to reclaim the poor as the top priority in the Kingdom proclamation. The concept gained momentum in the wake of Vatican II, but faltered under the restoration initiated by John Paul II. It never became a household word to rank-and-file Catholics.

In the gospels Jesus is repeatedly depicted as attacking the wealthy. "Woe to you, rich." (Lk 6:24) "How hard it is for the rich to enter the Kingdom?" (Mt 19:23) The singular issue for Jesus is greed (not sexuality). Jesus has to be recognized as the "Father of Class Warfare." Oddly, few wealthy people existed in his world. Today's "Occupy" movement identifies the American wealthy as "the 1 percent." It is questionable whether there even *was* a "1 percent" in Jesus' time. But he was outraged over the multitudes impoverished by Empire and Temple.

Liberation Theology critiques structures that maintain economic inequality. Again, it is not enough to *feed* the poor, but to also *ask why* they are poor. The goal is creating structural change, not handing out Band-Aids.

The preferential option for the poor is nonexistent inside American parishes. In some parishes where I was on staff, when the topic was raised concerning allocating funds for the poor beyond parish boundaries, it was often met with stiff resistance. No setting aside a portion of the budget, even 1 or 2 percent. Some (though remarkably few) parishes do engage in significant financial outreach. But most are content to spend their income on themselves—totally parochial, not catholic. Any outreach commonly touches those within their own community who might be poor. Thanksgiving turkeys and Christmas toys are staples. When raising funds for the international poor, countless times I was accosted by protests: "We have poor here." "Charity begins at home." "Let their own governments take care of them." Jesus' admonition to care for "the least ones" applies a triage approach—the least one comes first, wherever that one is. But few truly practice this. Most shrug and quote the fatalistic rejoinder, "You will always have the poor among you." (Jo 12:8)

Consequently, no widespread policy exists on the U.S parish level to follow the Liberation Theology approach and question structural inequity. If there were, many would probably balk, unwilling to challenge the status quo from which they benefit. Initiatives for economic justice within American society and around the world more frequently come from secular movements.

The poor are not a realistic priority for the RCC—there are just too many of them! It feels no urgency regarding the plight of more than 3 billion people living on $1-2 a day. There is always the next life for you, so let not your hearts be troubled.

Liberation Theology embarrasses the RCC with its insistence on this preferential option. Despite calculated attempts to suppress or even eliminate it, Liberation Theology remains a "still small voice" in the wilderness, the conscience of a lost Church. Members who seek to minister to "the least ones" commonly face insurmountable obstacles and little financial assistance. But governments often subsidize the RCC's bureaucratic ministry to the poor. In the USA, government grants provide two-thirds of the funding for Catholic Charities USA, says the CATO Institute. [149]

THE CHURCH AS MUSEUM
"I seldom go into a natural history museum without feeling as if I were attending a funeral." – John Burroughs

In the RCC's distorted perspective, buildings supersede individuals. Elaborate structures are built without regard for basic human needs of "the least ones." Topping even the Crystal Cathedral, a recent extravagance of the RCC is the Cathedral of Our Lady of the Angels, at $250 million. It was nicknamed "Taj Mahony" after Cardinal Roger

Mahony, who pushed for it in Los Angeles. Since clerics are forced to be celibate and are denied offspring, a magnificent edifice becomes a prelate's posterity.

The RCC has created an elaborate self-serving superstructure, an extensive network of parishes and dioceses, and a magnificent home office with elaborate archives and museums—all in need of constant upkeep. The cost of discipleship today is paying the utility bills and maintenance fees. Survival of the institution takes precedence over survival of the human race. Buildings are necessary to facilitate a mission, but they are a distant second to an engaged, prophetic community.

Catholics come to the Vatican not as pilgrims but as tourists, casual observers *oohing* and *aahing* over its elaborate displays of architecture and artwork. The cost of discipleship has been reduced to subsidizing an imposing edifice and splendid papal court, a legacy the Caesars would applaud. This does nothing to connect followers to their peripatetic founder, who lamented, "The foxes have dens, the birds have nests, but the Son of Man has nowhere to lay his head." (Lk 9:58)

Popes can write all the letters they want about obligations to "the least ones," but as long as they maintain their opulent lifestyles of pomp and privilege, they will not convince the world that they take to heart the teaching of Jesus. They mimic unscrupulous corporate executives—official proclamations are many, but no follow-through exists on the ground (parish) level. The witness to conversion toward a simple lifestyle is absent. Effectively, they witness *against* the gospels' proclamation of Good News for the poor. "These people honor with their lips but their heart is far from me." (Mt 15:8)

Popes seem to live by the words of the corrupt Pope Leo X, who realized an eschatological moment of glory when he exclaimed, "God has given us the papacy! Let us enjoy it!"

And the cost of discipleship to this marvelous papacy, tenaciously preserved by its occupants, is underwritten by simple, sincere members who provide the monumental funds necessary to shore up a lavish façade of faith.

Moynahan writes, "The Jesuit Francis Xavier sailed for India in 1541 with nothing but a few books and some coarse clothes ... Handsome and breezy, he laughed when he was advised to travel with a servant as befitted the dignity of a papal nuncio. 'Sire, it was that dignity that reduced the Church of Rome to its present state,' he replied. 'The best way of acquiring real dignity is to wash one's own underwear.'" [150]

I would update it as "to clean one's own toilet." I sometimes picture the pope on the papal bathroom throne to remind myself he is a mere mortal, and not to divinize any human. Some want to deny his humanity and deem a specialized status as "His Holiness," thereby removing him from equality with all people and injuring his own spiritual health. Theologian Bernard Häring advocated dropping this deference. The pope was supposed to be the Vicar of Peter but morphed into the Vicar of Christ. He now carries a superficial aura of divinity, like the Caesars. Imagining the pope on a toilet, or cleaning it, reminds us that we are all mere mortals. *"Inter faeces et urinam nascimur"* ("We are born between feces and urine").

Monks in a Zen monastery were dividing up household tasks. No one volunteered to clean toilets. Finally, the Zen Master announced he would take the job, because being a master means cleaning up after everyone. A graphic version of Jesus' dictum, "The greatest among you is the one who serves." (Mt 23:11) But who are the true servants in Rome's papal household? Religious women, acting as domestic laborers, like Vestal Virgins of the Empire.

Nothing like free labor to keep things humming. But it's totally unnecessary. The RCC can survive indefinitely on income from its vast and splendid collection of museums and libraries, stretching over nine miles. The monetary value is incalculable.

Revenues for the Vatican's 2010 fiscal year were down, but museum ticket sales were substantially up. The art pieces alone offer unlimited collateral, providing financial insurance far into the future. Popes have historically labored on expanding the Vatican libraries and museums, in some instances storing purloined artifacts that conquering Catholic warriors contributed to their ever-expanding collection.

197

Pope Nicholas V (1447-1455) was papal architect of the "church-as-museum" and founder of the Vatican Library in the mid-1400s. Apparently he missed Jesus' point about putting an end to the "theology of buildings." Jesus did not lament the loss of the Temple as the venue for the Divine Presence. "Not one stone here will be left upon another, which will not be torn down." (Mt 24:2)

On the contrary, Nicholas V claimed faith was found in stone: "If the common faith is reinforced and consolidated by great buildings, looking as an imperishable testimony to it, in such a way as to be able to survive as a Sacred Tradition in those who witness the buildings, both now and in the future, then *the world will embrace the faith with the most profound devotion*." (Emphasis added)

Contrary to Nicholas' assertion, the late Cardinal John Wright shared in the preface of a 1940s book the story of a young Parisian, shot during WWII while fighting in the streets of Paris as the Germans retreated. He is taken in by the sisters, into their convent courtyard on the Rue du Bac. As he lay dying, the nuns encourage him to make his peace with the "*Bon Dieu*" (Good God). The young man—who grew up in the heart of Paris, who daily eyed the cathedral of Notre Dame, the Sainte-Chapelle, the *Sacré Coeur* Basilica, and countless other monuments to God—responds in his dying breath, "Who is this Good God you speak of?" Great ecclesiastical buildings did not witness to his embracing the faith with the most profound devotion. Nicholas was proven fallible by this dying young man's words. [151]

Tourists to the Vatican today are understandably awestruck at the sight of the domes and columns of Bramante and Bernini, the breathtaking sculptures by Michelangelo, the hallowed atriums, the ancient tapestries, the magnificent paintings. The problem is their appreciation and wonder may not necessarily translate into acts of faith or justice or love.

The Vatican as magnificent museum boggles the mind, and stirs the heart. Again, as John XXIII eloquently protested, "We are not here on earth to guard a museum, but to cultivate a flourishing garden of life."

Of all the papal pronouncements in modern history, was anyone listening to *that* one?

CLOTHES MAKE THE MAN
*"For the longest time, I thought I was a boy. I really did.
I wore boys' clothes, played tag football." – Eliza Dushku*

No clerical accessory is more lampooned than the bishop's miter. The "pointy hat" is a staple of derision, but this doesn't stop conforming bishops from parading around in it. No bishop leaves home without it. In fact, if they do appear in public without the attire of the office, they will be reprimanded by the Vatican. When the bishop of Toowoomba, Australia dropped the Roman collar for a tie, the "temple police" reported him. Prelates are expected to import to impoverished, distant outposts the fanciful trappings of the papal court.

Prohibiting bishops from dressing like other men in their societies underscores their docility to papal power, and maintaining symbolic dress marks them as apart from—and superior to—other men. Actually, special costumes set clerics conspicuously apart from *all* members of the Body of Christ. Rather than uniting with fellow believers, they are separate, distinctive, and unique. One bishop encouraged parishioners to inform him if they saw priests in "civilian clothes." They must not be mistaken for one of the crowd. "Everything they do is for men to see: They make their phylacteries wide and the tassels on their garments long." (Mt 23:5)

The wearing of medieval-style vestments and kingly robes is symbolic of the RCC's refusal to change even its clothes to reflect a simple lifestyle. This underscores how resistant it is to abdicating power, liberating followers, and reading "the signs of the times." It is adamant in preserving its distinct garb, placing a select set of men a cut above.

Just imagine the astronomical amount spent over the centuries on ecclesiastical apparel. Gold and precious stones, embroidered garb, and luxurious furs are tailored into the finest linens and silks. Then again, the labor is free. Whole orders of religious women spend significant portions of their lives entirely devoted to the production of clerical dressmaking. It is unconscionable that a religious institution would have no qualms with conscripting women into cloistered communities to commit the best years of their lives as clerical seamstresses. In effect, they have become passive Vestal Virgins, submitting to male dictates in the name of the Lord, while prelates publicly bless these humble sisters for doing "God's work." Meanwhile human lives are cavalierly expended in the production of a questionable wardrobe.

The extravagant "things" the papacy has created for itself as props for the gospels are concrete examples of the opulent lives of the hierarchy, consuming incredible resources of human energy and financial expense. Apparently, elaborate costumes and over-the-top accessories are necessary in order to "do this in memory of me." These clerical outfits may be comical but they're also extremely expensive, running into thousands of dollars. The pompous Raymond Burke, upon being elevated to cardinal, reportedly purchased investiture robes that came in over $50K.

But money is no object. The wardrobe budget doesn't come from a cleric's pocket but from the pool of hard-earned dollars donated by the faithful, who have no say in such wanton expenditures.

It is forever Halloween in the RCC, and liturgical wardrobes are a costly extravagance. (Perhaps only Orthodox clerics out-dress the Romans.) Well, Vatican II did attempt to simplify clerical dress, such as discontinuing luxurious materials like handmade lace. But under John Paul II and particularly Benedict XVI, the "fashion pope," lace came back with a vengeance. Any respectable prelate wanting to be perceived as properly outfitted will boldly flounce about in public swathed in yards of lace, absent any male embarrassment. Even *haute couture* women today have virtually abandoned lace, save for underwear. Maybe only drag queens would appreciate clerical wardrobes (no offense to drag queens).

Amazingly, Roman clerics have no shame prancing about in garb most men would never be caught dead in. The off-setting attire they cling to tenaciously has little appeal for "lez get real" men. It's no wonder that the Roman liturgy has always drawn more women than men. Imagine Jesus traipsing about the desert dressed in satin and lace, about to address the starving crowds in the wilderness. They'd be thinking, "Who *dressed* this girl?"

Benedict XVI inspired the return of the *cappa magna*, made of watered silk with an overlay of ermine and a ten-foot train. Prelates have been publicly parading about in this outlandish garb since the pope signaled his preference for ancient and courtly dress. It makes for great theater—and wonderful photo opps for tourists—fitting for a cultural Church that preserves the vestiges of Europe from the Caesars through monarchical dynasties.

Snazzy wardrobe even inspired a future pope: "At the age of five, Ratzinger was in a group of children who welcomed the visiting Cardinal Archbishop of Munich with flowers. Struck by the Cardinal's distinctive garb, he later announced the very same day that he wanted to be a cardinal." (Wikipedia) In time, Benedict would inspire numerous clerics to embrace his penchant for luxurious and garish ecclesiastical fashions.

The costume became the inspiration, which became the reality.

ALL RIGHT, THEN, IS THE POPE GAY? DO WE CARE?
"I started being really proud of the fact that I was gay even though I wasn't." – Kurt Cobain

The recently deceased Italian journalist Angelo Quattrocchi rushed to press *The Pope Is Not Gay!* when Benedict XVI was to visit Britain, hoping to tap into the public pageantry and profit. To support his case, Quattrocchi raids Benedict's closet, casting suspicion that Benedict is guilty by association, paraphrasing the scripture, "By their fruits you will know them."

Gay blogger Andrew Sullivan, who is Catholic, observes this about Benedict: "At times, it seems to me, his gayness is almost wince-inducing. The prissy fastidiousness, the effeminate voice, the fixation on liturgy and ritual, and the over-the-top clothing accessories are one thing. But what resonates with me the most is a theology that … reflects a withdrawal from the world of human relationship, rather than an interaction with it." Sullivan acknowledges this is not inherently homosexual (and he should know personally) but adds that many repressed gay men try to avoid a life of pain when they "create a perfect abstraction of what it is, and what their role is in it."
152

This is the pope who declared that homosexuality is an "intrinsic disorder," without providing any scientific or psychological evidence, but only the subjective stroke of his pen.

While the RCC considers homosexual acts a sin, there was no tradition to define homosexuality itself as a "strong tendency ordered to an intrinsic moral evil," as Ratzinger wrote in his 1986 letter to bishops worldwide. This declaration reveals Ratzinger's subjective mindset. There is no way to empirically demonstrate it to be true.

Scholastic philosophy holds that something existing in the mind does not necessarily exist in the real world. There needs to be a foundation in reality (*fundamentum in re*). Ratzinger freely asserts that being homosexual means having an inherent evil, or an innate impulse toward evil. What he freely asserts should be freely rejected.

Additionally, while Sullivan argues the context of Ratzinger's behavior as questionably gay, Ratzinger's provocative proclamation arguably further underscores his being gay, as the 1986 assertion represents his personal projection. Modern psychology generally incorporates Sigmund Freud's finding that people project various characteristics onto others to reduce personal stress or guilt feelings, thereby protecting themselves. Projection is a defense mechanism. Even here, the projection has no foundation in reality, no "*fundamentum in re.*"

The incalculable harm Ratzinger unleashed in 1986 continues to devastate people struggling with sexual identity, self-image, and self-worth. Suicide is tragically the only answer for some individuals, lacking support, being ostracized, feeling they are lesser humans. They decide to take their life, which a Ratzinger Church deems as damaged goods. Ratzinger has a moral obligation to accept responsibility for the devastating impact his personal proclamation has had on countless lives, especially those of Catholics.

Ratzinger continues the tradition of Augustine, who viewed the person as defective because of original sin. Both believe God's creation is very flawed, not "very good." This has profound repercussions—people feel they are substandard, relentlessly questioning their self-worth, filled with anxiety that they can never measure up. A heavy load to carry. This theology of fear doesn't liberate anyone, doesn't lift any burdens. In the face of the mysteries of life, our only divine response can be compassion.

Contrast this Roman view with a Hindu one: "I once was speaking to a group of Hindus who wanted to understand evangelical Christianity, because rampant proselytizing was dividing their villages and splitting families down the middle. After the talk, a woman named Mohini came up to me. She asked, 'Is what you told us really true—that Christians believe children are born evil?' I explained again the doctrine of original sin. She was horrified. She said, 'When babies are born into Hindu families, we whisper to them: *You are perfect. You are a spark of the divine.*'" [153]

The issue is not whether or not Ratzinger is gay, but that anyone who *is* homosexual (or bisexual or transgender) *is not* damaged goods. Only a cosmic ogre, a monster god, would purposefully create defective creatures and then allow them to be the object of human persecution.

All human beings are sparks of the divine.

LONGING FOR ANOTHER SPRINGTIME OF HOPE
"No winter lasts forever; no spring skips its turn." – Hal Borland

John XXIII was all for nurturing the living today, not guarding artifacts of the past. People, not buildings, were his priority. His call to "open the windows" of the Church led to the II Vatican Council, where he prayed it would read "the signs of the times," and return to the Nazarene who proclaimed the Kingdom of God. John ushered in a springtime of hope for a wayward institution that had deviated far from the Jesus story.

In the 1960s, during the exuberant aftermath of Vatican II, I wrote an article noting that councils do not always succeed. I didn't realize how unexpectedly prescient I would be.

A 1985 piece by Italian journalist Giancarlo Zizola in *Magill* magazine detailed how the Reformation was being undermined: "He [JPII] plans to do nothing less than imbue the Catholic Church in the coming decades with the values of mediaeval Christianity. He himself and his own personality constitute a definite threat for the Church, the threat of interrupting the pastoral and cultural development which was (sic) promoted by the Second Vatican Council and by the work of popes John XXIII and Paul VI." [154]

So John Paul II teamed up with Cardinal Ratzinger, who became his behind-the-scenes enforcer (bad cop), while the pope played to the crowds (good cop).

During the second-longest papacy, while John Paul II was assiduously restoring the past, the clerical sexual-abuse scandal metastasized throughout the Catholic world. Distracted with his restoration, he ignored the victims. While Pius XII has been faulted for not intervening in the plight of the Jews in the grip of the Nazis, John Paul II needs to be censured for failing to rescue the lambs from the wolves of his own flock. Rather, Benedict XVI promoted him to be venerated as "blessed." Jesus was well aware of monumental human failings, even in his disciples, when he ordered Peter to "get behind me, you Satan!"

Now as pope, Ratzinger continues the Counter-Reformation efforts of his predecessor. He is virtually undoing Vatican II by incrementally dismantling practices that flourished from seeds planted by it. If he were to dispose of them *"en bloc,"* great alarm would be sounded. Instead, piece by piece, he restricts past freedoms, so only over a period of time will the widespread change be noticed.

The Ultramontanes (those who ascribe prerogatives and powers to the pope above all) were inspired by this papal restoration and resurfaced with a vengeance, faulting Vatican II for imprudence if not untruth.

But Jesuit scholar John O'Malley indicates otherwise, seeing Vatican II as "an unalloyed good, precisely because it marked a break with the past." As he puts it in *What Happened at Vatican II*, "At stake were almost two different visions of Catholicism: from commands to invitations, from laws to ideals, from definition to mystery, from threats to persuasion, from coercion to conscience, from monologue to dialogue, from ruling to serving, from withdrawn to integrated, from vertical to horizontal, from exclusion to inclusion, from hostility to friendship, from rivalry to partnership, from suspicion to trust, from static to ongoing, from passive acceptance to active engagement, from fault-finding to appreciation, from prescriptive to principled, from behavior modification to inner appropriation." [155]

Regrettably, the current power structure of the RCC vigorously disagrees.

In proclaiming the Kingdom, Jesus called for "*metanoia*" (change) from things as they are to what they might be. Since its marriage to Constantine, the RCC has been perceived by the world as wielding power, not serving but lording over.

While many members witness heroically to service, keeping alive the flame of the gospels, most hierarchs expect not *to serve* but to *be served*. And they make life miserable for those who attempt to serve. They hinder more than help, frustrate more than facilitate.

Analyzing the fallout from the sexual-abuse scandal in the Archdiocese of Philadelphia, writer Robert Huber is conscious of the cognitive dissonance: "That's why the Philadelphia archdiocese is now facing the greatest crisis in its history. It's a lot to ask of parishioners—to continue kneeling before a classic top-down power structure controlled by men who wear medieval robes and sit on thrones and rule with unquestioned authority. Especially when that authority so pointedly fails their children." [156]

Leonardo Boff provides arguably the most provocative analysis of the RCC in his writings. He was silenced by Cardinal Ratzinger, under whom he had studied for his doctorate. In his chapter, "The Power of the Institutional Church: Can It Be Converted?" he attempts to answer just that question.

Though he ends on a hopeful note, I doubt if twenty-five years later he would be as optimistic. Unfortunately, his 1985 book (*Church, Charism, and Power*) had limited circulation, mainly among academicians, and never reached a mass audience. [157]

MONEY TALKS
"Money, not morality, is the principle commerce of civilized nations." – Thomas Jefferson

The lack of an historical grasp of the Church among rank-and-file members enables it to surmount incredible scandals. The current clerical sexual-abuse scandal is only the latest episode that could cause its collapse. But Benedict XVI evidences a peculiar serenity in the face of impending demise. He envisions small groups beholden to the monarchial rule, with members who will be obedient, orthodox, unquestioning, and financially generous. A small number of affluent loyalists, unstinting in financial support, are preferred to a large number of wishy-washy commoners, providing only a pittance.

The RCC's *real* "preferential option" is the world's upper class. It has a long history of cultivating the powerful, the privileged, the moneyed. With few exceptions, these individuals and their organizations tend to resist change, preserving the status quo at all costs, as it is in their vested interests. They befriend the RCC, providing it financial and sometimes military and political support, and the RCC accommodates them. Both rely on each other to maintain the control of simple, sincere people, "the little ones." Corporations today are especially cultivated, the "new power body," having power to influence and control states because of their enormous wealth. Another rehash of the Golden Rule.

For twenty-four years I raised money for people in absolute poverty through several nonprofit groups. While these organizations accept the petty cash of small donors, they ultimately look to cultivate major contributors. It is the same with the RCC. It happily accepts the loose change of ordinary believers, but it fishes for the big bucks of major donors to fund its bureaucracy. The pennies of the pilgrims can't compare to the millions of the moneyed.

Founded in 1500s Europe, the Jesuits during their early years elicited the support of the wealthy to organize an educational system benefiting the males of this social class. Jesuits became confidants to the powerful. In contrast, the Spanish priest, Joseph Calasanz, opened Europe's first free schools in the 1500s, spending his life educating poor boys. A Roman cardinal was scandalized by his efforts. Once the poor were educated, who would do the menial work necessary to maintain society? Ultimately, Calasanz's vision was co-opted by the wealthy, and his schools eventually catered to people of means. And it was within his order where clerical teachers sexually abused children, then were routinely recycled, without reprimand, to abuse more.

In more recent times, new orders have surfaced—particularly Opus Dei, Communion and Liberation, and the Legion of Christ—that continue the tradition of singling out the powerful, privileged, and moneyed. Opus Dei has no open recruitment and is highly selective in seeking out those with something to offer in these categories. Its members worm their way into powerful positions for the benefit of the organization.

The Legion of Christ does the same. Its notorious founder, Marcial Maciel, was wildly successful in tapping into some of the wealthiest individuals on the planet, such as Mexican tycoon Carlos Slim Helu. Maciel was a particular favorite of John Paul II and many others at the Vatican, such as Cardinal Angelo Sodano, whose financial fiascos are detailed in Jason Berry's *Render Unto Rome*. John Paul's aide-de-camp, Stanislaw Dziwisz, now cardinal of Krakow, was the point man who received regular payments from the Legion of Christ and other influential visitors to the Vatican. Money buys access. Berry wonders, "Did Dziwisz salt away some for himself?" It begs the question. "In fact, you don't know where the money is going." [158]

The RCC has no moral qualms about accepting hefty donations even from non-Romans whose lifestyles and priorities are in opposition to Kingdom values. As noted, it made Rupert Murdoch a Knight of St. Gregory, despite his moral failings and shaky business ethics. He has been most generous to the Vatican and has donated $10 million to Cardinal Mahony for his California cathedral extravaganza. The Church is flexible toward the powerful, privileged, and moneyed, but it expects the rank-and-file to toe the line. Petty cash allows neither access nor knighthood.

Mother Angelica benefitted from the generosity of the elite. When she built her $42 million convent for her Poor (!) Clare community in Alabama, eight families provided the funds. She admonished those who thought their petty cash was used to build it. She was astute enough to realize she could find real money through a capital campaign from the conservative wealthy who assist those seeking to firm up the status quo. Dorothy Day of the Catholic Worker Movement could never drum up such wealth, as she questioned the status quo.

Faith is a free gift, but religion is expensive.

THE TRUE COST OF DISCIPLESHIP
"I have been my own disciple and my own master.
And I have been a good disciple but a bad master."
– Antonio Porchia

Sadly, the cost of discipleship today is maintaining a top-heavy, bloated bureaucracy—subsidizing a self-serving superstructure concerned with institutional expansion and self-preservation. But the true cost of discipleship, as intended by Jesus, is acting as a prophetic witness, speaking truth to power and accepting the consequences, all on behalf of "the least ones" of the world.

And this old world sorely needs a moral body that will prophetically and independently stand against all political and corporate abuse on behalf of the masses, who lack a structural organization against the powers of "this world." But the RCC is in bed with power, having more in common with Caesar than Christ. It is a Satan, a stumbling block to Jesus' prophetic proclamation. The Vatican, as is stands now, is a sign *against* the Kingdom.

"Go sell what you have, give it to the poor, and then come follow me." (Mt 19:21) Evidently, the papacy doesn't believe these words apply to it. It pretends to follow the one who had no place to lay his head, but is unwilling to sell off amassed treasures in its museums and banks, to give away its incalculable wealth. It has sold out to the powerful, the privileged, and the moneyed.

The unfortunate cost of discipleship today is the loss of disciples, the loss of credibility, and the loss of integrity. The RCC needs to have a huge yard sale in St. Peter's Square. It would be a start.

CHAPTER EIGHT

THE DARK SIDE:
EXAMINING THE WHOLE TRADITION

"Character, like a photograph, develops in darkness."
– Yousuf Karsh

Carl Jung knew all about life's shadow, life's darkness. In documenting a conversation with him shortly after WWII, A.I. Allenby offers this recollection: "[Jung] told me that he once met a distinguished man, a Quaker, who could not imagine that he had ever done anything wrong in his life. 'And do you know what happened to his children?' Jung asked. 'The son became a thief, and the daughter a prostitute. Because the father would not take on his shadow, his share in the imperfection of human nature, his children were compelled to live out the dark side which he had ignored.'"

The lesson here, the warning—for humanity and for the Roman Church—is not to ignore the dark side. Our true character is developed in our darkness. The RCC touts tradition as integral to its being, but it can be very selective, emphasizing the positive, burying the negative. As Jesus said, it is by the fruits that we'll be judged. Much of the RCC's tradition has brought forth bitter fruits. Its theology promotes an occasional "general confession," a review of one's past life. A confession is now necessary for the spiritual health of the institution itself, if it is ever to experience wholeness, to reconcile its cognitive dissonance, and to rediscover the Kingdom Jesus proclaimed.

IS THE ROMAN CHURCH PRO-LIFE? PRO-DEATH?
"Dying is easy, it's living that scares me to death." – Annie Lennox

Today's Church is adamantly and aggressively pro-life, narrowly focused on the fetus. Some would counter it is also against capital punishment. It supports life in *word*, but not always in *deed*. It continually harasses American politicians, mostly pro-choice Catholic Democrats, denying them communion, preventing access to its facilities, threatening excommunication. Though it is not even-handed with Republican Catholics who support capital punishment.

Supreme Court Justice Antonin Scalia has been outspoken in favor of capital punishment and has publicly dissented from the RCC. As reported by CBS News, in a 2009 presentation he "criticized his church's position against the death penalty, saying that Catholic judges who believe capital punishment is wrong should resign. The devout Roman Catholic said after giving it 'serious thought' he could not agree with the church's stand on the issue." He further told Georgetown students, "No authority that I know of denies the 2,000-year-old tradition of the church approving capital punishment ... I don't see why there's been a change." [159] Interestingly, no Roman clergyman has withheld him communion or called for his excommunication.

The Vatican, while in control of the Papal States, allowed capital punishment until the 1840s. In the new *Catechism*, the Church is not absolutely against capital punishment: "Following the lead of Pope John Paul II's *The Gospel of Life*, the catechism teaches that governmental authority has the right and duty to assure the safety of society, and to punish criminals by means of suitable penalties. This includes imposition of the death penalty if there is no other way to protect society." [160] The RCC does question whether exceptions are possible. But it doesn't slam the door on capital punishment.

Scalia makes a revealing historical statement when he says no authority denies the Church's tradition of approving capital punishment. He's wrong, and he's right. He's wrong in implying that Jesus would support capital punishment, particularly being an innocent victim of state power himself. (Scalia is an ardent advocate of the "original intent" of the Founding Fathers in the nation's legal documents, but he doesn't bring "original intent" to the scriptures to support capital punishment.) He's right in implying the RCC has not historically been pro-life. It repeatedly supported the taking of human life and only recently became an insistent "Johnny-come-lately" advocate of a narrow pro-life niche, the unborn.

Nothing rocks and roils Catholics today more than the issue of abortion. Yet the RCC refuses to make an infallible statement on abortion, even though it—of all institutions in the world—claims the power of infallibility. It allows endless accelerating strife without resolution, as members verbally and physically assault one another, as well as non-members.

John Paul II *almost* made an infallible statement on abortion; an early draft of his thoughts contained one. Cardinal Ratzinger intervened and stopped short of the "formality of dogmatization." His argument against formalizing it dogmatically undermines the reasoning Pope Pius XII employed when he declared Mary was assumed into heaven, body and soul. Pius claimed it was so evident from remote times that the obvious thing was to declare it infallible. On that issue, he embraced the formality of dogmatization.

While the Doctrine of the Assumption was neither a contentious nor contested belief, Pius XII deemed it important enough to make an infallible statement. Yet the issue of abortion continues to be relentlessly contentious and contested, because there is no unanimous and universal acknowledgement as to exactly when the fetus becomes a person. The RCC acts irresponsibly, *as if* its position on abortion (and birth control) is infallible, but without having the guts to formalize it.

The 2,000-year-old tradition of the Church that Scalia references is replete with an anti-life position. These days, it strongly asserts the *Magisterium* (Teaching Office) has been consistent throughout history. It *has* been consistent—in its inconsistencies! In the abstract it might have seemed consistent, but in practice and historical reality, it has left a bloody trail of pro-death policies and actions.

Benedict XVI laments the loss of the absolute, the constant relativizing of truths and beliefs. Yet the RCC has not held the Fifth

Commandment as an absolute. It has actively and passively participated in the taking of countless lives (innocent lives outside the womb) throughout history. When the clerical sexual-abuse crisis was cresting, the late Cardinal James Hickey wrote an op-ed stating that the Church did not fully understand the nature of pedophilia and relied on experts in psychiatry and psychology for guidance. This would become a hideous defensive mantra, an unbelievable *apologia* for celibate prelates who don't quite get it, who therefore are slow to act regarding pedophile priests.

So the RCC claims it didn't understand clinical pedophilia, the act of sexually attacking or raping a child. Does it also claim it didn't understand murder? How many centuries did it need for a learning curve? It repeatedly failed to acknowledge the Fifth Commandment as absolute. It constantly allowed or instigated killings, condoning even wide-scale destruction of life. Incongruously, it banned absolutely any deviation from sanctioned sexual activities, allowing no "parvity" of manner. Here it would be rigorously absolute.

The Sermon on the Mount moved beyond Moses of Sinai and the negative prohibitions of the Ten Commandments to a new attitude, emphasizing positive characteristics. It addressed not just egregious offenses such as murder but more common failings such as anger and arrogance. It instructed to turn the other cheek, walk the extra mile, love the enemy. New absolutes, or relative suggestions?

If the RCC historically failed to tenaciously practice the absolute of not taking a life, it can absolve itself because even Yahweh didn't hold absolutely to the commandment. In Exodus 20, Moses receives the command from Yahweh to instruct the Israelites not to kill. By Exodus 22, Yahweh can't follow his own commandment and announces, "My anger will flare and I shall kill you with the sword, your own wives will be widows, your own children orphans." (Ex 22:24)

A reading of the Jewish scriptures indicates Yahweh is on a killing spree, is a veritable serial killer, a mass murderer. He is evidently above the law he gave his Chosen People, just as kings, popes, and presidents consider themselves above the law. Passionately, Yahweh enjoins the Jews to kill, kill, kill! "Go now and put Amalek to the

212

sword, putting to the curse all they have, without mercy: put to death every man and woman, every child and baby at the breast." (I Sam 15:3)

Yahweh also orders the killing of unfaithful Samarians. "They shall fall by the sword, their little children dashed to pieces, their pregnant women disemboweled." (Hos 14:1). Here he violates the Geneva Convention of centuries later, which prohibits the killing of civilians. Yahweh is hardly pro-life, disemboweling pregnant women! Whose job is it to remind Yahweh, "Thou shalt not kill"?

It was Yahweh who instituted the first pogrom of ethnic cleansing by ordering the Jews to rid the Promised Land of its inhabitants, the new planters. This same land today is the site of history's longest unresolved bloody contest over territory, the result of Yahweh's provocative instigation.

These instances are but a sampling of the murder and mayhem that ensued after Yahweh gave Jews the commandment, "Do not kill." The evidence reveals this Yahweh didn't intend to be taken absolutely seriously. This Yahweh is a terrorist. "I will bring terror on you from all those around you, declares the Lord, the Lord Almighty." (Jer 49:5) Is Yahweh an historical witness to the concept that there are no absolutes, that all is relative? Is this a God to seek, to believe in, to obey and love? Can this be the God of Abraham, Isaac, and Jacob? The God of Jesus?

If the RCC were to repudiate this Yahweh and witness to the revelation of the "New Moses" (Jesus) of the "New Mount Sinai" (the Sermon on the Mount), to love the enemy, a step would be taken so the human condition could be disarmed, and paradise restored.

Unfortunately, the record shows the RCC has been on the side of cruelty, revenge, and murder in its treatment of the enemy. It has not been absolute in following "Do not kill" or "Love the enemy." Again, it claims tradition is equal in importance to the scriptures, but its tradition is extremely disturbing.

Throughout history, the RCC methodically executed people who dissented from its interpretation. It casually took life in abundance

213

rather than imitating Jesus, who came to give an abundant life. (Jo 10:10) It failed to enforce the "Gamaliel Principle," conveniently forgetting this part of its tradition. One would think the reprieve Gamaliel granted would have been burned into its consciousness. But no. As early as 386 CE in Trier, Germany, Christians set fire to a group of their own, tragically charging their fellow Christians with heresy, coldly imposing the same penalty that Nero had ordered. [161]

Hollywood has made countless films of Christians being fed to the lions or being forced to fight gladiators till death. The perception remains that many pious Christians met their deaths in Roman arenas at the hands of barbaric pagans. Wikipedia states, "The first documented case of imperially supervised persecution of the Christians in the Roman Empire begins with Nero (37–68). In 64 CE, a great fire broke out." Nero conveniently used Christians as scapegoats, throwing them to the lions. And Roman emperors did at times persecute the growing Christian community, though not as often as the movies imply.

With the advent of Constantine, Christians became favored over pagans, providing the Church financial support and promoting clergy to public positions. The Emperor Theodosius I made Roman Catholicism the official state religion. It wouldn't be long before Christians turned with vengeance on the pagan populace. The fourth century marked the decline and eventual demise of paganism in the Empire—by brutal and violent means.

Christianity became a classic example of the oppressed becoming the oppressors. No longer a religion of invitation, it evolved into one of forceful imposition. Book burning purged pagan texts that might adversely influence readers. It is still popular today, its latest supporter being extremist "pastor" Terry Jones, who burned the Koran and caused the deaths of at least twenty-four innocent bystanders worldwide.

Given the green light as the state religion, the RCC moved beyond burning pagan books and destroying pagan statuary, and began eradicating recalcitrant pagans themselves. The fourth century was a nightmare for pagans, who were forced to go underground to avoid Christian attacks. "The triumph of Catholic Christianity over Roman paganism, heretical Aryanism and pagan barbarism," asserts J.N. Hillgarth, "was certainly due in large part to the support it received, first from the declining Roman state and later from the barbarian monarchies." St. Augustine encouraged Christians to smash all tangible symbols of paganism they could find. (Wikipedia)

Christian texts entirely suppressed this treatment of pagans while exaggerating its own persecution by pagans. In 353 CE, the Emperor Constantius ordered the death penalty for worship through sacrifice and "idols." St. Ambrose influenced Theodosius I to issue his infamous decrees (389-91 CE), declaring an extensive war on paganism. One might compare this analogously to the Nazis' war on Jews, to their systematic imposition of laws that devastated Jewish life in the Third Reich. Where might Nazis have found their model?

Mandatory worship was enforced, state subsidies to pagan clergy were ended, copyists of pagan texts were threatened with having their hands cut off if they dared pass on pagan tradition. Intolerance was the new order as emperors became Christian converts and zealously promoted their new-found "faith." In 784 CE, an estimated 4,500 Saxons were beheaded when they refused baptism. Some scholars argue over the true number, but not the event.

Only two choices existed—baptism or death. An either/or option, as the RCC embraced intolerance to the extreme.

Bishop Bartolome de Las Casas, the missionary advocate of Native American Indians, had little support from the institution or his fellow Catholics: "We should realize the truth that in forty years some twelve million souls … have died unjustly and tyrannically at the hands of Christians." Conquistadors sometimes hanged their victims in two rows of six with a single gibbet at the end, "in honor and worship of our savior and his Twelve Apostles." [162]

What "faith" did these Christians bring to the New World? To whom, exactly, did they believe the Fifth Commandment applied?

When the RCC realized what a friend it had in Constantine, it began an historical rapprochement with political leaders. If it couldn't dominate them, it would develop symbiotic relationships wherever expedient. Access to one person with power meant more than allegiance to millions without it: "The example of Constantine, Theodosius and Justinian, who were seen as 'godly emperors ... serving the church and crushing its enemies,' was cited repeatedly by Christian authors who endorsed religious persecutions. When Louis XIV of France issued the Edict of Fontainebleau in 1685, revoking the Edict of Nantes and persecuting the schismatic Christian Huguenots, he was saluted as a 'new Constantine' by Jacques-Bénigne Bossuet." Bossuet was a renowned French bishop. (Wikipedia)

The Christian scriptures acknowledge that disciples of Jesus may be persecuted. And the Beatitude "Blessed are they who are persecuted for the sake of righteousness ..." admits the possibility of torture, but certainly does not suggest to respond in kind, nor initiate it. "But I say to you, love your enemies, bless those who curse you, do good to those who hate you, and pray for those who spitefully use you and persecute you, that you may be sons of your Father in heaven; for He makes His sun rise on the evil and on the good, and sends rain on the just and on the unjust." (Mt 5:45)

It is unfathomable to conceive how early Christians would fail to grasp this essential teaching. It is more understandable today, though, since it was *never* a priority in the RCC catechesis.

Early Christians were not only intolerant of pagans and Jews, but vindictive toward *other* Christians who held different interpretations of the arguably controversial understanding of who precisely Jesus was. The fourth and fifth centuries were times of bloody religious warfare. The Roman Empire was besieged from without by barbarians, and from within by theological dissenters.

Philip Jenkins describes the violent mayhem then executed against other Christians: "Jerusalem was occupied by an army of (Monophysite) monks; in the name of the one incarnate Nature, they pillaged, they burnt, they murdered; the sepulcher of Christ was defiled with blood ... On the third day before the festival of Easter, the patriarch was besieged in the cathedral, and murdered in the baptistery. The remains of his mangled corpse were delivered to the flames, and his ashes to the wind; and the deed was inspired by the vision of a pretended angel ... This deadly superstition was inflamed, on either side, by the principle and practice of retaliation: in the pursuit of a metaphysical quarrel, many thousands were slain." [163]

This was insanely beyond loving the enemy, turning the other cheek, walking the extra mile. What did these "Christians" not understand about the commandment incorporated into their belief system from Judaism, "Thou shall not kill"? It certainly was not an absolute belief in practice. While the nature of Jesus was argued and contested, how could the clear instructions not to kill, but to love one another, fail to influence their thoughts and actions?

JEWS AS THE TARGET OF INTOLERANCE
"Why don't Jews drink? It interferes with their suffering."
– Henny Youngman

Jews—neither pagans, nor infidels, nor Christians, but the tribe from whom Jesus sprang—became a special problem when it came to tolerance. Very few Jews ever accepted Jesus as the Messiah, since Jesus was a Jew before the word *Christian* was uttered. How were non-accepting Jews to be treated?

St. Paul was emphatic about the bond with Israel. "I say then, God has not rejected His people, has He? May it never be!" (Rom 11:1) If the average Christian was unaware of the commandment, "Do not kill," fewer were aware of Paul's passion for his fellow Jews. Ordinary people didn't read the scriptures, but more likely prelates did, and they should have questioned the all-out persecution of Jesus' people.

The brakes were put on proceeding with total annihilation of the Jews, as other groups, but their presence prevented the existence a pure Christian tribe. In time, they were labeled with the popular slur "Christ-killers." But even if some felt they did deserve that label, wasn't the Christian message to love the enemy?

Jews particularly feared Holy Week because for centuries they were described in Catholic liturgy as "perfidious" (until John XXIII removed this in 1960). Jews would lie low during Holy Week, lest some cleric would rouse his people to retaliate against Christ-killers: "For centuries, the Jews of Europe dreaded the cry of 'Christ-killers,' which preceded the rampaging mob murdering, raping, and burning their homes, particularly in the pogroms in eastern Europe between the 1700s and World War II." [164] Incredibly, Benedict XVI restored the term *perfidious Jews* in the Tridentine Mass liturgy of Holy Week, at least until an international outcry caught his attention.

The relationship between Catholics and Jews was indeed ambivalent, and unfortunately became more malevolent. Preaching of tolerance toward Jews diminished because of Jesus' origins and attempts to downplay his background. Centuries of negative attitudes about Jews went unabated, defined by pogroms, confinement to ghettos, and in some locations selective taxes and levies.

Pope Paul IV forced Roman Jews into a ghetto, requiring that they wear distinctive clothing. The Nazis had only to follow papal tradition in devising their treatment of Jews.

Anti-Semitism has deep roots in Christian tradition, going back to the scriptures, where Jewish religious leaders are consistently depicted in a negative light. Christian writers and prelates would expand on this, and a high point of anti-Semitism would be reached by Martin Luther: "Although Luther did not invent anti-Jewishness, he promoted it to a level never before seen in Europe. Luther bore the influence of his upbringing and from anti-Jewish theologians such as Lyra, Burgensis, (and John Chrysostom, before them). But Luther's 1543 book, *On the Jews and Their Lies*, took Jewish hatred to a new level when he proposed to set fire to their synagogues and schools, to take away their homes, forbad them to pray or teach, or even to utter God's name. Luther wanted to 'be rid of them' and requested that the government and ministers deal with the problem. He asked pastors and preachers to follow his example of issuing warnings against the Jews. He goes so far as to claim that 'We are at fault in not slaying them' for avenging the death of Jesus Christ. Hitler's Nazi government in the 1930s and 40s fit Luther's desires to a tee." [165]

The treatment of Jews in the West exposed the failure of Jesus' teaching to take deep root. His parables of tolerance, such as the weeds and the wheat growing together till harvest, were totally ignored. Instead, the intolerance implanted in earnest during the Constantine era, when the RCC gave up its prophetic birthmark, would blossom into a poisonous jungle.

If, during the time of their Diaspora among Christians, Jews had had a positive experience, who knows how many would have been receptive to Jesus' message of the Kingdom of God? But followers didn't abide by the Kingdom teaching to love one another, even enemies, revealing the seed failed to fall on fertile soil.

If the Jewish experience in the West had been positive, who knows if a separate state of Israel would have been needed? Many Jews were not originally ardent Zionists, but the Holocaust fired them up, leading to bitter suspicion toward those who preached a message of love while acting on behalf of evil. The intolerance they experienced is seen today in the treatment of Israelites toward Palestinians— another sad example of the oppressed becoming oppressors.

The genius of Judaism is its ability to survive the loss of the Temple, centuries of displacement, punishments and genocides, while remaining vibrant and strong to the present, without a bureaucratic structure of a papal curia to preserve its message and community. Makes one pause and wonder where the Spirit might be.

IS THE ROMAN CHURCH A PEACE CHURCH?
"What really breeds violence is political differences. But because religion serves as the soul of community, it gets drawn into the fracas and turns up the heat." – Huston Smith

If the Jesus story is to be believed, Jesus refused to use violence to defend himself. Why?

At his arrest, a disciple tries to defend him with a sword and Jesus rebukes him. "Put your sword back in its place," he commands, "for all who draw the sword will die by the sword." (Mt 26:53) Though innocent, and in danger, he says *no* to violent response. Rather than take life, he allows his life to be taken.

This rejection of violence has never been accepted as an absolute by most disciples, only by the exceptional few. Christians don't embrace pacifism and rarely question the use of violence against others. Only a miniscule number reject the use of force. It is their vigilant witness that tends the flame of the Kingdom's message in the Sermon on the Mount as a powerful alternative to the ready use of violence.

If the Fifth Commandment and the Sermon on the Mount were relentlessly reinforced as absolutes among members, this might have mitigated the widespread acceptance of violence as a necessity, a stock response. The RCC tradition from the Constantine period reveals a long history of military involvement. The papacy's utter dependence on military support sent a distorted message, as did its blessing of forceful conversion by the sword.

Violence was the norm. Christians took the cue from their leadership. In the Dark Ages following Constantine, the West was in a constant state of warfare. About 989 CE an attempt to quell the violence occurred with the emergence of Peace and Truce of God movements. But they had little impact upon Christians who dominated society.

Before Constantine, while not pacifists, at least Christians were conflicted about serving in the Roman military. But with the advent of Constantine and the favor he granted persecuted Christians, they were less hesitant. The alignment with power was complete; members could be relied upon for military service.

St. Augustine gave impetus to the use of force and coercion to compel others to conform, advocating that state power use violence against recalcitrant people. His promotion of a "just war" conditioned the RCC to acquiesce to centuries of warfare in societies in which it dominated. It released the brakes on warfare as it debated whether a particular one might meet the standards of a "just war." Which military action did the RCC canonize as meeting the standards of a "just war"? Historically, it was largely an academic exercise.

Empires depended on military strength for their staying power, so the RCC built armies to maintain institutional survival. If it could not subject the political order to be subservient, it would get the political order to serve its vested interests. With the shift of the Roman Empire to Constantinople, Rome fell into decline. The RCC stepped into the vacuum in Italy, effectively donning the apparel of the Empire, becoming the *de facto* empirical presence that offered a sense of structure and stability to a threatened populace. Most popes came from Roman families who wielded the remnants of power and fought to extend boundaries beyond Rome.

Author Derek Wilson claims what the RCC lacked was military muscle: "What they needed was a loyal son of the Church who had the backing of a strong army." The only feasible candidate who filled the bill was Charlemagne. [166]

Pope Leo III crowned Charlemagne as Roman Emperor. The act of the pope crowning the king symbolically positioned Charlemagne as subject to the pope. (A thousand years later, Napoleon, aware of this subjugation—the papacy as overlord—would crown *himself.*)

With the patronage of Charlemagne, a pattern was set. From then on, popes were not reluctant to organize armies to protect their vested interests. Repeatedly, they looked to the intervention of armies to defend Rome and its Italian territory. While popes were all for the persecution of heretics, they could be ecumenical in military matters. Pope Innocent XI backed (some say funded and blessed) the Protestant William of Orange against Catholic monarchs James II of England and Louis XIV of France.

As early as 849 CE, popes supported a papal navy to repel invaders. It limped along till it was scuttled by Leo XIII in 1878. Jesus called his apostles to be fishers of men. At best he might have blessed a fishing fleet, but not an armada.

English historian David S. Chambers began his research in Italy and at the Vatican in the 1950s, developing a niche interest in the papacy and warfare. The result was *Popes, Cardinals and War,* published in 2006. The sensationalism of his study is subdued by serious scholarship, casting light on a disturbing dark side of the RCC. It is a hard read, not simply because of the unsettling history of a warlike papacy, but because the facts are delivered in a dry, dispassionate, constrained manner that demands the reader's sheer willpower to keep going. It portrays a troubling segment of Church tradition that the RCC, on its own, would never bring to the light of day. In this matter, exorcism is long overdue.

It is only in his very brief epilogue that Chambers expresses any personal or emotional response to a religious institution that promoted a Prince of Peace when so many of its clerical princes were anything but peaceful.

221

Again, cognitive dissonance failed to be experienced in high places. Chambers laments, "We have yet to hear a word of recantation or apology for the centuries of warfare." [167] He feels the virus of violence lingers in the RCC. "Fortunately, one can leave to the imagination what might have happened, had events turned out differently in the twentieth century."

Unfortunately, few may be willing to read Chambers' academic research, for which the Vatican can thank its lucky stars. He concludes his epilogue by stating, "This book … has aimed to show the Roman Church's leadership being drawn, almost inevitably into processes of war rather than peace." [168] Extremist papists (Ultramontanes) may scream *"Anti-Catholic!"* without studying the historical record. But I encourage those who want substantive facts to tackle Chambers' text.

I could not write a better synthesis of his work than this unsigned description offered on Ebooks.com: "Can Christian clergy—supposedly men of peace—also be warriors? In this lively and compelling history D.S. Chambers examines the popes and cardinals over several centuries who not only preached war but also put it into practice as military leaders. Satirised [sic] by Erasmus, the most notorious—Julius II—was even refused entrance to heaven because he was 'bristling and clanking with bloodstained armour [sic].' *Popes, Cardinals and War* investigates the unexpected commitment of the Roman Church, at its highest level of authority, to military force and war as well as—or rather than—peace-making and the avoidance of bloodshed. Although the book focuses particularly on the fifteenth and sixteenth centuries, a notoriously belligerent period in the history of the papacy, Chambers also demonstrates an extraordinary continuity in papal use of force, showing how it was of vital importance to papal policy from the early Middle Ages to the nineteenth century. *Popes, Cardinals and War* looks at the papacy's stimulus and support of war against Muslim powers and Christian heretics but lays more emphasis on wars waged in defence [sic] of the Church's political and territorial interests in Italy. It includes many vivid portraits of the warlike clergy, placing the exceptional commitment to warfare of Julius II in the context of the warlike activities and interests of other popes and cardinals both earlier and later. Engaging and stimulating, and using references to scripture and canon law as well as a large range of historical sources, Chambers throws light on these extraordinary and paradoxical figures—men who were peaceful by vocation but contributed to the process of war with surprising directness and brutality—at the same time as he illuminates many aspects of the political history of the Church."

Slowly, more studies of the papacy's propensity for military power are emerging. Robert Royal's *The Pope's Army: 500 Years of the Papal Swiss Guard* as well as David Alvarez's *The Pope's Soldiers: A Military History of the Modern Vatican* were published since Chambers' book. Possibly these works represent a harbinger of further scrutiny of an institution in which Jesus' kingdom teaching failed to be embraced seriously and unequivocally at the top.

I contend the dark side of the RCC underscores its similarity to Caesar. Pope Julius II is the poster-prelate for warfare. One story has Julius ask Michelangelo, "What is that under my arm?" Michelangelo replies, "A Bible, your Holiness." The pope roars, "What do I know of Bibles? I am a warlord; give me a sword instead." [169]

The RCC still supports military activity despite occasionally denouncing a war, as JP II did with Bush's war on Iraq. The American hierarchy, however, formed no chorus condemning this war. To me, this reveals the political nature of the papacy. A pope may decry a particular war but marshals no legion of hierarchs to join collectively, instead allowing the politics of war to play out locally. There is no official Catholic resistance to war. The violence of war has yet to be exorcised from the RCC. Politically, it seeks to cover all the bases, to avoid burning any political bridges. Because it insists on being treated as a political *and* a religious organization, the RCC fails to act as an unequivocally moral institution. Sadly, too often, too many positions are filtered through political considerations.

I admit my knowledge of the history of world religions is extremely limited. But to me, Islam and the RCC are identical in their use of warfare to defend and expand their "exceptionalism." But did Islam's religious leaders actually take up arms? It would be interesting to investigate whether they donned the garb of the warrior and led military assaults, as did the RCC. And I suspect that the histories of

Hinduism and Buddhism reveal few if any religious leaders who acted as commanders or even cheerleaders for warfare.

When it came to war, popes, bishops, abbots, and clergymen led the way. In warfare, the RCC remains exceptional.

THE CRUSADES
"During the crusades all were religious mad, and now all are mad for want of it." – J.G. Stedman

Since the historical record reveals no tolerance for differences of opinion and belief among Christians within the Empire, it is easy to grasp how the RCC would be intolerant of foreign belief, as in Islam. The Church was threatened by Islam, doctrinally and militarily. Islam was aggressive, relying on military might to extend its conquest. It had been repelled in 732 CE, but now in the tenth century it was on the move toward Constantinople. Pope Urban II responded to a plea from an eastern emperor for military support to check the advancement of militant Islam. But he gave it a religious twist. "I, not I, but God exhorts you," he proclaimed in launching this plan. Crusades became a bloody way of life for the Church, beginning with the First Crusade in 1095 CE and continuing into the fifteenth century.

In mobilizing the nobility and knighthood of Europe to mount a crusade in 1095 CE against the infidel Muslims (with the rallying cry *"God wills it!"*), Pope Urban II punctured the new wine skins of the Sermon on Mount, voiding their contents. God was now forced to be on the side of Christian aggressors.

Urban II redirected the military infighting and feudal violence rampant in Europe at the time, coalescing warring factions of a splintered Christendom toward one goal—hating the outsider, the Muslim. This military strategy has lasted throughout history, diminishing internal turmoil by directing it to an external "enemy," real or fictitious.

Islam today has an historical memory of the bloody Crusades, not the Sermon on the Mount. Evangelization from the West came by force, not invitation. It learned nothing of an alternative power to restore

224

paradise, but only brute force that would stoke the fires of hell here on earth. Christian militancy attempted to trump Islamic militancy.

Today, people in the West find it abhorrent that some Muslim extremists embrace terrorist tactics as a ticket to Paradise. In his time, Urban II motivated the religious illiterate by guaranteeing their engagement in a holy crusade would be their heavenly voucher, absolving all their sins and opening the doors to eternal paradise without having to pass through purgatory: "Crusaders who killed Jews and Muslims earned forgiveness for all their sins and were assured of a place in paradise *after* death, not after baptism." [170] Killing others became a new opportunity for grace, salvation.

One theologian who provided theological support for the Crusades was Bernard of Clairvaux, considered a reformer and a saint: "Bernard coined the term *malecide* (killing an evildoer) to describe the Crusades, in place of *homicide* (killing a human being)." [171]

This allowed for a simple progression of Augustine's assertion that error had no right. Now, for Bernard, the one who was in error had no right to life. Preaching malecide to Crusaders eased their conscience, reassuring them they were doing good by participating in a "holy war."

Bernard's malecide teaching took root. His influence in demonizing "the other," hence manufacturing a reason to eliminate this enemy, endures to this day. If we view "the other" as an evildoer, that other—like evil—has no right to exist. Why hesitate in erasing evil people from the earth? "Evil, be thou my good!" [172]

Originally, a Crusade was invoked to repel advancing Muslims, but it was redirected into military actions against various ethnic groups. The ensuing crusades were religiously sanctioned. Death and destruction was the pattern. Violence was a way of life. An apparent lack of cognitive dissonance was felt from acknowledging the Sermon on the Mount (let alone the Fifth Commandment) while massacring Muslims, Jews, and Christians.

These centuries of bloodbaths can only render a verdict that the RCC was *not* pro-life. Scalia is vindicated!

The failure to take the Holy Land from the Muslims reinforced the RCC's will to solidify the internal unity of the Holy Roman Empire against future assaults by Islam. Heresy was seen as a virus undermining the unity of faith, therefore of the Holy Roman Empire. The Albigensian Crusade, launched in 1209 CE, intended (among other things) to eradicate a growing dissident movement. When preachers of the RCC were unable to convince Cathars to reject their heretical beliefs and practices, Pope Innocent III, who had previously decreed heresy as "treason against God," now bestowed a special indulgence on those who joined the military campaign against heretics. He had no problem marshaling an army. Crusades and inquisitions were twinned in the papal move to eradicate the Cathar heresy in France.

At the town of Beziers, France, the crusaders demanded 200 heretics be handed over. Locals protected them and allowed them to flee to sanctuary in churches, thinking these Christian crusaders would never violate the sacred precincts. They were mistaken. The leader, Arnald-Amalric, ordered his men to "kill them all; the Lord will look after his own." They broke into the churches and massacred even women suckling infants. Arnald happily reported to Pope Innocent III, "Today, your holiness, twenty thousand citizens were put to the sword, regardless of age or sex." [173] And, he should have added, regardless of allegiance as Romans or Cathars. And Arnald-Amalric was an abbot.

Numerous smaller Crusades took place, lost to historical footnotes, marked by the same pattern of violence against those who resisted not only the doctrines of the RCC but the authority of its prelates: "Between 1232 and 1234, there was a crusade against the Stedingers. This crusade was special, because the Stedingers were not heathens or heretics, but fellow Roman Catholics. They were free Frisian farmers who resented attempts of the count of Oldenburg and the archbishop Bremen-Hamburg to make an end to their freedoms. The archbishop excommunicated them, and Pope Gregory IX declared a crusade in 1232. The Stedingers were defeated in 1234." (Wikipedia)

The total number tortured and murdered during numerous Crusades held under the auspices of the Church is known only to God.

226

Apologists for the RCC seek to downplay the actual number. Regardless, the fact remains that the RCC was *not* a pro-life institution. It failed to publicly and vocally witness against the taking of even one life, let alone consistently intimidating and threatening others with torture and execution, in effect belying a pro-life tradition.

Popes would not only organize troops to do battle against enemies without and within, but would don military garb and lead forces into the fray themselves, particularly Pope Julius II. As the name he took indicates, he was enamored with the glory of the Roman Empire. Ross King describes Julius' military exploits, in one instance consecrating a huge wheel of bread as the Body of Christ to precede his army into battle. Not only was this sacrilegious, but it underscored the belief that popes could do as they pleased, accountable only to their God—the divine right of kings and popes.

Michelangelo, though dependent on Julius II for art commissions, penned his view of popes:

> *Of chalices they make helmet and sword*
> *And sell by the bucket the blood of the Lord.*
> *His cross, his thorns are blades in poisoned dipped*
> *And even Christ himself is of all patience stripped.* [174]

He was well aware of the cognitive dissonance.

INQUISITIONS AND COMPLIANCE WITH STATE POWER
"Fear is the path to the Dark Side. Fear leads to anger. Anger leads to hate. Hate leads to suffering. I sense much fear in you."
– Yoda, at the Jedi Council

It is the inquisitions that most notoriously reveal that the RCC was not pro-life. They utilized instruments of torture, consigning countless people to death merely because they dissented from Church teaching, failed to observe Church practices, or happened to be Jews or Muslims.

On the way to the bonfires, the RCC disingenuously tried to wash its hands of mass murder. As Moynahan points out, "It sought to preserve the principal, *Ecclesia non novit sanguinem* (the Church does not shed blood). This provided some form of theological fig leaf, since laymen carried out the actual executions, but it was, of course, the grossest hypocrisy. No churchmen exonerated the Jews on the grounds that they had merely handed Jesus to Pilate for sentencing, and that Roman soldiers had performed the crucifixion." [175]

Jesus dissented from Torah Law by offering his own interpretation, irking the religious leaders of his day and eventually being dragged before the Roman court. The Romans weren't interested in theological squabbles. It is only when charged with "stirring up the people" that they perceived he might threaten the order of the empire and therefore needed to be eliminated.

If the RCC meditated on the unjust suffering and death of its founder, Jesus, how could it mete out torture and death to others who dared to interpret its dogma and practice? Did it even *believe* the Jesus story? It acted more like a threatened empire than a mirror of the Kingdom of God.

The Spanish and Roman inquisitions would mar the history of Europe and bequeath a legacy of an institution that terrorized people. When Europeans remember their history, it is not difficult to understand why the RCC continues to decline there.

The RCC was perceived as a formidable power constantly entangled in a web of political alliances. Members who advocated nonviolence were rare, as the institution had no catechesis on any level to encourage individuals to "put back the sword." The opposite, unfortunately, was the reality, as it obligated members to support rulers militarily. The RCC could be relied upon to convince compliant members to participate in military endeavors.

In modern times, the RCC has been dependable in delivering its members to serve in the military, regardless of which side. There would never be a Church-wide reflection on whether any particular war was a "just war." Perhaps detached academics and churchmen might speculate at a distance from the blood and gore of war. Meanwhile the Vatican delivers its members to unquestioningly do their civic duty.

If a Catholic were to question the morality of a war, it would have to come from personal initiative. In a Church that promotes a theology of fear, members are too inhibited to question an authority over them. And that authority would never encourage them to trust their conscience, independent of its external and eternal control.

Ben Salmon was an American Catholic, though few Catholics or Americans have ever heard of him. He was a rarity among American Catholics, being a conscientious objector during WWI. He applied for conscientious objector status, "something the U.S. government made provisions for among historic peace churches. Roman Catholics were not included for the church taught and adhered to a 'just war' theory." [176] He subsequently was found guilty and initially sentenced to death, which was commuted to twenty-five years in prison. He had frequently attended daily mass but would be denied the sacraments while in prison and expelled from the Knights of Columbus. He ultimately would be committed to St. Elizabeth's Hospital for the Insane in Washington, D.C. It would be the fledgling ACLU that took up his cause, not his Church, which closed its eyes and distanced itself from him.

Though limited by an eighth-grade education and scant resources, he wrote a 200-page manuscript while in prison critiquing the Church's "just war theory" and declaring, "There is no such animal as a 'just war.'" He based his belief and reasoning on the Kingdom teaching of the Sermon on the Mount, something the hierarchy and theologians were strangely unable to reach, understand, preach, or even remember.

Salmon was a solitary soul, at odds with his own country and Church and the tradition of supporting military involvement. In 1918, Cardinal Farley of New York remarked that "criticism of the government irritates me. I consider it a little short of treason. Every citizen of this nation, no matter what is his private opinion or his political leanings, should support the president and his advisors to the limit of his ability." [177]

In 1918, the RCC in America was under scrutiny by the Protestant majority, suspicious of whose allegiance members would put first— loyalty to the American Constitution, or to the papacy? Cardinal

Farley may have bent over backwards to promote unquestioning allegiance to the president, but he was more representative of the long tradition of the RCC to support the military of whatever government to which it sought an alliance.

Salmon was one of only four known Catholic Americans who declared themselves conscientious objectors during World War I. Through its long history of involvement in warfare, it was an accepted fact that its members would be totally compliant to serving in the military of any country in which they were citizens, regardless of whether the war was "just" or "just another war."

In World War II, Franz Jägerstätter, an Austrian farmer, refused military service under the Third Reich. He received no support from the hierarchy and was beheaded. Also a man of limited education, he concluded Hitler's wars were immoral, something educated Roman hierarchs and theologians were either unable or unwilling to admit. Obviously, if they concluded the wars were immoral, there would be severe repercussions, as in Jägerstätter's case.

Besides, the RCC had signed a Concordat with the Nazi regime, and would be faithful to it, not prophetic against it. It had made the pact with Hitler in order to protect its institutional interests. Catholics could only conclude that if their holy institution had no moral qualms about Hitler's wars, why should lowly members contest them? More Jehovah's Witnesses resisted disproportionally military service than Catholics in the Greater Reich.

While the RCC has supported the "just war" position for centuries, it routinely assigned clergy as chaplains for the military even when battles weren't raging. A declaration of a "just war" was not necessary to assign chaplains; they were standard components of the war machine even in "peace time." The RCC even walked the extra mile for the military in organizing and staffing military prep schools, conditioning young people for future military needs. There was never any catechesis for its young members to question the morality of participating in warfare altogether.

While the RCC would counter chaplains are provided for the spiritual well-being of its members in uniform, it never considered their spiritual well-being might be better served without donning a uniform and bearing arms. For centuries the papacy had been reliant upon military assistance for its institutional interests. It had conditioned itself to the idea that the use of force was inevitable. It was blind to the cognitive dissonance that the Kingdom teaching of the Sermon on the Mount might arouse. And as long as that teaching was not an absolute, the RCC relativized its stance.

The RCC was so fond of the military that patron saints were delegated to it. When someone posted a question on the website ask.com, "Who is the patron saint of the military?" a respondent offered this summary: "Here are several possible patron saints of the military. St. George, Martin of Tours, St. Sebastian, and St. Maurice are all patron saints of soldiers, while Joan of Arc is the patron saint of American soldiers. Saints Brendan, Erasmus, and Nicholas of Myra are the patron saints of sailors. Michael the Archangel is the patron saint of paratroopers. As you can see, our warriors have a lot of saints looking out for them!" No heavenly rest for saints deployed to watch out for the warriors.

The United States is the most recently organized empire in the history of humanity. When President Eisenhower left office he warned of the military-industrial complex that would undermine American democracy. His prescient judgment of it is now the engine that drives the USA, one upon which an incredible number of citizens are reliant for their livelihood. The conservative Rutherford Institute describes how Eisenhower's warning has been thoroughly ignored: "The American military-industrial complex has erected an empire unsurpassed in history in its breadth and scope, one dedicated to conducting perpetual warfare throughout the Earth. For example, while erecting a security surveillance state in the U.S., the military-industrial complex has perpetuated a worldwide military empire with American troops stationed in 177 countries (over 70 percent of the countries worldwide)." [178]

American citizens have a vested interest in the continuance of the military-industrial complex. They feed off the military machine. Currently, 48 percent of the nation's budget is siphoned into the military, affecting enlisted and retired members. In the private sectors, the U.S. is the world's largest arms exporter (30 percent). [179]

Many Americans support the military-industrial complex because they are in some way dependent upon it for their daily bread.

The RCC will not challenge the priorities of the American empire. If anything, it will remain supportive through passive complicity. The hierarchy is reluctant to challenge the war machine because the majority of Christians support it. In this instance, the hierarchy follows the lead of its members. It supports the status quo. To do otherwise, it would dare to be prophetic. The War Resisters League reflects more the Kingdom of God than the Roman hierarchy.

The RCC can be safely anti-abortion and remain nonthreatening to the empire. The empire casts a benign eye at this pro-life position. But if Roman hierarchs were to question not whether a particular war was a "just war" but if *any* war was *ever* justified, the wrath of the nation and its military would come crashing down on their pointy miters. If the RCC stopped supplying chaplains, it would be labeled traitorous and unpatriotic, causing Cardinal Farley to spin in his grave. Were it to make conscientious objection part of a parish curriculum, its nonprofit status would be in jeopardy.

Local pro-life committees are the latest thing. The RCC has directed its parishes to organize these groups, which remain largely focused on the future of the fetus. Not being a "peace church," it failed to engage pro-life committees or provide a catechesis for parishes to consider nonviolent alternatives to conflict, primarily military in nature. No way. This would be too prophetic for the RCC. While every Christmas it drags out Jesus as "the Prince of Peace," it's all a sham. There is no real-time effort to work with members in promoting that peace, in developing nonviolent methods to resist evil. It is too compliant to a military legacy and culture to undergo such a conversion. Catholics have been conditioned to accept the legitimacy of violence, and might overwhelmingly balk at pursuing peaceful resolutions to conflict. The theology of fear triumphs once again.

Very few American Catholics have publicly resisted military power. The Berrigan brothers were notable among the few. The hierarchy distanced itself from members who witnessed against the use of force and violence. Archbishop Raymond Hunthausen and Bishop Thomas Gumbleton were effectively shunned by their fellow hierarchs. Fr. John Dear, S.J., did jail time for his protests. Fr. Roy Bourgeois and his organization, SOA Watch (School of the Americas Watch) represent the strongest resistance movement of RCC members. But the bishop of Madison, WI, Robert Morlino, unashamedly doing the bidding of Empire, is on the board of the SOA organization, renamed Western Hemisphere Institute for Security Cooperation (WHINSEC). Many, notably religious sisters, have been jailed for their protests against its training in torture through the American military.

Overwhelmingly, most Catholics would not identify with these dissenters. Rather, they would have no qualms in accepting the Military Ordinariate, a Vatican-sanctioned apparatus that complies with state power by providing clerics to support the military.

Who needs a church that's really an extension of a government? The spirit of Constantine is alive and well!

TORURE: FAILURE TO MEDITATE ON THE INNOCENT JESUS
"Well, to the people who pray for me to not only have
an agonizing death, but then be reborn to have an agonizing and
horrible eternal life of torture, I say, 'Well, good on you.
See you there.'" – Christopher Hitchens

Look at the historical facts. The RCC has not been a "peace church" since Constantine, due to championing "just wars" and employing military power for its security. But this pales in comparison to its historical sanctioning of a more horrific form of force—torture.

If members believe Jesus was tortured by Roman soldiers prior to his execution, it defies the imagination how they don't recognize the cognitive dissonance at the torture of human beings, innocent or guilty. This reflects a failure to mediate what happened to the innocent Jesus. Once again, do they even *believe* the Jesus story?

To my knowledge, no species in the animal kingdom willfully tortures others, save humans. Torture is more reprehensible than even killing. It is a sadistic mind that finds pleasure in causing another person to suffer, to prolong the agony. The not-so-innocent Pope Innocent IV (1243-1254) issued a papal decree authorizing the use of torture. "*Ad extirpanda*" (To extirpate) is labeled "perhaps the most terrible of all Bulls in the history of the Inquisition" by researcher Jonathan Kirsch. [180] In issuing it, Innocent IV absolved the Roman Empire of its treatment of Jesus.

The RCC contends its tradition is parallel to the gospels, or even has priority over them. Lamentably, a central part of this tradition was the authoring of its infamous "how-to book," *The Hammer of Witches*. Actually, more than one manual of torture was circulated, detailing horrific techniques, mechanisms, implements, and practices, with instructions employing them to force victims to recant.

The Hammer of Witches was commissioned by Pope Innocent VIII in 1486. This nefarious work of two Dominican inquisitors, Heinrich Kramer and Johann Sprenger, became a bestseller, reaching twenty-eight editions by 1600. [181] One can only deduce how extensive and receptive the audience was. *The Hammer of Witches* apparently inspired other torture manuals.

Book burning started in the thirteenth century, and by the mid-fourteenth century the RCC released the *List of Prohibited Books*, a list of authors and publications members were forbidden to read under pain of excommunication. Ironically, no gory training manuals made the hit list. Without endangering their souls, members could safely indulge their sadistic fantasies by reading step-by-step instructions on torturing their fellow human beings. This was undoubtedly a comfort to the Marquis de Sade, who purchased copies for his like-minded friends.

The manufacturing of instruments of torture became a lucrative business for artisans who fashioned devices to apply pressure on victims to confess. The RCC created a niche market for the torture industry. Today, bloodcurdling artifacts are displayed in specialty museums from Amsterdam to Vienna to Wisconsin Dells, WI.

Torture has been kept alive through the centuries with greater degrees of sophistication. Unfortunately, the tradition of the RCC bequeathed to modern times manuals and the mechanics of torture. Stalin, Hitler, and Hirohito "benefitted" from this legacy of inflicted suffering. The manuals have been conveniently updated to include refined methods of torture employed even by our own country. Waterboarding, a traditional standby, remains one of the favored means of inducing torture, even as many here continue to debate whether it even *qualifies* as torture. Ask the victims.

The RCC's new-found pro-life position may expect to convince others to protect the unborn, but it has a sordid tradition of torturing and killing the already born. If we are unable to protect the already born, we will hardly convince anyone to protect the unborn. For we go from the known to the unknown, from the *seen* to the *unseen*, from one who already is to one who might possibly be.

Would that the unique Jewish commandment, "Thou shalt not kill," had been embraced as absolute at all times, in all places, by all persons. Paradise here would have been restored.

But exceptions make the rule, even by Christians here in the USA, from the massacre of Indians, to the lynching of blacks, to the fratricide of the Civil War, to the participation in wars of aggression, to the dubious honor of being one of few civilized nations enforcing the death penalty. Militant conservative Christians are passionate about posting the Ten Commandments in every public venue, but do not necessarily believe in the Fifth one on the list.

In practice, to kill is a relative command based on one's subjective decisions. Pope John Paul II liked to boast of a "culture of life" (apparently as opposed to a "culture of death").

This is a new-found slogan, inconsistent with Roman tradition. The RCC boasts of the importance of tradition, but its tradition of violence underscores its moral failure and deviation from what is uniquely new wine in the Jesus story—the teaching of the Sermon on the Mount. "But I say to you, love your enemies and bless the one who curses you, and do what is beautiful to the one who hates you, and pray over those who take you by force and persecute you." (Mt 5:44) Paul also served this new wine. "Repay no one evil for evil but give thought to do what is honorable in the sight of all." (Rom 12:17)

It is the tradition of the RCC that presents the strongest evidence indicating it has *not* cultivated a "culture of life."

While all religious (and non-religious) groups have morally failed in some ways, the RCC is singular in the extent of suffering it has caused the world. Its morbid tradition can't be surpassed. For two millennia, leaders and followers betrayed the basic teaching of their inspired leader. This continues today in those desirous of revenge, bellicose supporters of war and military intervention. How could so many spread so much evil, so much hate?

ROMAN EXCEPTIONALISM
"I have learned to keep to myself how exceptional I am."
– Mason Cooley

In today's political discourse there is frequent mention of American "exceptionalism." Of course, it's all a matter of interpretation. Frenchman Alexis de Tocqueville is considered the first to reference it here. He saw this experiment in democracy as "exceptional" in its sense of equality, populism, individualism, and freedom. Nowadays, neoconservatives here have viewed America as a "city on a hill," exempt from historical forces influencing other countries. Of course, neocons are quick to call other citizens unpatriotic if they don't happen to share this perspective.

According to Wikipedia, *exceptionalism* refers to "the perception that a country, society, institution, movement, or time period" is "unusual or extraordinary in some way" and thus does not need to conform to common rules or general principles. In this sense, the term has a wide application, "reflecting a belief formed by lived experience, ideology, perceptual frames, or perspectives influenced by knowledge (or lack thereof) of historical or comparative circumstances." (Wikipedia)

Without using this exact term, the RCC has consistently in its tradition considered itself exceptional over *all* world religions, not just other Christian denominations. "Outside the Church, there is no salvation" (*"Extra ecclesiam nulla salus"*) was an expression coined by Cyprian of Carthage in the third century. Until Rome and Constantinople split in 1054, the expression was embraced by Christians in the West and East, validating Christianity as the one-and-only vehicle in the search for universal salvation. (This begs the question. Who says everyone actually *searches* for salvation?)

The Romans seized upon this expression with fervor, applying it to themselves and excluding the Orthodox. Beginning with Innocent III in 1208, Roman pontiffs underscored their organization as exceptional. Boniface VIII (1302) was more vehement in making the argument: "We declare, say, define, and pronounce that it is absolutely necessary for the salvation of every human creature to be subject to the Roman Pontiff." Interestingly, salvation was suddenly delivered not through the Church but the Roman Pontiff.

Centuries later, Pius IX would meld salvation and pontiff in his boast, "I am the Church!" And in recent times, John Paul II reiterated this in the encyclical *Dominus Jesus*. All other religions are insufficient for one or more reasons, so it claims. It is not that Christianity is exceptional, but that the Roman Catholicism *alone* is exceptional. Boniface would have understood.

In his sweeping documentary, *Catholicism*, Fr. Robert Barron unfortunately glosses over the dark side of RCC tradition. "A handful of people did terrible things," he admitted in an interview with Tim Drake, senior writer and host of *Register Radio*, "but we have 2,000 years of beauty, art, architecture, liturgy, and the saints." [182]

Were the "handful" a dozen, a thousand, a million? And this so-called "2,000 years of beauty" renders the prophetic Jesus more akin to an aesthete who inspired a religious art form. Since Barron dismisses the dark side of the institution, one should question his historical credibility.

Leaving aside the argument as to whether the RCC alone is exceptional in offering the singular authentic means to God, it *is* entirely exceptional in having established inquisitions spanning centuries of its shadowy history. The organized structure of inquisitions struck fear into the minds and hearts of members, and many non-members who were at times more terrified than members.

Orthodox hierarchs had no comparable apparatus to terrorize people in its jurisdiction. Among Christians, the closest contenders were some Protestant leaders, notably John Calvin in Geneva with his reign of terror. Queen Elizabeth I of England persecuted Catholics, though primarily because they were a political threat. Pope Pius V (1566-1572) issued an encyclical against her, intimating her overthrow. She responded by ridding England of papists.

But no Christian group could match the centuries of bloodcurdling inquisitions that the RCC maintained and institutionalized, even creating their creepy bureaucratic headquarters—the Congregation of the Holy Office—in the shadow of St. Peter's. The inquisitions would encompass the terror, torture, and death of innocent individuals under the auspices of this "Holy Office." Apparently no cognitive dissonance was noticed in the use of the word *holy* when naming this terrorist organization.

Christianity is one of the three religious groups that comprise the People of the Book; Judaism and Islam form the trinity of belief, the concept of one God. Yet Judaism and Islam never created inquisitional bureaucracies. They were not bloodless in dealing with unfaithful members, and they may have documented brutal instructions to deal with them, but they never organized a systemic bureaucracy to spread terror among their own membership, and beyond.

As for Hinduism, Confucianism, and Buddhism, there is no historical record of any organized punitive system or institutionalized bureaucracy like the RCC's Holy Office (which continues today under the guise of the Congregation for the Doctrine of Faith).

When it was established by Paul III in 1542, he defined its mission: "To maintain and defend the integrity of the faith and to examine and proscribe errors and false doctrines." One could hardly argue with this bland, generalized statement. Any group has the right to define itself and determine if its members satisfy its requirements and goals. The problem with the RCC's mission here is not with the ends, but the means. It would not be satisfied to simply shun or dismiss an unfaithful member (or non-member), but insisted on subjecting such an individual to incredulously cruel and inhumane punishments, beyond comprehension. Death would be a welcomed exit.

The institution that implemented this hell on earth believed its founder was innocent, yet suffered and was executed. It failed to sense any cognitive dissonance between mourning his death and ordering countless deaths of other innocents, without compunction. No accurate account remains documenting the exact number of those interrogated, tortured, or murdered through these horrifying mechanisms. Inquisition panels operated quite a sophisticated bureaucracy that kept meticulous notes, though numerous records were lost to the vicissitudes of history.

From the existing records an estimate could be attained. But would any particular number act as a "tipping point," forcing the Vatican to confess its shame over the historical demonization and bold-faced unfaithfulness to its founder? And what would that number be?

Evidently, John Paul II had some misgivings about Catholic exceptionalism in light of its history of terror and execution, when Vatican archives were opened to allow researchers to comb the records. In 2000 (the Jubilee Year), he became the first pontiff ever to publicly acknowledge the profoundly tragic effects the inquisitions had on world history and the institution. But he could not bring himself to single out any pope or ecclesiastical leader who had blood on his hands.

And I purposely say "on *his* hands" because women were totally out of the leadership loop (and therefore uninvolved in inquisitions, torture, and murder on behalf of the "holy" organization). The ongoing violence was another manifestation of uncontrolled males.

History's female members are virtually the only innocents. Well, and children. But John Paul II had described these horrendous crimes as departures by some of its "children." The invoking of the word *children* when describing perpetrators of such incredulous violence is mindboggling.

Instrumental in opening the Vatican archives was Carlo Ginzburg, a Jewish-Italian historian. At the public ceremony acknowledging the sins of Church Fathers, John Paul II spoke of being "sorry" over this historical failure. Cullen Murphy documents Ginzburg's response: "Ginzburg said, 'This is all very well.' He said, 'What I didn't hear the pope say today, and what I haven't heard anybody in this discussion say, is that the Catholic Church is *ashamed* of what it did. Sorry is easy. I want to hear the Catholic Church—I want to hear the pope—say he is ashamed.' There was a tremendous round of applause from the historians. Not from the theologians." [183]

Ginzburg would never hear those words uttered by the pope, nor by any hierarch on behalf of the pope. They are exceptional!

As the 2000 millennium approached, to his credit, John Paul II made a *"beau geste"* to address the sordid history of the RCC, despite resistance from the Curia. He apologized for 100 wrongdoings involving individuals and groups that devastated millions. An historical precedent it was, but more ritual than reform. The Vatican fell short of implementing new policies to prevent similar abuse (unlike modern Germany, which has been extremely proactive in acknowledging its shameful history, instituting laws to guard against the reoccurrence of blatant anti-Semitism).

From the list of 100, here are some notable and notorious sins committed by the RCC (according to a Wikipedia list): "the persecution of the scientist Galileo Galilei; involvement with the African slave trade; burnings at the stake and religious wars following the Protestant Reformation; execution of John Hus; injustices against women, violation of their rights, and historical denigration; inactivity and silence during the Holocaust; violating the rights of ethnic groups and peoples, with contempt for their cultures and religious traditions; the Crusades; abuses against indigenous peoples of the South Pacific; and massacre of Aztecs and other Mesoamericans by the Spanish." All in the name of Holy Mother the Church.

To cite one wrong from John Paul's dirty laundry list, a sign of true conversion would have been demonstrated were it to include women in the governance of the institution. Without advocating for women priests (as I advocate for no priests *at all*—male or female—but only disciples), I believe it could easily have admitted females to substantive positions on par with males. The College of Cardinals is the inner circle of advisors to a pope, an entirely human construct. If historically even teenagers (the pope's nephews) were created cardinals, surely women of wisdom should be included today. Yet the Vatican adamantly refuses to be inclusive of both genders. Women dominate membership within its community, yet they are negligible in its hierarchy. At any Sunday liturgy across the USA, easily two-thirds of those present are women. But in the offices of leadership, they are absent. The RCC constantly claims it is not a democracy. Unfortunately, it is an authoritarian structure. All power remains exclusively in a miniscule group of members—male clerics. They resist any attempt to allow other members to share authority despite Vatican II's emphasis on collegiality.

Even within the male clerical elite, only the hierarchy has effective power. Lay male members are excluded as are women, even religious women who dedicate their lives wholly to the institution.

There cannot be a more egregious departure from Jesus' Kingdom priority of service as the antidote to the corruption of power than this fierce resistance to share. If all members had participated collegially, the abuse of power would have been restrained and the history of the RCC since Constantine would have reflected light rather than darkness. Without balance in the exercise of power, it will continue to corrupt absolutely.

In these declining days of Benedict XVI, the world is witnessing in the Vatican a power struggle among male clerics who want to ascend the throne of papal omnipotence. The image now displayed is that of *"Pontifex Maximus"* (the "Supreme Pontiff," a title Caesar held), not *"Servus Servorum Dei"* ("the Servant of the Servants of God").

The American Shakers were inspired by the scriptures' teaching of equality, and opened leadership roles equally to women and men. How were they able to drink this new wine, when the Romans never even put the bottle on the table?

Years ago, a priest friend boasted he was a "feminist." I was taken aback. I thought only *women* were feminists. He explained that he supported the efforts of women to gain equality in church and society, both of which in fact claim equality of persons—in theory, at least.

Isn't equality a Kingdom value? Yes, but in practice it was gradually suppressed (without acknowledging the cognitive dissonance), while the second-class status of women was passively accepted, as most females themselves succumbed accordingly to male dominance.

Currently, Democrats and Republicans are battling over a supposed "War on Women" in American society. But an older and longer "War on Women" still marches on in the RCC.

Women lack any significant governing authority, and if a rare woman accedes to the role of diocese chancellor, she finds herself under the thumb of a priest. Catholic women have, until only recently, remained extremely compliant to male superiority within the tribe.

One exception is seen in women religious who took Vatican II to heart and began to define their own roles within the Church. They blazoned new spheres of competence and leadership, becoming some of the earliest CEOs in America. They diversified their activities and moved well beyond enforcing the *Baltimore Catechism*. They fanned out into American society, particularly fulfilling the Kingdom initiative of identifying with "the least ones."

Ultimately, this would set them on a collision course with displeased hierarchs, who preferred that women religious be "back in the burqa" and handmaidens to father.

The Leadership Conference of Women Religious (LCWR) is the largest organization of women religious in America, representing more than 80 percent of the nation's 57,000 sisters. Its homepage boldly states its mission in brief bursts of rolling type: "We embrace our time as holy, our leadership as gift, and our challenges as blessings ... led by God's spirit and companioned with one another ... we believe God's call is written in the signs of the times ... inspired by the radical call of the Gospel."

Well, the Vatican has not been happy with such assertiveness on the part of these educated "uppity women." Instead of targeting American bishops for their failure to protect children from priest predators, the Vatican instigated an investigation exclusively of American women religious!

This action reveals the arrogance and abuse of raw male clerical power.

The Vatican accuses the LCWR of "radical feminism." It simply lobs this verbal grenade at its members, a scatter shot to put them on the defensive. One would think, given the history of misogyny in the RCC, verbal restraint might be in order. The Vatican does not define its choice of words, simply implies a negative assertion. "Radical masculinism" ought to be tossed back at it. What I mean by "radical masculinism" is the historical male abuse of power whose last vestiges are found in places like Saudi Arabia and the Vatican. Given the societal strictures of Jesus' time, he could only, through today's lens, be viewed as a "radical feminist," a subversive revolutionary. No wonder some wanted him out of the way, just as some today dismiss the LCWR.

The RCC in America has a human face only because of women religious. Its other face, as mirrored by bishops, shows brute force. Bishops have the canonical power (since males wrote the canons) to enforce their edicts, but lack the moral power to persuade the masses. If the RCC is to regain any moral legitimacy here, it will only occur through female members rejecting the brutal imposition of the male principle. What is happening now is a violent affront to the ethical and spiritual self of women, a form of "moral rape," imposing male will on resisting females.

If the RCC is to be saved, it will be under the leadership of women. Men had their chance. They ruled for centuries and all they have to show for it is the abuse of power.

Meanwhile, John Paul II redefined the mission: "The duty proper to the Congregation for the Doctrine of the Faith is to promote and safeguard the doctrine on the faith and morals throughout the Catholic world: for this reason everything which in any way touches such matter falls within its competence." This paints an absurdly broad stroke. *Those who have the power have the power to determine what touches such matters.* Wonderful!

Today the RCC cannot continue its legacy of torture or sentence anyone to death. At worst, it can excommunicate a member it deems a threat to its doctrine and morals. Did this decision to eliminate the means of torture and death come from an internal conversion? Or from external pressures from more enlightened secular, humanistic, democratic forces?

This exceptionalism of the RCC represents just another failure of its moral authority. As a result, knowledgeable people are further encouraged to act as their own moral authority, faithful to their own conscience. The centuries of its inquisitional exceptionalism, the control over the minds and hearts of its people, reflects an empire, a totalitarian state.

Historically, the wrongs the RCC inflicted came from its use of force, both physical and mental, and its reliance on governments to enforce its perverted version of morality. But today's democratic societies are not so accommodating.

Nonetheless, it continues to coerce high-profile members in politics and education by enforcing its morality with the threat of excommunication. In the light of its dark tradition, the Vatican needs to exorcise its theology of fear and convert to a *praxis* of love. But no signs since the millennium falderal and its proclamation of a New Evangelization indicate anything but business as usual.

The RCC maintains its tradition is combined with the gospels and constitutes the deposit of faith. But its irrefutable tradition consistently initiated and condoned violence. The modern Vatican cannot suppress this horrible reality. It would be as if Germany today were to deny the Holocaust was initiated and enforced by German citizens.

In a sense, one shouldn't be surprised by these horrendous actions. Since Constantine, the RCC purposefully operated as a political empire. And what do political empires do? They brutally extend and maintain power and control. Once the Vatican became political and forsook its prophetic and empowering message, it is no surprise that its actions were of an institution more reflective of Caesar than of Jesus.

And in that sense, the Roman Church is still exceptional today.

CHAPTER NINE

CONVERSION:
RECOVERING THE KINGDOM

"If we are to go forward, we must go back and rediscover those precious values—that all reality hinges on moral foundations and that all reality has spiritual control." – Martin Luther King, Jr.

Writing in 1985, Leonardo Boff was hopeful about the future of the RCC, observing that Abraham's wife Sara was sterile in her advanced years but became fertile and brought forth new life, a new generation, in her son Isaac. At that time Boff wrote optimistically, but he finally opted out of the RCC, frustrated by its resistance to substantive change. He later wrote that its true identity "is not in a past that it often vainly tries to restore but in a future that is still to be revealed." [184] The restoration of John Paul II was just under way, and now under Benedict XVI, the past had returned with vigor.

I am less optimistic than Boff. The RCC focuses on itself, not the Kingdom. Above all, it clings to power and vehemently resists authentic service. Jesus must have seen this coming—Peter was the obstacle he called "Satan." Almost humorously, Luther called the RCC "the whore of Babylon." Compared to Jesus' label of Peter, Luther's pronouncement sounds charitable.

Though not optimistic, perhaps I'm hopeful. The fact that tension exists indicates the dream of the Kingdom still appeals. As Dr. King reflected, "Our lives begin to end the day we become silent about things that matter." It is in giving a damn that we witness to hope. This saying was mentioned early in the book: "The Church is always being reformed." Would that it embraced its status as a work-in-progress rather than posturing as a triumphant empire! Those sharp words of Enda Kenny mentioned earlier ("the dysfunction, disconnection, elitism, the narcissism, that dominate the culture of the Vatican") were not Irish bluster. This has been the Vatican for centuries. As long as it clings to Constantine, it is a Satan, a stumbling block to the Kingdom being realized.

The problem is the tendency to equate the *institution* with the *kingdom*. Consider again Fuellenbach's words, noted earlier: "The Church is not the Kingdom now, because *the Kingdom makes itself present outside the Church as well*. Her mission (church) is to serve the Kingdom and not to take its place." (Emphasis added)

Being in solidarity with individuals and groups that reflect truly spiritual values sustains one's hope for a greater realization of the Kingdom. Amazingly, the past century saw a flowering of groups especially reflective of the Kingdom, even when the RCC was not. Hope springs from being in their company. Meanwhile, the theology of fear maintains anguish over attending mass (physical presence suffices) to avoid mortal sin and eternal torture. But being Kingdom-focused might mean finding a more productive use of time, pursuing a Kingdom value instead of sitting in a pew. Nonetheless, the RCC continues to unleash a theology of fear on unsuspecting, naive people. It needs to be converted to the Kingdom.

CAN THE CHURCH BE CONVERTED?
"Power based on love is a thousand times more effective and permanent than the one derived from fear of punishment."
– Mahatma Gandhi

Can the Church look clear-eyed at its underlying power and convert it from fear to love? Any conversion that occurs in the RCC will come from below, not from above. Its leadership has held control for centuries and has failed to be converted to seeking the Kingdom first. The last hurrah for its salvation will come only from those without institutional power when they awaken to realize they are the salt and the light of the earth.

Despite the papacy's efforts to crush Liberation Theology, it remains a viable vehicle to galvanize those committed to Kingdom values. It engages people in critical thinking and provides leaven to impact society substantively, not superficially. "A day is coming when people will worship in spirit and in truth." (Jo 4:23) That day arrives when more individuals, whether official "believers" or not, internalize values that reflect the Kingdom and act on them in building a community of hope for humanity.

Increasingly, non-church organizations and groups are in the "business" of serving others. In their work for the well-being of others, these secular groups are a sign of the Kingdom.

Rotary International's motto is "Service Above Self." There is no better summary of the Kingdom teaching. And Rotary is truly catholic, as it encourages its members to intervene in meeting the needs of "the least ones," the vulnerable of the world. As an organization, it has spearheaded the eradication of polio throughout the world. The seed has, fortunately, found fertile ground *outside* church walls.

"Perfect love casts out fear." (1 Jo 4:18) But the RCC *instills* fear.

Perfect fear continues to cast out love!

These new attitudes in the Beatitudes reject revenge and violence, which throughout history stemmed from the bitter fruits of fear. They encompass the equality of all persons.

The RCC offers lip service to equality while maintaining a rigid hierarchy of important *persons* rather than important *functions*. It favors the good old boys. It keeps women subservient. And it treats children as nonpersons. (Clerical sexual-abuse crimes were widespread because children were viewed by the clergy as silent abstractions, neither seen nor heard.) The equality of all people bends toward human solidarity, transcending limitations imposed by family, tribe, and nation. Kinship through spirit, rather than through blood and tribe, defines the future.

The RCC's lust for power renders null and void Jesus' teaching of service as the antidote to power. It rejects Paul's insight, "To serve is to reign." It doesn't want to kneel humbly *before* others, but prefers to stand in a commanding position *over* others.

The Roman Catholic Church, in emphasizing *Roman* over *Catholic*, thrives on religious exceptionalism and maintains antagonism between non-believers and believers of every hue. It seeks to impose its beliefs regardless of others' beliefs and values. It needs a conversion to truly serve, to go beyond simply preaching. It resists Paul's warning, "Lest preaching to others, I myself become a castaway." (1 Cor 9:27) An institutional castaway, a museum of antiquity.

Today's adults are growing and maturing in their beliefs, living increasingly by internal values and attitudes, not conforming simply to external laws and customs. But the RCC is uncomfortable acting as a fellow pilgrim with all persons of goodwill, unwilling to join the journey to live in spirit and truth.

Whether Jesus existed or not, whether he was both divine and human or only one or the other, isn't as important as the gospels attributed to him. They offer a message about living life, right here right now, in a new way.

The duration of ministry attributed to him was so short there was little time to sow seeds, and many of those planted have yet to mature. But they have been planted in the proclamation of the Kingdom. The message of the Kingdom is hope for humanity, believers and non-believers. It offers nourishment for a human spirit that hungers for more than bread.

As an atheist friend acknowledged, "I live by the gospel teaching, 'Whatsoever you do to the least ones.'"

The RCC hierarchy has forgotten about seeking the Kingdom of God first. We need to take it upon ourselves to rediscover the seminal concepts of the Kingdom teaching, to discern what is truly new wine, while being mindful the gospels contradict themselves in places, contain inaccuracies, and carry unnecessary baggage.

Despite their limitations, they do serve new wine.

NEW WINE, NEW ATTITUDES, IN THE BEATITUDES
"'Blessed is the man who expects nothing, for he shall never be disappointed' was the ninth beatitude." – Alexander Pope

Is there anything unique in the Kingdom that can't be found elsewhere?

In each section of this chapter, I offer an element that reflects the original seeds in Jesus' proclamation:

• The Beatitudes

• The rejection of violence and revenge

• The priority of the person and equality of all

• Human solidarity above family, tribe, nation

• Service as the antidote to power

• Overcoming fear through critical thinking

• The praxis of love

The RCC has emphasized the Ten Commandments more than the Eight Beatitudes. Christians in the USA wage battles to position the Commandments in public places but show zero interest in exhibiting the Beatitudes. If quizzed, many Catholics would fail to identify any Beatitude but would score better with the Commandments, since the RCC drummed these into them as children.

The Commandments are essentially external norms, speaking of fear, roaring "Thou Shall Not ..." and demanding tribal conformity.

The Beatitudes are essentially internal values, speaking of freedom, transcending tribal limitations, engendering challenges to the human spirit, inviting participation and internalizing new attitudes as groundwork for a common, hopeful future.

These attitudes are universal in scope, but it takes a personal conversion to embrace them.

REJECTION OF VIOLENCE AND REVENGE
"While seeking revenge, dig two graves—one for yourself."
– Douglas Horton

When we feel wronged, we defend ourselves with the Old Testament quote, "an eye for an eye." But the Kingdom teaching would disarm us. "You have heard that it was said, 'An eye for an eye, and a tooth for a tooth,' but I say to you, do not resist an evil person; but whoever slaps you on the right cheek, turn the other to him also." (Mt 5:38)

But when Moses advocated "an eye for an eye" it was actually a moral advance. Prior to him, there was little sense of proportionality but only full-throttle revenge. Many Catholics are more Jewish, as they prefer an eye for an eye. And many Jews, too, reject Moses' teaching of proportionality, to walk the extra mile. In the current Israeli-Palestinian conflict, Jews do not act proportionally in response to Palestinian violence, are not reluctant to return superior power and force. They have stockpiled weapons of mass destruction, disproportionally arming themselves against their neighbor, reverting to a pre-Moses mentality.

Jesus rejected instruments of violence. "Put your sword back into its place; for all those who take up the sword shall perish by the sword." Yet some hierarchs claim he was referring to this one particular occasion. Jesus claimed he could summon a division of angels to defend him, but allowed that his life be taken rather than take life. Yet, he says, "Do not think that I came to bring peace on the earth; I did not come to bring peace, but a sword." (Mt 10:34) This is often quoted to counter the nonviolent side of Jesus. The context, however, shows him willing to cause division for the sake of the Kingdom, whose values are often in conflict with the status quo, the culture, the family. His moral and prophetic sword will not destroy but save lives.

Some Samaritans once refused Jesus entrance to their village on his way to Jerusalem. James and John wanted to command fire come down from heaven to consume them. Jesus rebukes James and John, whom he called elsewhere "sons of thunder," claiming, "The Son of Man did not come to destroy men's lives, but to save them." (Lk 9:56) He handled the situation nonviolently, simply circumventing the village and its inhospitality.

As noted, the RCC historically engaged in acts of violence and revenge, witnessing against the Kingdom. Only a few members like Salmon and Jägerstätter heroically resisted violence and revenge. Yet entire Christian sects managed to avoid violence and revenge throughout their histories. Today in the USA, the "Catholic left" resists the American military machine (with virtually no support from Roman hierarchs here, who align with the state).

The piety presented in the Stations of the Cross has the faithful meditate on the suffering, the torture, the eventual murder of Jesus, one totally innocent. But this meditation does not necessarily lead to a profound rejection of the violence in torture and killing. And if the Sermon on the Mount has no effect, surely the old wine, the Fifth Commandment, should put the brakes on.

This is the enigma of Jesus—his refusal to take a life, even in self-defense, while allowing his own life to be taken. "No one takes my life from me but I lay it down of my own accord." (Jo 10:18) The RCC has been a strong supporter of self-defense, condoning the taking of life. It does not encourage members to reflect on Jesus' rejection of self-defense even while it preaches that they live in imitation of him.

The U.S. in particular, a "Christian" nation, is adamant in supporting gun laws for self-defense. The RCC is frightened of challenging the easy accessibility of guns or the nature of firearms protection laws. Currently, the U.S. has the highest rate of gun ownership in the world, at 88.8 firearms per 100 citizens, for a conservative total of 270,000,000 guns in a population of approximately 311 million people. [185]

And the U.S. is the leading manufacturer and exporter of weapons. To publicly question this nationwide engine of death would be divisive, but prophetic. Of course, it would rankle countless individuals who support an incredibly unrestricted and virtually unregulated gun culture. If the RCC were to mobilize members at the parish level against arming for self-defense, in light of Jesus' refusal to defend himself, it would be tantamount to drawing the metaphorical sword, causing division within the household of the institution and the households of members. But isn't this a necessary division if the goal is to reduce firearms?

251

Fear drives people to arm themselves, even when risk analysis indicates the actual level of danger is minimal. A culture of fear drives people to think and act irrationally. And the RCC itself is driven by fear of being prophetic on the issue, even though acknowledging Jesus' rejection of self-defense is crucial in grasping him and his Kingdom message.

The dark side of violence in the RCC's tradition is a virus that has not been exorcised, rendering the institution a barrier to progress, not light and salt for humanity in initiating disarmament. Paradoxically, secular organizations are more prophetically attuned to the Kingdom message as they work efficaciously to put down the weapons for the sake of life.

PRIORITY AND EQUALITY OF ALL PERSONS
"All the people like us are We, and everyone else is They."
– Rudyard Kipling

Most societies are hierarchical. They maintain a pecking order—an individual is assigned a place and largely remains confined to it, with little chance of upward mobility. Equality comes more easily in societies threatened by their environment. Inuit Eskimos had no personal pronouns, as the severity of existence demanded they all watch out for one other, and the common life became the natural priority. But in most societies, hierarchies evolved and equality devolved.

Jesus replaced the hierarchy with the individual. That was his big thing. He made the person absolute. The person was the new wine, towering over Torah Law.

St. Paul, the observant Jew, wrote in Romans, "But now we have been released from the Law, having died to that by which we were bound, so that we serve in newness of the Spirit, and not in oldness of the letter." (Rom 7:6)

The RCC rejected this new wine by clinging to Canon Law and Natural Law, which often decided against the person through rigid interpretation. As always, it gave priority to the letter of the law rather than the spirit of the law, but "it is the spirit that gives life." (Jo

6:3) The RCC may publicly proclaim the theory of equality, but its heart is in its practice. And in practice, it maintains inequality.

Jesus was clear and direct in teaching the divine didn't dwell in a building but in a person. Still, the RCC keeps alive its "edifice complex," obsessed with extravagant structures. To place value on the person—*every* person—is to appreciate the divine in the human rather than in the manufactured magnificence. This new wine of equality and priority of the person is far from being consumed.

But what if Catholic hierarchs held out their glasses and got drunk on this wine? They might then notice that their splendid buildings are empty while "the least ones" are exposed to the vicissitudes of the weather, while innumerable children are aimless on roads and streets, while the people are desperate and need shelter. Does anyone at the Vatican see this?

Imagine St. Peter's as a dormitory for the homeless, as an inn for the one who had "no place to lay his head," for whom there was "no room in the inn."

Societies also value buildings over humans. An organization that builds homes for paralyzed veterans attempted to construct one in a Georgia community. The neighborhood association blocked construction after months of negotiations, with the excuse the house would lower property values. The veteran's family decided not to live in a community that valued a building more than a person, in this case, a person who became paralyzed protecting this nation, and this subdivision. [186]

In April 2012, a group called Occupy San Francisco encamped in a vacant building owned by the Archdiocese of San Francisco, and about seventy-five were arrested. The protesters hung a banner outside the building: *Give us this day our daily bread, and forgive us our trespasses.* They reportedly planned to use the building as their headquarters for providing social services. "There is no reason why any building should be vacant when people have no housing," one protestor told a *San Francisco Chronicle* reporter. "We ask that the archdiocese do the right thing and allow these services in these buildings." [187]

Many organizations espouse the equality of the person in theory, but when push comes to shove, not in practice. Capitalism controls the world's economy, making profit the bottom line, the absolute, no matter the cost to humans. In capitalism, the person is the means to the end. In the Kingdom, the person *is* the end.

Including women, foreigners, children, sinners, and the unclean in his company made Jesus the target of the ruling class. In John's gospel, Jesus meets a Samaritan woman at a well at high noon. This simple story has surprising depth. Jesus flaunts the status quo by engaging with a foreign woman who, it will be revealed, has had five husbands. His embrace of her as a person defies the norms and customs of society.

He is willing to go against the grain, defy convention, revealing every person is of value in the Kingdom.

On the flip side, the RCC staunchly defends the patriarchy that Jesus strongly opposed. Its hierarchy remains the last all-male bastion of dominance in the West. The only female residents of the Vatican are servants, domestics, religious women who do the housework. Only the Greek Orthodox Mt. Athos outdoes the Vatican—women can't even visit there.

Roman Catholicism increasingly has more similarity to Islam (with its male-only clergy) than even Judaism (with female rabbis among conservative, reformed, and perhaps even Orthodox Jews). As recently as Holy Thursday 2012, Benedict XVI adamantly rejected the possibility of women serving equally as priests. This continual and stubborn refusal to accept the gifts of women underscores inequality as the norm of the RCC, in direct opposition to Kingdom teaching. Benedict XVI apparently doesn't see the cognitive dissonance. He still blames Jesus for wanting only male priests.

In the early community of Jesus, the marginalized were attracted to an unusually open community. Though, as Bart Ehrman points out, some early opponents rose up among the pagans, such as the second-century critic Celsus, who "denigrated the religion on the grounds that it was made up largely of children, slaves, and women (i.e., those of no social standing in society at large)." [188] Paul championed

254

equality in leadership roles, declaring, "There is neither Jew nor Greek, there is neither slave nor free, there is neither male nor female; for you are all one in Christ Jesus." (Gal 3:28) While Paul offered this new wine, the RCC emptied the wineskin, maintaining its strict patriarchy. Today, the Vatican decries "cafeteria Catholics" because they seemingly pick and choose their beliefs. Is there not some projection going on here? Vatican hierarchs pick and choose which scriptural texts suit their positions, which parts of history will be revered, which beliefs will be held up as sacrosanct.

Our natural inclination is to imagine some people as superior to others, causing us to project significance on them and invest power in them. A mother said to a daughter setting off into the world as an adult, "Remember, you are no better than anyone else, and no one else is any better than you." It is hard to sense such "equality of persons" in a world based on disparity of wealth, power, and status.

Fr. Fernando Montes, rector of a Chilean university, denounced and labeled as "a dictator" Fernando Karadima, a prominent priest charged with child sexual abuse who had developed a popular cult following. Montes condemned conditions that "favored an environment for committing abuses," warning of the danger of divinization and sacralization. "The person in authority is not just an authority, but is transformed into a sacred being, who cannot be touched, who cannot be criticized," he said, providing "an enormous opportunity to redefine the way of exercising authority." [189]

Of all the powerful people on earth, no one is more "sacralized" than the leader of the Roman Catholic Church. The pope alone among all priests ("Fathers") would become the ultimate object of devotion (the "Holy Father"). The poetic language of the Good Shepherd parable underscores the intimacy existing between shepherd and sheep. But the RCC *created barriers* between shepherd and sheep. Language and imagery more reflective of the Roman Empire than scripture describes the papacy. Eventually the pope would be crowned with a tiara like a potentate, hoisted upon a *"sedia gestatoria"* (throne), and carried through the streets above the masses, which were made to genuflect and kneel as if before a divine king, Caesar. But he was merely a man. How could he not feel "special"?

THE THEOLOGY OF FEAR

Will Benedict XVI take the next step in upgrading papal majesty by restoring the *"sedia gestatoria"*? If so, it would paint a rueful picture of cognitive dissonance.

At a March 2012 conference, retired Bishop Robinson lambasted such sacralizing and its influence on the hierarchy's response to widespread clerical pedophilia. "The roots of the decades-long clergy sex abuse scandal lie not in any set of rules or practices, but are found deep in the culture of the church itself," which refuses to admit its contribution to the crisis, he said, as noted by the *National Catholic Reporter*. When studying this abuse, "we must be free to follow the argument wherever it leads" instead of deciding in advance that our findings must not demand change in any teaching or law, he insisted. "We must admit that there might be elements of the 'Catholic culture' that have contributed either to the abuse or to the poor response to abuse."

As reported, Robinson then identified many of these elements, including a hierarchy that maintains a "culture of obsessive secrecy," a "mystique" attached to priests that render them "above other human beings," and a "creeping infallibility" of papal decrees. All this has led to Robinson's "profound sense of disillusionment with the whole response of the church, particularly at its highest levels." [190]

The RCC clings to hierarchy, imbues priests with special powers, "sacralizing" them above members. It contends it is not a democracy. It should be *more* than a democracy in championing the equality of the person, no matter how lowly. For in democracies, capitalism has undue influence and jeopardizes the equality of persons. It is getting more difficult to believe in "one man, one vote."

Sexual and gender equality don't sit well with the RCC. They might remain at the center of a universal and worldwide battle, but it aggressively resists granting such equal status, aligning itself with religious groups of the same mindset—fundamental and evangelical Christians, Orthodox Jews, conservative Muslims. Such religious groups are too often wedded to cultural traditions, unwilling to read "the signs of the times" and transcend the past. Rather than headlights for humanity, they are broken taillights.

Simply put, many individuals, for many reasons, still reject the notion of equality. They would view this Kingdom value as a threat to the status quo. Not surprisingly, the Kingdom is often found *outside* the religious sphere. In promoting equality on many levels, democratic societies are witnesses to the Kingdom.

People are obviously "unequal" in terms of talents, abilities, and opportunities. But this does not make them "unequal" in terms of personhood. The gifts one has should not create a sense of superiority over others who have different or lesser gifts. Paul holds all the various manifestations are ultimately for the common good. (1 Cor 12:7) As an analogy, he shows how the parts of the human body function together as a unit. One part, he says, cannot say to another, "I don't need you."

SOLIDARITY OVER FAMILY, TRIBALISM, AND NATIONALISM
"Nationalism is an infantile disease. It is the measles of mankind." – Albert Einstein

The word *catholic* represents an exciting, embracing concept. It speaks to a collective and all-encompassing spirit, an opening to the world. Loyalty to a tribe shuns one's embrace of the world. People have an innate desire to belong. A tribe, like a family, is a harbor in a tempestuous world. Human history, though, has been racked by conflicts between tribes struggling for dominance. Even if people experience tensions within their tribe, when the tribe is threatened, they default to joining with it.

The Jewish tribe has been extraordinary in its ability, despite incredible pogroms, to survive and continue to influence well beyond its numbers. The Jewish scriptures strengthen group cohesion when the tribe is threatened to be fragmented from within or without, and the Ten Commandments are the linchpin to tribal cohesion. Judaism holds Jews together as a tribe, whether they practice their religion or not. It keeps fresh their history and tradition. Unfortunately, an observant member who leaves Orthodox Judaism is not simply shunned, but considered dead.

It is extremely difficult to leave any tribe. Restrictions are both internal and external. Historically, people were firmly fixed by their geography. But in modern times, people are often freed of geography and able to migrate beyond, leaving their tribe behind. In open, democratic, pluralistic societies, people are exposed to a variety of human experiences, allowing for the possibility of assimilation into a new tribe.

Jesus deviated from tribal loyalty without leaving his geographical location. His acceptance of Samaritans, the heretical offshoots of Judaism, did not win him points with his fellow tribal members. He was risky. To use the "Good Samaritan" as a model for his contemporaries was extremely provocative toward his fellow Jews. Palestine in his time was under the heel of Rome. Rebel movements were advocating violence to overthrow the Romans. If anything, Jesus warned his followers not to join rebel movements.

If Jesus were a "revolutionary," it was not due to violent confrontation with the dominant powers. Revolutionary change comes without resorting to violence, as seen today in South Africa, Eastern Europe, India, and recently parts of the Middle East. To identify Jesus as a revolutionary does not mean he approved of violence. Yet in some minds, like Benedict's, *violence* and *revolution* are synonymous.

Nonetheless, the Jesus movement *was* "subversive." He employed parables to encourage the masses to question the status quo and its commonly held beliefs, such as sickness being a personal failure, or wealth being God's special blessing. Jesus' inclusion of women and foreigners did not sit well with the patriarchal tribal hierarchy. If he were a loyal tribal member, he would not have encouraged open inclusion, but enforced group cohesion. Inclusion is new wine, stretching boundaries beyond tribal limits. He doesn't restrict loyalty to one tribe only, but extends his attention and care to all beyond. New Zealand poet Eileen Duggan in her poem *Nationality* describes how Jewish Jesus was, and how he expanded beyond this identity, ending with, "O ye, with frontiered hearts, consider, if you can, it was not only life he gave up but country for man!"

The ultimate showdown between Jewish and non-Jewish followers of Jesus is described in Galatians. Did they have to be circumcised first before being allowed as members? Peter wasn't able to make an infallible pronouncement on the controversial issue. A majority led by Paul overruled him. This new religious tribe of "The Way" was not based on blood relations but on free and voluntary relationships. Its members expanded beyond Palestine into the entire world to preach the Good News. Those who heard them were invited to drink this new wine freely, not by force.

This was a radical break from tribalism. The Kingdom teaching on the equality of the person was proclaimed as Good News to the world by disciples no longer constrained by tribal limitations. Membership was a free and voluntary act. The poisoned old wine of history was forced, but that didn't stop the RCC from serving it. Christians, like Muslims, traveled the world making disciples— unfortunately often by force. Priests accompanied Conquistadors to the New World and "converted" hapless natives—usually with the sword.

In *The Nicene Creed*, it is proclaimed, "And I believe in one holy catholic and apostolic church." There is no reference to anything *Roman*. But it is the *Roman* Church that reasserted religious tribalism, attempting to subject all to its interpretation of the Jesus story. It historically squashed cultural expressions of neighboring communities. The Roman model was to be stamped on every new community that would emerge beyond the pale of Rome.

In the sixteenth century, creative Jesuits brought to the court of the Chinese Emperor the "Good News," the message of the Kingdom, hoping to translate it into the Chinese culture, adapting what was compatible with the Kingdom message. But eventually Rome totally suppressed the so-called "Chinese Rites." The institution in China had to look exactly like the institution in Rome. Rome was imposing an absolute structure; these Jesuits were introducing the Kingdom message.

Within the RCC, a branch identified as "Eastern Catholics" trace their history and tradition back to apostolic times. While many are aligned with the RCC, they are treated as second-class members. If the Roman Church joined with the Orthodox Church, it would have to be humbled as merely "one among equals."

Many Roman Catholics are unaware of these sister churches and may be surprised at some Eastern practices that Rome hasn't been able to suppress (particularly their unbroken history of a married clergy). Though this topic is a non-issue for Eastern Catholics, it is debated *ad nauseam* among Romans. In the 1920s the Roman hierarchy in the USA, dominated by Irish bishops, requested that the pope *not* allow married Eastern Catholic clergy here. They would only confuse members and act as visible witnesses to what Roman priests were denied.

John Paul II and Benedict XVI made a concerted effort to end ecumenism embraced by the Vatican Council. In 2000, they issued the encyclical *"Dominus Jesus."* It politely dismisses (instead of hurling the *"anathema sit"*) other Christian sects and other world religions, while identifying itself alone as offering Jesus as the way to salvation, to God.

These hierarchs are afraid that the RCC would be seen as *just one* among all Christian denominations, and *just one* religion among all religions. The idea of "one among equals" is abhorrent to the RCC. Theologians who dared to be inclusive and ecumenical were hauled in by the Grand Inquisitor himself, Ratzinger, to recant or be rubbed out of the membership.

Religious tribalism is no less problematic than tribalism itself. It encourages competition rather than cooperation with other religious tribes, group solidarity rather than human solidarity. Currently, Christianity and Islam are aggressively competing to become the biggest religious tribe. Historically, they have been violently antagonistic. Should we not expect more violence as the two continue to compete?

In an interview, literary scholar Regina Schwartz observes that "the Bible is full of violence against peoples, and as the most influential book in the West, it ... has left us a legacy of intolerant thinking about other peoples, and it has authorized such intolerance as the will of God," which now affects religious, racial, and ethnic conflicts around the world. When asked why she feels violence is a legacy of monotheism, she replies, "Monotheism is a rich, complex concept with a multifaceted history. But one aspect of monotheism has been complicit with violence: the demand of allegiance to one principle, or one god, is aggression to those who have other allegiances. Unfortunately, the injunction 'Thou shall have no other gods before me' turns into intolerance for other people who may have other gods, or principles, or beliefs. It says in Exodus, 'Whoever is for the Lord come to me ... Gird on your sword, every man of you, and quarter the camp from gate to gate killing one his brother, another his friend, and another his neighbor.' While organizing a people under one principle seems like an effective way to create a positive identity, it can also create destructiveness and division, insiders and outsiders." [191]

In today's global village, the "exceptionalism" of the RCC allows it to rigidly view itself as distinctive, unique, and superior to the rest of humankind. In doing so, it rejects "human solidarity" as a witness to the Kingdom.

No doubt about it, the Vatican has clout.

At the 1994 UN International Conference on Population and Development, the Vatican attempted to prevent an overwhelming majority vote supporting women's empowerment, particularly involving access to contraceptive methods and reproductive health information. The Holy See has had "Permanent Observer Status" at such UN gatherings since 1964 (recently upgraded to "Enhanced Observer Status"). It speaks at General Assembly meetings, *unlike all other world religions and NGOs* (which have only Consultative Status).

It digs in its heels and maintains an absolute position that resists dialogue. And it relentlessly demands that its absolute position be accepted and implemented. Amen.

If all world religions were allowed such a platform, a new Tower of Babel would be built, because many (not all) would extend their interpretations of morality to the others—by imposition, not invitation.

The Samaritan woman's encounter with Jesus at high noon eventually led her to raise concerns about true worship. Her renegade Jewish tribe clung to Mount Gerizim, not Jerusalem, as the place of true worship. Jesus responded it was neither, stressing that a day would come when believers would worship not in a place, not within a specific religion, and not in an external way, but internally in spirit and truth. This new wine has yet to be imbibed with gusto by many who cling to their place of worship and prefer the taste of the familiar.

The larger form of tribalism today is "nationalism," in which a person's country has top priority. Particularly in the USA, not to put country first is to be labeled unpatriotic. To espouse human solidarity is asking for trouble. This revolutionary teaching of Jesus will continue to bring conflict into households and communities. When he instructed followers to bring a sword, it was a metaphor for being ready to divide relationships. If one rejects the racism of tribal members, it causes division. How many are willing to risk creating conflict? When tribal members demand America first, before any sense of human solidarity, how many are willing to openly dissent?

The Kingdom revisits family loyalty. Before loyalty to tribe or nation, loyalty to family historically had the strongest hold, and still does in many places. In some aspects of Arabic culture (among others), disgrace to a family must be avenged. If a woman should marry or have sex with someone not of the family's choosing, she brings dishonor to the family, and death may be her punishment. It's not unlike the family conflict in *Romeo and Juliet*.

Family, like everything in life, is a double-edged sword. We can't choose family members like we choose friends. While some families have incredible harmony and cohesion, more suffer from dysfunction and alienation. We've been taught that we *must* have positive feelings about family even when they don't exist. Blood is thicker than water—but blood clots! Sometimes the greatest act of charity toward family members is polite distance.

Most people, nonetheless, cling to a mythical sense of family strength. A Keene, NH man who was battling child custody issues for ten years doused himself with gasoline and set himself ablaze, creating a deadly political protest. In his lengthy last testament, sent to the local newspaper, he pleaded with his children to always remain tight: "You are to stick together no matter how old you get or how far apart you live. Because it is like Grandma always said. The

262

only thing you really have in this world is your family." In his despair, he felt he lost the only family he could ever have. Had he realized there was more to life than blood relationships, he might not have left his children a nightmare legacy. [192]

Blood can become sacred, an end to itself rather than a means. But family is just a starter-kit. If people can bond beyond simple blood relationships to find kinship of spirit, it is to be celebrated. Relations that are chosen rather than inherited are less likely to carry the negative baggage of unfulfilled expectations, and more likely to nurture growth in the participants.

In Kingdom teaching, *family* means a new kinship of spirit. It allows us to get past the idea of "absolute" ethnic or religious tribal membership. Human solidarity with all people enables us to transcend the limitations of our blood, nation, and religion.

The instruction to leave father, mother, brother, and sister for the gospels' sake has been misrepresented by many. Modern cults often intimidate new members to brutally break ties with families. (That alone should sound an alarm to back out of such organizations.) The RCC throughout history advised those with vocations not to look back once they entered religious life. Initiation ceremonies entailed lying prostrate and shrouded in black, symbolizing death to family and to the world. Many who entered religious communities never saw their families again, or only rarely. My father was dying when I was in the seminary, but my superior denied my request to visit him. It was inhumane, but I was so indoctrinated into obedience I never considered defying him.

The Kingdom is not about alienating others, or severing ties, or burning bridges, but choosing personal values, savoring relationships. It is not about isolating or separating ourselves from one another, but deepening our sense of community.

As noted, when Jesus was in someone's house and was told his mother and brothers were outside wishing to see him, he looked at the people in the circle and announced that those who hear the word of God and do it are mother, brother, sister. (Lk 8:21) It was not a *rejection* of his blood relations but an *extension* of them.

SERVICE AS AN ANTIDOTE TO POWER
"Service to others is the rent you pay for your room
here on earth." – Muhammad Ali

"Power tends to corrupt, and absolute power corrupts absolutely." Lord Acton's famous dictum was occasioned on his return from Rome, where the reigning pontiff, Pius IX, had forced through the I Vatican Council (1870) the concept of "papal infallibility" in faith and morals. Acton, not impressed with the papacy, was moved to comment on the corruption inherent in power—no less in the RCC, and perhaps more so!

Pius IX is to have uttered, "I *am* the Church!" making himself absolute. Jesus' call to service evidently eluded him.

Admittedly, the idea of performing service—especially for men—was new. "You know that the rulers of the Gentiles lord it over them, and their great ones exercise authority over them. It is not to be this way among you, but whoever wishes to become great among you shall be your servant, and whoever wishes to be first among you shall be your slave; just as the Son of Man did not come to be served, but to serve, and to give his life a ransom for many." (Mt 20:25) Jesus addresses this to males, who alone had power; females were merely service providers.

The RCC claims he ordained "priests" at the Last Supper, but he actually confirmed male "disciples" to embrace service as the antidote to the corruption of power, which was (and still is) largely a male prerogative.

The subsequent lust for power by clerics, beginning with Constantine, would peak with the phenomenon of "prince-bishop"— a position combining both secular and religious authority. Priests were vassals to bishops, who were vassals to the pope, maintaining a medieval power structure. Until modern times, the clergy were power figures in the community. The French Revolution would topple the favored position of clergy as part of the privileged First Estate, outranking even the nobility of the Second Estate (and of course the masses, who remained on the lowest rung, the Third Estate). The papacy hated Revolution leaders for usurping its privileged role, but in this instance, those leaders were more reflective of the Kingdom of God.

Despite this dethronement in the French Revolution, the papacy and its clergy made their way back into power-and-privilege positions. Today's bishops and cardinals mimic this court royalty. Fancy titles abound: *My Lord, Your Grace, Your Excellency, Your Eminence.* Some bishops inscribe on their "Episcopal Coat of Arms" (a graphic medieval symbol of courtly power) Jesus' words, "I have come to serve, not to be served." (Mt 20:28) Strange. Their extravagant lifestyles are upheld by a retinue, a court of attendants to grant their every wish. In the age of unprecedented corporate power, they are inaccessible CEOs, hardly shepherds one with the flock.

Constantine—not Jesus, the Christ—had the greatest impact on the imperial RCC: "In the realm of high politics, Constantine was not the pupil of the Roman Church but its instructor." [193] He was a good tutor. Eventually, the Church became exactly what Constantine was.

A *New York Times* article traced the money trail forged centuries ago: "In the Middle Ages, all authority was male and monarchical, so the pope became a king. His multiple realms had all the appurtenances of a medieval monarch—armies, prisons, spies, torturers, legal courts in papal service. The money flowed in from many sources—as conquest, as tribute from subordinate princes (secular and religious) or from the crops on farm lands held by the pope, who was not accountable to anyone for use of these funds. When normal sources did not satisfy papal ambition, clerical underlings invented new kinds of revenue—like the granting of time off in Purgatory for cash contributions during life ('indulgences' for sale)." [194]

In the eighth century, the papacy acquired the Papal States in central Italy. It claimed title from the so-called Decretals of Isidore and the Donation of Constantine, both spurious documents. These forgeries were not debunked until 1440, and the Papal States were not dissolved until 1929, when the RCC got an even better deal. Italian dictator Benito Mussolini signed the Lateran Treaty with the Church, granting it parcels of land, but more importantly, creating "the State of Vatican City."

In one sense, the RCC is more politically powerful than ever. The papal Diplomatic Corps, unknown to most Catholics, is its political muscle. Since it is a purely political entity, *any* Catholic—male or female—technically qualifies. But it remains a privileged caste, composed entirely of ordained male clerics. Despite a desperate shortage of priests around the world, the Vatican has no qualms about using them as international ambassadors. And perhaps the priests themselves prefer the glamour of political life to the tedious role of parish priest. The Diplomatic Corps allows a select cadre of clerics to escape a parochial life of confecting sacraments. It is definitely an upward career move within the hierarchy.

Diplomacy has been an unsavory element of Catholicism. Cardinal Eugenio Pacelli (subsequently Pope Pius XII) was the diplomatic envoy representing the papacy, the Vatican's Secretary of State, who signed the Concordat with Hitler's Third Reich. A career diplomat, he was more concerned with moving up the ranks to secure his future than taking up the cross to prophetically challenge power.

A diplomatic chapter yet to be revisited is the role of the Vatican's mission in Rwanda, Africa's most Catholic country. Rwandan bishops publicly decried the use of condoms, but not tribal warfare. The Vatican was well aware of the antagonistic build-up to the massive genocide of 1994, but it failed to alert the world. What, then, is the point of papal diplomacy?

The Diplomatic Corps ultimately spreads the theology of fear worldwide—overseeing clergy, enforcing compliance to papal pronouncements, expecting strict adherence to its interpretation of dogma and morality. In particular, the Corps monitors bishops with an unwritten mandate to diligently enforce the Vatican's version of sexual morality. Even though technically they are there as a political liaison, they provide dual roles for the Vatican.

The pope wears two hats—spiritual and political—when he visits another country. The spiritual hat is well-known, often put forth as the only reason for the pope's visit. The political hat allows for immunity otherwise denied someone with a purely religious role. Catholicism is the *only religion in the world* that is both a political state and a spiritual entity.

The papacy claims it needs special status as a state to protect itself from the changing political tides of Italy. Yet the headquarters of the Orthodox Church remains in Istanbul (since the fall of Constantinople in 1453), a tiny Orthodox minority among an overwhelming Muslim majority. It speaks well for both that despite periodic conflicts, they coexist.

If all world religions had political states whereby they could exchange diplomats with all sovereign nations on earth, it would mean the demise of any authentically independent spiritual movement (but at least it would level the playing field). And as long as the RCC persists in claiming both political and spiritual entities, it cannot authentically fulfill either role. In attempting to be a political *and* a moral authority, it is neither.

LIBERATION FROM FEAR THROUGH CRITICAL THINKING
"There's less critical thinking going on in this country on a Main Street level—forget about the media—than ever before. We've never needed people to think more critically than now, and they've taken a big nap." – Alec Baldwin

At the beginning of Jesus' public ministry, Luke has him borrow Isaiah's words as his mission statement: "The spirit of the Lord is upon me, because he anointed me to preach the Good News to the poor. He has sent me to proclaim release to the captives, and recovery of sight to the blind, to set free those who are oppressed." (Lk 4:18) Jesus is depicted as coming with Good News of liberation for the oppressed. But rather than spreading the liberating spirit, the RCC oppressed its members with the theology of fear.

Roman theology historically has been in the hands of an elite group of academicians and professionals, and members were expected to swallow whole what was handed them, without their participation, once filtered by the hierarchy. Traditionally, priests preached resignation to "God's will," reinforcing the belief that the world's unequal distribution of wealth and power comes from heaven. Peasant societies indoctrinated this way tended to internalize a fixed and fatalistic view of the universe with symbols and rationalizations. But Jesus challenged people to rely on faith (imagination) rather than fatalism (resignation).

Liberation Theology emerged with Vatican II. It is not just another dictation from the top down, but a grassroots effort from the ground up. It mirrors more directly the revolutionary mission of the Jesus story. It engages ordinary members in reflection and application. The teacher is the pupil, and the pupil is the teacher.

Jesus, as a Jewish layman, criticized interpreters of the Torah Law for their harmful influence on the masses. Liberation theology criticizes both society and religion for their unjust structures. Unlike academic theology, it focuses on solidarity with people, especially "the least ones," in its insistence on a "preferential option for the poor." It brings the Kingdom into the reality that is here on earth—creating a stark contrast to the otherworldly Roman theology that orients people to an afterlife. And it threatens those who think they are in control.

It wasn't long before John Paul II and Cardinal Ratzinger forcefully acted to dismantle and diminish its growing influence, particularly in the Southern Hemisphere. They attacked it under the guise of its use of Marxian principles to explain the plight of the poor. But Liberation leaders were not shy about opposing the complicity of the RCC, reflecting the spirit of Jesus with his compassion for the masses, victims of the Jewish hierarchy's abuse of power.

Archbishop Dom Helder Camara of Recife, Brazil provided a simple but brilliant summary of Liberation Theology and its precarious political position in his famous statement: "When I feed the poor, they call me a saint. When I ask why are they poor, they call me a Communist."

In its essence, Liberation Theology has three major aspects: "an interpretation of Christian faith out of the suffering, struggle, and hope of the poor; a critique of society and the ideologies sustaining it; and a critique of the activity of the Church and of Christians from the angle of the poor." [195] It is built on real-life practice rather than dogmatic purity. The "powers that be" are threatened by such radical reflection, when it organizes people into small groups, treats them like adults, and encourages critical thinking. This the RCC assiduously avoids, preferring the spoon-fed education for children and the issuance of sanctioned interpretation for adults. As an institution, it provides no leadership to develop critical thinking among its members. If anything, it blocks or suppresses any such attempts through its ongoing censorship.

Someone coined the phrase *pew potatoes* to describe passive postures that don't demand engagement. In the liturgy people are subjected to a monologue, usually "official" teaching. Thinking is like exercise; it takes effort. As Henry Ford remarked, "Thinking is the hardest work there is, which is probably the reason why so few engage in it." Effectively, Roman hierarchs admonish members to "leave the thinking to us."

In 1983 at Port-au-Prince, Haiti, John Paul II began promoting "The New Evangelization," but this remained a vague slogan. He asserted it wasn't a new message, when a new message was *exactly* what was needed! That message should have publicly repudiated the theology of fear and salvaged a spirituality based on rediscovering the values of the Kingdom.

John Paul II highlighted the need for lay members to be in the vanguard—but how? All power in the RCC remains in the hands of clerics, and clerics are disinclined to follow lay persons unless they have real authority, and there isn't one lay person with any authority over a cleric!

A Vatican meeting in June 2011 addressed "the distinction between religious life and the lay state, including insistence that laity who are in charge of a movement or association may not exercise formal ecclesiastical jurisdiction over priests and religious." This was meant to rein in and reorient clerical dominance. [196] But clergymen aren't going to be enablers of new movements. They're relegated to acting as sacrament dispensers, save for a few maverick priests. Clergymen generally aren't creative or innovative. It's really not their fault. Seminary indoctrination effectively stymied all that long ago. Obedience was paramount, and weeding out those questioning authority was the reason for the long preparation.

A 2011 *Rolling Stone* investigation of the sexual-abuse scandal revealed a trove of hidden documents indicating the hierarchy's tolerance of pedophile priests and conspiracy to cover up their crimes. The article reports that William Lynn, a high-ranking monsignor who kept the secret files, reportedly acted as the Philadelphia Archdiocese's "sex-abuse fixer, the man who covered up for its priests," and would become "the first Catholic official ever criminally charged for the cover-up." (Lynn was found guilty of felony child endangerment in June 2012 and faces up to seven years in prison at his July sentencing.) He was no lone wolf. He reported directly to the cardinal (Cardinal Anthony Bevilacqua, mentioned earlier, who died in January 2012), was "simply a company man, a faithful bureaucrat who did his job exceedingly well." He was encouraged by his superiors, who received orders from *their* superiors, "an unbroken chain of command stretching all the way to Rome." Such loyalty is fostered in the seminary, "a form of military-style indoctrination, molding men to think institutionally, not individually. 'It's like a brainwashing, almost,' says Michael Lynch, who attended St. Charles for nine years but was rejected for priesthood after repeatedly butting heads with his superiors. Lynch recalls a priest barking at his class, 'We own you! We own your body, we own your soul!'" [197] Spiritual slavery, perhaps?

This "brainwashing" molds men for a lifetime of submission to the hierarchy. At ordination, priests must take an oath of obedience to the bishop and his successors—essentially blind obedience. One's superior is the "*vox Dei*," the voice of God. To disobey him is to disobey God.

The RCC is still big on oath taking, promises, and vows. In Matthew 5:34, Jesus counsels not to swear any oath. Rather, one's *yes* should be *yes*, and one's *no, no*.

The Kingdom emphasizes personal integrity rather than oaths, promises, or vows of loyalty to another. Fear sends us into hiding, protective of our life and any perceived threat to it. But it means living the life of a prisoner.

Critical thinking won't allow us to hide. It forces us to stand on our own two feet. It demands courage, taking the consequences when we let our *yes* be *yes*, and our *no* be *no*. It means being vulnerable, allowing truth to be ultimately liberating.

If there is to be a "New Evangelization," priests must be free to question, analyze, even doubt. This is precisely what the Vatican resists, not unlike Duvalier of Haiti. Priests are ill-equipped to lead others in critical thinking, stuck in their own deep-seated indoctrination and lacking the energy or willpower to overcome the past and look to a new future. It is easier to preside over others with prescribed rituals.

Following Vatican II was a refreshing springtime of hope that members would share in a conciliar model of community. It was short-lived. Practically the moment he became pope, John Paul II began to restore structures prior to Vatican II, those now abetted by Benedict XVI with his personal "reform of the reform."

So, nothing changes. The RCC lives on as a clerically run institution, though more culturally bourgeois. It caters to the middle and upper classes, which rely on its sacraments as comfortable rites of passage and public displays of faith, as pleasant and peripheral functions, not true priorities in their lives. In return these members silently agree not to rock the boat, not to think about structures that keep the powerful powerful and the poor poor.

Ah, how the Roman Church resists the liberation of the Kingdom.

THE PRAXIS OF LOVE
"There is only one terminal dignity—love." – Helen Hayes

What else is new, unique, in the proclamation of the Kingdom of God? It is the praxis of love, the practice of inclusive love of friend and enemy, neighbor and stranger. Who would advocate something so irreconcilable, so at odds with human instinct? Who would dare to embrace this seemingly inconceivable proposition? More often, lowly members rather than powerful elites.

The "practice" of love might lead to "perfect" love. We become better with practice, ending up in a different place from where we started. This challenge to love beyond self-interest is not easily achieved. Self-love is the starting—and ending—point for most of us. An inclusive love seems like an impossible dream, the domain of a few.

First, growing into perfect love has to be a personal goal. Sadly, the Roman catechesis did not define life's primary motivator as the pursuit of love, but the avoidance of hell. Overcoming the theology of fear and responding to the challenge of perfect love requires a quantum leap. Consider Augustine's famous ode to God, "Late have I loved you, O Beauty ever ancient, ever new, late have I loved you!" Coming out of the tunnel of fear to see the light of perfect love may not happen overnight, possibly only after a long journey.

To paraphrase Augustine, *Late have I loved love!* To arrive at perfect love is the journey's end, the Kingdom fully revealed and experienced. But the journey can only begin when one rejects fear as life's primary motivator.

Witnesses of perfect love are often not so-called "spiritual leaders," but "simple practitioners." A striking example comes from an unassuming black woman in South Africa. After apartheid, during which the majority blacks were politically, educationally, and economically dominated by the minority whites, a Truth and Reconciliation Commission convened to ensure justice and allow both sides to be heard. Author Andrew Harvey documents this story: "The Commission brought an elderly black woman face to face with the white man, Mr. Van de Broek, who had confessed to the savage torture and murder of her son and husband a few years earlier. The old woman had been made to witness her husband's death. The last words her husband spoke were 'Father, forgive them.' One of the members of the Commission turned to her and asked, 'How do you believe justice should be done to this man who has inflicted such suffering on you and so brutally destroyed your family?' The old woman replied, 'I want three things. I want first to be taken to the place where my husband's body was burned so that I can gather up the dust and give his remains a decent burial.' She stopped, collected herself, and then went on. 'My husband and son were my only family. I want, secondly, therefore, for Mr. Van de Broek to become my son. I would like for him to come twice a month to the ghetto and spend a day with me so that I can pour out to him whatever love I have still remaining with me. And finally, I want a third thing. I would like Mr. Van de Broek to know that I offer him my forgiveness, because Jesus Christ died to forgive. This was also the wish of my husband. And so, I would kindly ask someone to come to my side and lead me across the courtroom so that I can take Mr. Van de Broek in my arms, embrace him, and let him know that he is truly forgiven.' The assistants came to help the old black woman across the room. Mr. Van de Broek, overwhelmed by what he had just heard, fainted. And as he did, those in the courtroom—friends, family, neighbors, all victims of decades of oppression and injustice—began to sing 'Amazing Grace.'" [198]

Remarkable in her witness to perfect love, thankfully she is not "our tainted nature's solitary boast."

In October 2006, at a one-room schoolhouse of an Amish community in Lancaster, PA, a lone gunman took children hostage, ultimately shooting ten girls and killing five, before he shot himself. The immediate response of the Amish community stunned the world. According to Wikipedia, "A grandfather of one of the murdered Amish girls was heard warning some young relatives not to hate the killer, saying, 'We must not think evil of this man'... A Roberts family (the murderer's family) spokesman said an Amish neighbor comforted the Roberts family hours after the shooting and extended forgiveness to them. Amish community members visited and comforted Robert's widow, parents, and parents-in-law. One Amish man held Roberts' sobbing father in his arms, reportedly for as long as an hour, to comfort him. The Amish have also set up a charitable fund for the family of the shooter. About 30 members of the Amish community attended Roberts' funeral, and Marie Roberts, the widow of the killer, was one of the few outsiders invited to the funeral of one of the victims. Marie Roberts wrote an open letter to her Amish neighbors thanking them for their forgiveness, grace, and mercy. She wrote, 'Your love for our family has helped to provide the healing we so desperately need ... Gifts you've given have touched our hearts in a way no words can describe. Your compassion has reached beyond our family, beyond our community, and is changing our world, and for this we sincerely thank you.'" (Wikipedia)

How many Roman Catholic parishioners would show such incredible, spontaneous forgiveness as this Amish community did? Understandably, its members reacted so because the Amish make the Sermon on the Mount central to their communal reflection. In them, the seed found rich soil and produced abundant fruit. And how many

Roman Catholic victims would show spontaneous love as this South African woman did? The author notes that what struck him most was the murderer fainting, "the sacred power ... fell on him like invisible lightening from a dimension of pure love he might never have begun to suspect existed." [199] Perfect love?

These are not medieval tales or ancient parables, but contemporary incidents, evidence that modern individuals and communities can extend perfect love. An Internet search of people who have forgiven murderers will reveal news stories of inspiring individuals who love perfectly. The Kingdom is rising leaven in our midst. Google it!

Jesus' tribal members did love, but only their own. His new wine offered a different flavor. "But I say to you, love your enemies, do good to those who hate, bless those who curse you, pray for those who mistreat you. Whoever hits you on the cheek, offer him the other also; and whoever takes away your coat, do not withhold your shirt from him either. Give to everyone who asks of you, and whoever takes away what is yours, do not demand it back. Treat others the same way you want them to treat you. If you love those who love you, what credit is that to you? For, even sinners love those who love them." (Lk 6:27)

To love your enemies is to be defenseless, vulnerable. When the RCC yoked itself to Constantine, it sold its birthright to the Kingdom of God and reinvented itself as a Kingdom of Power. Well, it got what it wanted. It is widely viewed today as one of the world's most powerful institutions. This brings up the ultimate question: What is the essence of the Kingdom teaching, and how can it be distilled?

There is a classic tale of a gentile who approached a rabbi and said he would convert to Judaism if the rabbi would teach him the whole Torah while he stood on one foot. The rabbi waved him away with his cane. He then went to the famous rabbi Hillel with the same request. Hillel replied, "That which is despicable to you, do not do to your fellow. This is the whole Torah, and the rest is commentary. Go and learn it."

Can the complexity of human morality be reduced to a positive slant, a "Do unto others" response? God is not even mentioned here, only self and others. The Letter of John states if one says he loves God but hates his brother, he is a liar. If one can't love the known, how can one love the unknown, the unseen? As we all know, many supposedly religious persons loudly and publicly proclaim their love for God, all the while distaining others. "I thank You that I am not like other people: swindlers, unjust, adulterers, or even like this tax collector." (Lk 18:10) Conversely, others make no public pronouncements about their feelings for an unseen God, yet embrace even their enemies. They act in spirit, veritably true worshipers.

A lawyer tested Jesus with a pop quiz. "What is the greatest commandment in the Law?" Jesus replied, "You shall love the Lord your God with all your heart, and with your entire mind. This is the great and foremost commandment. The second is like it. You shall love your neighbor as yourself." (Mt 22:34) Joining love of God, neighbor, and self into one triangle of love is significant. It's easy to say you love God; loving another person is the rub. The cartoon strip "The Wizard of Id" depicts the court preacher in the pulpit proclaiming love: Love one another, love your enemies, love is the answer, blah, blah, blah. As the people leave the royal chapel, he greets them with a Cheshire cat grin, saying to himself, "This is the part I hate!"

If one were to ask a member of the RCC how Jesus' teaching could be distilled while standing on one foot, love would hardly be the spontaneous answer, as the theology of fear dominates the heart and mind. But any Christian community's "reason for being" should unequivocally be the primacy of love. Fear inhibits most members, so they would hardly speak spontaneously of love. More likely they'd respond, "I'll have to think about that." When instead it is the primacy of fear, one wonders whether that community is under the control of sinister powers. Bring in the exorcists?

Clemens Forell was a captured World War II German soldier sentenced by the Soviets to a Siberian labor camp. He and his fellows lived and worked in a mine. Prisoners talked of escape but the obstacles seemed insurmountable—the likelihood of being shot, the distance to Germany (5,000 miles), the hostile terrain full of wild animals, the need for navigational aids, the lack of food and water. Fear paralyzed them—except for Forell. Motivated by love for his family, he took the risk and endured incredible hardships in his solo odyssey, finally reaching home. "Love conquers all!" His story was the subject of a German film, *As Far as My Feet Will Carry Me*. None of his fellow prisoners returned, apparently dying in the desolate mine, victims. Forell could also have died at any time during his awesome journey, but it would have been as an agent, not a victim. His risk for the sake of love freed him from the fear of death.

"No one takes my life from me. I lay it down of my own accord." (Jo 10:18) When we rise to the challenge to experience perfect love, we unleash an unknown potential within. But first we must exorcise the theology of fear, which blocks love's possibilities. To love inclusively, even the enemy, will cause a firestorm. Many Christians prefer Moses' moral proportionality, an eye for an eye, rather than the Kingdom's challenge to walk the extra mile. To love is to be vulnerable. Empires are about strength, supremacy, domination— not vulnerability.

So who will direct this much-needed conversion? Again, Bishop Robinson: "It is surely simple fact that the People of God as a whole would never have got us into the mess we are in ... the pope and the bishops have lost credibility, and it is only the People of God who can restore it to them." [200]

Teilhard de Chardin, who experienced the wrath of the RCC, nonetheless was able to envision a glorious future. "Someday, after mastering the winds, the waves, the tides, and gravity," he said, "we shall harness for God the energies of love, and then, for a second time in the history of the world, man will have discovered fire." [201]

"I have come to cast fire upon the earth; and how I wish it were already kindled!" (Lk 12:49) Perfect love is the Kingdom realized.

The Kingdom reveals good news. All are capable of perfect love.

CHAPTER TEN

SPIRITUAL BEINGS:
AWAKENING TO WORDS MADE FLESH

"We are not human beings having a spiritual experience.
We are spiritual beings having a human experience."
– Teilhard de Chardin

What compels us to live beyond automatic responses to our instincts? What causes us to pause, reflect, and consider something more than satisfying material needs? Certainly, the material world has an enormous impact—it's the engine that drives us to pursue our daily bread and cake.

But after we've satisfied our appetite, why are we hungry still, for something more?

THE INSATIABLE HUMAN SPIRIT
"The fact that logic cannot satisfy us awakens an almost insatiable hunger for the irrational." – A.N. Wilson

After a prolonged period of fasting during his desert experience, Jesus was hungry, naturally. Then he was improbably tempted to turn stones into bread. But, we are told, he realized that one does not live by bread alone. (Mt 4:4) Rare is the person who denies that.

The food pyramid created by the federal government is dwarfed by the human needs pyramid created by psychologist Abraham Maslow.

277

Of the five levels in his hierarchy, bread is the minimal and most basic need, on the bottom of the pyramid. The other levels represent largely non-material desires and possibilities. We stretch and aspire for something that transcends our grasp. We reach relentlessly.

As Robert Browning poetically put it, "Ah, but a man's reach should exceed his grasp. Or what's a heaven for?"

Yet humans have needs that the material world alone cannot fully satisfy. The creative instinct transcends apparent limitations in the pursuit of something greater, better, fuller. The unquenchable human spirit, driven toward the unrealized, the unknown, is never satiated.

"The spirit blows where it will."

From antiquity, this spiritual quest for "something more" expressed itself in religious traditions that attempted to make sense of existence and quell the deepest hunger within. These traditions inspired creativity, tapped the imagination, looked to the future. But the dark side of religious traditions surfaced in time, working against their better angels, becoming tribal, insulating and compelling followers to think and act within limited confines, bridling the human spirit.

For Jesus, *faith* was about imagination, seeing beyond the limitations and fears of the present. The Kingdom of God proclamation was about imagining the impossible here, on earth. Fear would be the obstacle to overcome.

For Catholicism, *faith* became a set of doctrines and dogmas that effectively limited human reach in the hope of aspiring to something more. They put the brakes on individual creativity for the sake of tribal conformity.

Jesus evidently aspired beyond the limitations of his religious tribe; otherwise, why did he continually question its traditions and practices?

The reach of his Kingdom proclamation stretches the imagination to conceive of a different life here.

FORMAL RELIGIONS AND THE "NONES"
"I do benefits for all religions—I'd hate to blow the hereafter on a technicality." – Bob Hope

Historically, formal religions evolved slowly to deal with the non-bread issues. Hinduism was first to organize around a set of principles or beliefs, without a single person to identify as its founder. It is difficult to pinpoint its origins. Estimates vary from 5,000 to 2,000 years before Jesus would appear.

Unlike the RCC and its obsession with order and control, Hinduism seems chaotic. Yet it remains remarkably free of any inquisition, censorship, or centrality of power. Its beliefs and traditions vibrantly nourish about 900 million today. Practically leaderless, it thrives as the third-largest religion in the world, without evangelizing efforts or military backup for its maintenance and expansion. While the powerhouse RCC and Islam are very aggressive, laid-back Hinduism employs little coercion.

The RCC is insistent in enforcing its tradition, removing any person or idea (even violently) deemed less than purely orthodox, however narrowly defined. As discussed earlier, the latest Vatican pronouncement, in April 2012, targeted American religious women, judging them as deviating from the *Magisterium* and giving them a five-year ultimatum to get in line. There was no parallel pronouncement judging the practice of American bishops, on whose watch countless children were raped or molested. Pure doctrine trumps pure practice, once again.

The RCC fears its belief system and tradition will be diluted and lost without firm and unquestioned adherence to its *Magisterium*. While it preaches that unity is the work of the Spirit and not human effort, it acts contrary to its own pronouncement—imposing human intervention to force *conformity*, then calling it *unity*. Does the RCC have the humility to learn from Hinduism?

With a world population expected to approach 10 billion by 2020, the majority of people still identify with some formal religion, though this trend is waning.

The newest, most explosive category is "No Religious Denomination" or "Nones" (secular / nonreligious / agnostic / atheist).

The "Nones" classification is the most rapidly growing in the USA, ranking third behind Catholics and Baptists, with continued expansion worldwide. This is historically incredible. Never have so many people freely identified with this group.

A 2007 report on the largest religious groups said Christianity claims 2.1 billion followers, Islam 1.5 billion, "Nones" 1.1 billion, Hinduism 900 million, Chinese traditionalism 394 billion, and Buddhism 376 million. (Judaism is down the list at 14 million.) [202]

Those less constrained by tribal religious beliefs are apparently drifting into the Nones, especially in pluralistic and educated societies where they are free to choose without being shunned. Most people maintain connection to a religious tradition because of birth into a religious tribe. Interestingly, the Nones largely see this as an individual decision, and are less likely than others to impose their "belief systems" on offspring.

If atheism is rising, is God dying? Sara Robinson, who has been dubbed "one of the few trained social futurists in North America," analyzed this question and arrived at some provocative findings that give pause. [203] For one, atheism is growing in some locations, while God is winning out in others. Europe, most Christianized in the West, finds declining emphasis on God among its citizens. Canada is a close second. The Southern Hemisphere is God's biggest booster, housing growth not only for the RCC and Christianity, but also Islam. Robinson anticipates the possibility that "conflict and competition between the conversion-oriented faiths could eventually lead to political disruptions and military confrontations." [204] Interestingly, one phenomenon discovered here is that affiliation with a specific religion, particularly in Africa, is more defining than affiliation with a tribe or nation.

Earlier, I questioned Europe's diminishing interest in God and the RCC, and gave a guess. Robinson provides a more educated guess that the history of religious wars exhausted Europeans, who now view religion as too divisive.

MEMBERSHIP AND THE NUMBERS GAME
"Anyone who thinks there's safety in numbers hasn't looked at the stock market pages." – Irene Peters

An indelible mark on a soul at baptism stamps it *Roman Catholic* for all eternity, creating a "permanent record" that will never be destroyed. Someone who leaves the RCC is excommunicated, carrying a "grave sin" which, if not forgiven, means everlasting damnation. [205] This individual is considered "lapsed" but is *still* subject to Church rules and regulations—once a Catholic always a Catholic!—and *still* amasses mortal sins. Though baptism is very rarely a personal decision, one is forever stuck through time and eternity with the RCC membership card and all that it entails—at least according to the issuer of the card.

The census of the 2011 *Annuario Pontificio* (Pontifical Yearbook) says Roman Catholics numbered about 1.181 billion in 2009 (up from 1.166 billion). The RCC arrives at this by including *every person ever baptized*, active or not! What a disingenuous way of playing the numbers game. If the Vatican were forthright, it would acknowledge its active membership is barely a third of the 1.181 billion.

Some European countries tax citizens for their religious denomination. The state essentially collects taxes for churches, mosques, and temples. Individuals can petition to have their names removed from the state roster as Roman Catholic, and the tax will no longer be distributed to the RCC. They would be off the governmental rolls—but still on the baptismal registers.

THE SEARCH FOR AUTHENTIC SPIRITUALITY
"Religion is for people who are scared to go to hell.
Spirituality is for people who have already been there."
– Bonnie Raitt

John XXIII called the II Vatican Council an "*aggiornamento*," an "opening to the world." His first letter was a dramatic departure, addressed to "all people of goodwill" rather than members only. Critics would claim the membership decline is due to John and Vatican II. But the anti-birth control position initiated by his successor, Paul VI, was roundly rejected by more educated, less fearful people who had the guts to follow their conscience. And the Vatican's arrogant mishandling of the ongoing clerical sex-abuse scandal continues to drain membership.

People are looking for a spirituality not found in the legalistic, narrow, moralizing institution that denies their serious input. Without calling for another council, John Paul II and Benedict XVI set a personal agenda to close the window to the world (triple-glazed it) and restore the pre-Vatican II Church. They resisted "the signs of the times."

So, many simply and quietly walk away. (Though the hierarchy contends they're not off the hook.)

Ironically, Benedict XVI doesn't lament the loss. Even before becoming pope, he serenely envisioned a smaller, leaner RCC. The *New York Times* (and many others) referenced a 1997 interview in *Salt of the Earth* (Ignatius Press), when he said, "Maybe we are facing a new and different kind of epoch in the church's history, where Christianity will again be characterized more by the mustard seed, where it will exist in small, seemingly insignificant groups that nonetheless live an intense struggle against evil and bring good into the world—that let God in." Many argue he wants "a more fervent, orthodox, evangelical church—even if it drives people away." As Ratzinger, he predicted that someday "the West will tire of secularism and spiritual loneliness" and will "discover the little community of believers as something quite new," as hope for them, as "the answer they have always been looking for." [206]

Someday the West will tire of secularism and spiritual loneliness? The West has *already* tired of pious hypocrisy and moral corruption. The West is distrustful of an institution that obstinately refuses to face reality and has little to offer those pursuing an authentic spirituality. The West remembers when the Church acted as Caesar more often than Christ in burning heretics, initiating crusades, launching inquisitions. The West has lost its faith in an organization that forgot Christ, that indeed mocked him.

Benedict vaguely refers to little groups struggling against evil, but doesn't define what *evil* is. The RCC's current concept of evil revolves around abortion, contraception, homosexuality, and same-sex marriage. Perhaps some of its members wage "an intense struggle against evil," but its leaders were unable to see unspeakable evil in their own midst—its clergy raping and defiling its own vulnerable children. They closed their eyes to this evil, even conspired to hide it, until exposed by the news media.

Unfortunately, Benedict XVI sees evil as having the wrong thoughts or doctrines, which he has pursued with zeal as the Grand Inquisitor. When did he call before his tribunal those who failed to act compassionately, to act prophetically and justly, in the name of Jesus of Nazareth? He defines evil as the absence of pure doctrine, not pure practice. He operates in a land of his own fanciful imagination, having lived a cocoon existence as an academician and privileged prelate, not incarnated among the people as a simple equal.

Regardless, Benedict is optimistic that obscure little groups fighting evil will suddenly be rediscovered. If this were ever to happen, Zoroastrianism would fit the bill. Older than Christianity, it remains today largely unknown but views itself as a force for good battling evil. Author Mary Boyce claims that "Zoroastrianism is the oldest of the revealed world-religions, and it has probably had more influence on mankind, directly or indirectly, than any other single faith." [207]

Christians often posture self-righteously, insisting that Jesus is the Way, the Truth, and the Life, and that no one can be saved without accepting him as their personal savior. Evangelicals feel obliged to confront others, asking if they're born again or if they've accepted Jesus. In *Time* magazine's coverage of Pastor Rob Bell's book on hell (*Love Wins*), a respondent sounded off: "Hell is easy to define. It would be spending eternity with evangelicals." [208]

No matter what fundamentalists and evangelicals say, the RCC ups the ante. It asserts it *alone* is the direct way to Jesus, it *alone* is the One True Church. (Islam is arguably the strongest contender in the righteousness competition, as most other world religions are less interested in evangelizing.)

Such absolute dogma no longer sways the masses. The Pew Survey provides evidence. In the USA, the RCC "has experienced the greatest net losses as a result of affiliation changes. While nearly one in three Americans (31 percent) were raised in the Catholic faith, today fewer than one in four (24 percent) describe themselves as Catholic." [209] Immigrants, mainly Hispanic, staunch its loss of Caucasians who have veered off the path to Rome.

While many are becoming Nones, this doesn't mean they lack spirituality. Some Christians like to label them as *secularists*, implying they have no values. In doing so, they dismiss the teaching of Jesus to "judge not lest you be judged." (Mt 7:1) Perhaps they find it difficult to believe people can be good without God. Like Augustine, they feel people need divine grace before they can make the moral and honorable choice.

The monk Pelagius and his followers felt otherwise. People can choose good without grace, as creation itself is of God's doing, according to monotheists (the "one God alone" crowd).

Nones may take considerable criticism from believers, but they don't spend much time returning fire. They tend to live and let live, encouraging everyone to follow their conscience. That would be blatant relativism in Benedict XVI's mindset. But John Fuellenbach would maintain that Nones are not necessarily out of sync with Kingdom values because, as he says, "the Kingdom makes itself present outside the church as well." [210]

Jesus anticipated the day when people would worship together in spirit and truth, stressing prostitutes and sinners would enter the Kingdom of God and "you yourselves [religious leaders] shut out." (Mt 21:31)

As Augustine observed, "How many sheep there are without, how many wolves within!" [211]

In the USA, atheists arguably still lag behind blacks, Jews, and homosexuals in being treated as equals. "Rarely denounced by the mainstream, this stunning anti-atheist discrimination is egged on by Christian conservatives who stridently—and uncivilly—declare that the lack of godly faith is detrimental to society, rendering nonbelievers intrinsically suspect and second-class citizens." [212]

Most people look for meaning and value within their short lifespan, before worrying about whether there is or isn't anything or anyone in the Great Beyond. Some are content to live without reflecting at all. As Tennyson wrote, "Ours not to reason why, ours but to do and die." [213] Or, as Frost put it, "Live your damned life as though it matters. And why? Because it *is* a damned life. Because, at core, it *doesn't* matter." [214]

Many *do* make it matter. They have overcome fear of the future and seek a qualitative existence right here. Humans are inherently spiritual. As an anonymous author wrote, "Man transcends his finiteness in the very act of being aware of his finiteness." The relentless hunger for more meaning, more beauty, more discovery is driven by the restless human psyche. And Chardin's empowering words that opened this chapter tell us we are "spiritual beings having a human experience."

People feel less constrained to be committed to a particular religious tribe today as to the spirit within themselves, the truth, wherever they might find it. When released to exist in open, educated, democratic, pluralistic societies that foster exploration—both inner and outer—the human spirit is irrepressible.

Certainly for multitudes of people, the "purpose driven life" is defined by the pursuit of material success, conspicuous consumption, power and status, and the imposition of ego. They experience no transcendence in life, only material reality. They can be found in religious organizations that provide a veneer to hide these base impulses. At the end of his life, Cardinal Wolsey, Henry VIII's chancellor, is said to have uttered, "If I had served my God half so well as I have served my King, He would not have abandoned me now."

Others are bold enough to publicly witness their chosen values, like the disciples of Ayn Rand. Transparency is always more laudable, whatever the source, than the cloak of transcendence.

Still others take a path where acquiring goods is not everything, moving beyond self-centeredness, seeking solidarity with others even if these "others" include all life on earth, and the earth itself.

They embrace the commonwealth, the common good, the common hopes of humanity. Surrounded by the self-inflicted atrocities the world has created, they put the brakes on humankind's darkest impulses. Evidently, the "ten just men" Abraham desperately sought to save Sodom and Gomorrah have been found—and they include women!

Creation and civilization trudge forward even when overwhelmed by the savagery of world war, ethnic cleansing, and genocide. International tribunals for justice spring up as permanent, albeit fragile, shoots on the world's landscape. There is growing awareness that human complicity damages the environment, that capital punishment is anti-life, that sex education and birth control reduce the need for abortion, that war is obsolete, that international economic justice is for everyone—all marks of the Kingdom.

A new spirituality is being forged, a new wine is being produced at the ground level.

"NEW MONKS" AND "THE OTHER"
"We have wasted our spirit in the regions of the abstract and general just as the monks let it wither in the world of prayer and contemplation." – Alexander Herzen

The RCC's tradition forged a different "spirituality," one that encouraged retreating from the world to remote monasteries and convents to contemplate God, essentially rejecting the Incarnation, the marriage of human and divine. The world was evil; run from it to save your soul. Virginity and monasticism became ideals. Religious routines occupied the day—repeating rituals, chanting psalms, meditating silently, reciting prayers, fasting. Somehow through these acts, a union with God would be achieved that mere mortals would never otherwise attain.

This variety of spirituality could be found only in celibate communities. It was an exercise in religious elitism, a rejection of the idea that God saw *all* that he had made and it was *all* good. Spirituality for the masses was reduced to pious practices, pilgrimages, and sacraments (often under penalty of mortal sin).

286

Spirituality was dictated from above; movements from below were suspect. Rather than enabling followers to discern their innate gifts as contributions to the common good, the RCC reinforced their disposition toward evil.

Monasticism—a withdrawal from the world—was promoted. The virginal life of the monk and nun became a higher state than marriage. The solitary life vertically focused on God became an ideal, though antithetical to the concept of the Incarnation.

Wordsworth wrote of the idyllic life of monks:

> *Nuns fret not at their convent's narrow room;*
> *And hermits are contented with their cells.*

Such is a serene and safe lifestyle, lacking the true asceticism of those who leave security for insecurity, for the sake of humanity, for the Kingdom.

The monastic life *can* be very much a part of the world when persons commit themselves to the use of their gifts for the sake of the common good. Suffering is mitigated not by reciting repetitive prayers but by finding practical applications to eliminate or contain the forces devastating humanity. "*Ora et labora.*" Pray *and* work.

Today's "new monks" more accurately reflect the Kingdom's presence.

Consider Nathan Wolfe, a virologist who tracks emerging infectious diseases before they begin to kill. Like monks of old, he left the comforts of home and travelled to remote parts of the world, but he did so to collect blood samples and chase down outbreaks. In pursuit, he almost died of malaria. Or Esther Duflo, an MIT economist who left the safety of the ivory tower to gather real data, to see what actually works in alleviating poverty. In the process she overturned conventional wisdom by moving into unchartered terrain, interacting with the poor themselves. Or Marie Colvin, a journalist who risked covering wars to alert the world to the victims of violence, losing an eye in 2001 by shrapnel in Sri Lanka, killed in February 2012 by military mortar in Syria.

Can anything be more monastic, spending enormous amounts of time studying retrieved specimens, or living with the poor and sharing their hardships, or risking the fire of warfare to inform the world? Can such lives not be but godly? These are the "new monks," those who subject themselves to a severe but authentic discipline.

These "new monks" are engaged with the world, not withdrawn from it. They are passionately concerned about the common good. Their involvement reflects the Kingdom *and* the Incarnation, using talents for the sake of others. It is not enough to give out Band-Aids to those suffering, smugly satisfied with treating the side effects of evil rather than remaining ever vigilant, even restless, until its causes are addressed and persons are made whole. This demands a discipline that no simulated asceticism—no monk or nun withdrawn from the world or resigned to a routine of ritualized prayers—could ever achieve. It is a healthy rather than a warped channeling of energy.

Most people, lacking supreme talents and amazing gifts, are challenged to act extraordinarily in their ordinary existence, witnessing to a spirituality that is other-oriented. Easier to count the stars than the persons on the planet burdened with someone or something in their lives that saps them of every ounce of energy every waking moment. So many are thrust into situations that would make them cry for escape, release.

Yet most do not abandon their burdens but remain, heroically tending to the demands of others or the fate consigned them. They need no faux religious practices to have union with God. Their unrequited love is the deed that no treatise on love can describe or match. Theirs is a witness to authentic spirituality.

When Jesus yoked love of neighbor to self and God, it was "new wine." Jesus revealed repeatedly that the "neighbor" wasn't just the tribal member, but the outsider, even the enemy, within and without. In John's letter he pushed the envelope. The emphasis isn't first on love of God, a God no one has seen, but on love of a neighbor we can see. If we can't include this person, any pretense about loving God renders us liars. "Orthodox Catholics," prompted by recent popes, perceive the modern age has lost its sense of transcendence, especially of God. Hence, the Vatican's pushed to compel an archaic liturgy, with language jarringly distinct from the vernacular—the "vulgar" language people speak normally—to create a sense of transcendence. But what act demands more transcendence than to view and acknowledge others—particularly persons of disrepute, loathsome ones, our enemies—as dwelling places of the divine? How many "orthodox Catholics" would encounter an intimidating murderer, tattooed and branded, bulked up to beat anyone in his path, and have a transcendent experience of the divine dwelling in him? Countless times a day we are confronted with such moments, in persons we find challenging for a multitude of reasons. "If anyone says, 'I love God,' and hates his brother, he is a liar; for he who does not love his brother whom he has seen cannot love God whom he has not seen." (1 Jo 4:20)

How we approach and regard "the other" reveals whether we are one with God. If we don't love the one right in front of us, how can we say we love the God who is unseen, as 1 Jo 4:20 challenges? The treatment of "the other" is the heart of Kingdom teaching.

The burden is on believers. Do believers truly love others, especially the unlovable, the despicable, the enemy? If *not*, no need to praise the Lord. And if *so*, no need to praise the Lord, for the Lord is already praised when the other is included. Believers need to confront their fellow members who debase others through militarism, racism, sexism, and economic inequity, rather than worrying about praising the Lord.

A priest shared a story of traveling with a group of pilgrims to the Holy Land and handing out room assignments. A white woman was to share a room with a black woman but locked the door on her, declaring she wouldn't sleep with a "nigger." Both baptized and equal members of the Body of Christ, both on a tour to walk in the footsteps of Jesus.

Exclusion comes in many forms. Christians have created a special religious language, viewing others as outsiders because they don't understand it. Rather than using a separate vocabulary and speaking exclusively to insiders while alienating outsiders, Christians should take the initiative to speak an inclusive language of love, truth, and justice that all people of goodwill understand, encompassing whoever is "the other."

In referring to ancient dates, the religious reference *AD* ("*Anno Domini*," or "in the year of the Lord") should give way to the more catholic *CE* ("Common Era"). This would be an act of true inclusion, signaling a desire for universal dialogue instead of widespread division. Unfortunately, a militant Christian minority would take up arms to defend the term *AD*, as if defending the Lord himself.

If Christians drank the new wine, this would underscore that Kingdom values are found not so much in words but in deeds. The new wine of authentic spirituality is living for others, and that stretches the parameters of our heart. Believers and Nones can walk side by side in common spiritual pursuit.

This authentic spirituality transcends religious tribes. Of course it's easier to love one's own, but "if you love those who love you, what reward will you have?" (Mt 5:46) And this wouldn't be the way of the Kingdom.

WHY CATHOLICS NEED TO BECOME CATHOLIC
"He was of the faith chiefly in the sense that the church he currently did not attend was Catholic." – Kingsley Amis

The word *catholic* indicates a global perspective transcending family, tribe, nation, and corporation. It seeks common ground, common good, common life with all. Focusing on *Roman* rather than *Catholic* reflects the fear of losing some sort of religious "exclusivity," religious "exceptionalism." But the new wine of Jesus is *all about* losing the old way of life, about dying to old ideas. "Unless a grain of wheat falls to the ground and dies, it remains alone, but if it dies, it bears much fruit." (Jo 12:24)

Some contemporary atheists have become militant, evangelizing as aggressively as some Christians. They make convincing arguments attacking the suppositions and superstitions that abound among Christians unwilling to skeptically analyze their institutionalized belief systems. Unfortunately, some Christians feel threatened when they—or their dogmas—are simply questioned. They are unable to proceed with certainty and confidence in resolving dilemmas about what they feel and believe, and cannot produce empirical data to support their claims. They've been put on the defensive. They're now experiencing the other side of prosthelytizing. The new wine Jesus serves allows us to cease being afraid and let go. This is not a Jim Jones "Kool-Aid" but a drink to new life for all, nurturing spirit and truth. Illuminating dialogue is liberating for everyone.

Many Nones accept some type of theism, but do not expend enormous amounts of time and energy trying to discern God's nature or God's will. We need to first understand not God but our own humanity, that which is visible rather than invisible. As Alexander Pope said so well, "The proper study of mankind is man." Endless speculation about a deity distracts us from understanding others and interceding in their lives. Better to spend time on humanity, which is begging for intervention and for salvation, here and now.

In Buddhism, speculation about God is a low priority. Scholar Richard P. Hayes writes of the Buddha's "well-known aversion to speculative views concerning matters that are beyond man's ken." He notes that focusing on "whether the universe is beginning-less or had a definite point at which it came into being" is "a distraction from pursuits closer at hand." In fact, "the attitude of the Buddha as portrayed in the Nikāyas is more anti-speculative than specifically atheistic." [215]

In Catholicism, spirituality is centered on reception of the sacraments, particularly mass attendance, under threat of punishment. Rather than opening opportunities to grow in the spirit, the very existence of the sacraments ironically paves the way to eternal damnation. Spirituality becomes a legalistic practice rather than a transcendent experience. *Free sacraments without sin!*

"The wind blows where it wishes and you hear the sound of it, but do not know where it comes from and where it is going, so is everyone who is born of the Spirit." (Jo 3:8) The RCC emphasizes the external rather than the internal. It stresses performing outer rituals, which leads one to a spiritual dead end, rather than conforming to the inner spirit, which leads one to unimaginable places.

Many Catholics are intent on pursuing the mystery of an invisible God, rather than finding the divine in other humans. Some even object to the mass as translated into the vernacular and feel only the Tridentine expression is authentic. An Ohio newspaper reported on the resurgence of the Latin mass: "Scott Wilson, who lives in Beavercreek, said those who attend Holy Family are in search of a spiritual experience that is meaningful, serious and reverent. 'They are tired of mediocrity. They want authenticity,' he said. 'We are surrounded by a materialistic culture, a fake world. They want truth and want to take their lives seriously. This Mass is focused on God, not on man.'" [216]

This sentiment represents an escape from the world rather than an engagement with it, when dialogue may be painful and difficult. It is a return to vertical relationships with God exclusively, when Vatican II sought to reorient us toward horizontal relationships with one another.

For many religionists, mythological explanations suffice. They provide a meaningful structure around which to order life, explain what happens at the end of life, are easily understood and accepted but rarely questioned. They provide comfort. This is understandable, given the vagaries of human existence. The conflict arises when we seek to impose our values on others.

For Christians, there is tremendous solace in the belief of a resurrection and the hope of being reunited with loved ones someday. But the teaching of a place of eternal torture and punishment is equally a part of the Christian package. Some Christian tribes deemphasize it while others keep it in the forefront as a cautionary tale. If, as Prothero pointed out, religious tribal members are highly illiterate regarding their own belief systems, they will hardly understand or investigate those of others. But it is the "Nones" who score highest, as they are personally driven to decide on (rather than inherit) a belief system.

The last closet being emptied contains the incredible number of Nones throughout the world who are no longer hesitant or fearful in admitting they believe in no religious tradition. The fear of retribution, so intimidating in the past, is now gone in much of the world. Salvation comes through education and investigation, through democracy and pluralism, through openness and inquiry. People are less often victims of tradition than agents of their own future, their own heaven or hell.

The dividing line for the fate of humanity may be drawn between those desperate for certainty, both now and in the future, and those willing to live with uncertainty. The latter overcome fears that have always plagued humanity. Once they are no longer imprisoned by fear, people think clearly and creatively, act more consciously for the common good. And they subconsciously take to heart the enlightenment of Jesus. "Do not fear; you are worth more than many swallows." (Lk 12:47) Ultimately, self-esteem does not require external approval.

The future is a place where people will decide for themselves what to believe or not, whether to believe or not. If the Christian message has any validity, it will be in the concept of the prodigal father. He allows his children to discover for themselves what is out there in the world, and they know they will always be welcomed home unconditionally, and should be ready to party upon returning!

This image of a prodigal God that Jesus offered clashes with the historic Judeo-Christian concept, handed down over the centuries, of a harsh and punitive God. To accept a prodigal God is to reject a fear-mongering God. Yet many still cling to this ogre.

As recently as Easter Sunday 2012, Anne Graham Lotz, daughter of Billy Graham, reiterated twice on *Meet the Press,* "The fear of the Lord is the beginning of wisdom." (Pro 9:10)

Anne's wine cellar seems to be stocked with vintage fare. No new wine there.

AFTERWORD

SEEDS OF TRUTH:
FINDING FERTILE GROUND

*"The Heart is a good fertile ground. Anything planted there—
Love, Hate, Fear, Hope—will surely grow and bear fruits. It is
for us to decide what to plant and harvest." – Anonymous*

In *Practicing History: Selected Essays*, historian Barbara Tuchman counsels a writer to "quit before you're finished!" She learned the expression from her father. When she was a teenager going out on a date, she asked him, "How far can we go?" He replied, "Quit before you're finished!"

That works for writing, too. No one has the last word. I believe it is vital to speak one's thoughts, even if incomplete, ragged and jagged. To add them to a never-ending dialogue about what is not of bread alone.

Of all the world's organizations, religious institutions should be the most receptive to, and welcoming of, a person searching for and speaking the truth. They may claim to nurture the intangible, the thoughts and concerns of members, but in reality can be as repressive as totalitarian states.

Millions, perhaps billions, are inhibited from publicly expressing their thoughts, fearful of repercussions from those in power. The dark side of humanity is maintained by stifling free inquiry.

But the gnawing words of Jesus empower us with the startling pronouncement that *we will know the truth and the truth will set us free.* He dared to voice a revolutionary perspective, but it did not come without personal cost. Those who speak the truth of their understanding share not only kinship, but also retribution.

Institutions rarely welcome questioning. They maintain thought control. They are vigilant in suppressing contrary views and opinions—blocking the ongoing struggle for a free press, controlling media, filtering information, creating public opinion.

Fortunately, much of the world's population today has been liberated by the Internet, an increasingly accessible vehicle that encourages individuals across the planet to freely search, investigate, learn, speak, and debate.

A late friend, Mary Murphy, was in her nineties and computer illiterate though aware of the Internet when she asked me one day, "Emmett, do you think the Internet is the Holy Spirit?" She startled me. Of course, I asked her what she meant. She responded, "It seems to bring people all over the world together. Isn't that what the Holy Spirit is supposed to do?" Listen to wisdom.

Sara Robinson finds that the spiritual marketplace has gone global through online access and social networking. The result is a religious cross-pollination, "a trend that could move us toward a sort of syncretic, celebratory sharing of traditions that could be healthy for everyone." [217]

Roman hierarchs would be alarmed, clinging to "exceptionalism," resisting change altogether. They would quickly quote Hebrews 13:8, "Jesus Christ is the same yesterday and today and forever," implying no change, no new perspectives, no interpretations. They would not be comfortable with Heraclitus' insight that there is nothing permanent except change.

If a body is alive, it is dynamic. Once it becomes a cadaver, it is static (though even a dead body moves through stages of decay). So, we need to know. Is the Body of Christ alive? Or is it a cadaver?

The dark side of the RCC has refined the control of thought and its expression through many centuries of inquisition, censorship, indoctrination, condemnation, and punishment of those who—like Jesus—would reinterpret tradition. Self-censorship has now become ingrained. Even its theologians generally write and talk only to their own class. Liberation theologians are the exception, as they seek to engage all people in a communal quest for truth.

The RCC's control is incessant and relentless. One of Benedict XVI's first acts was to sack the editor of the U.S.-based opinion magazine, *America*: "Jesuit officials in Rome said Thomas J. Reese, S.J., resigned as editor in chief of *America* magazine after repeated complaints from then-Cardinal Joseph Ratzinger, who objected to the magazine's treatment of sensitive church issues." [218] This was not an isolated incident but the continuation of a tradition of repression, honed through centuries of experience. In 2012, two priests—Gerard Maloney, the editor of a tiny (6,500 subscribers) Irish Catholic publication, *Reality*, and Tony Flannery, a writer—were silenced by the Vatican for questioning some of the tradition in published articles.

Self-censorship successfully permeates the RCC's many media organizations. It's extremely difficult to initiate a dialogue when a powerful institution rigidly maintains a monologue, including control and censorship of all publications. Does *Pravda* come to mind? The institution insists that dogmatic and moral positions are not open to review. They're settled. I find it unsettling that the power clerical elite alone determines what is settled and what is not.

An appealing aspect of the Jesus figure is his audacity to question authority, to reexamine tradition. It is easy to imagine a contemporary Jesus using the Internet and any other means available to spread his message of liberation. But even his divinity failed to save him from the abuse of power. What will save a mere mortal who questions authority nowadays?

The human spirit cannot be forever smothered. Two strains define human history—suppressing or stimulating the human genius. Powerful forces, even religious, have obstinately sought to suppress this drive. But the spirit is tough, persistent, resilient. It blows where it will. Ours is a history of transcendence. This speaks to the spirit within more than the material without.

"We are spiritual beings having a human experience." Perhaps this is why Sara Robinson concludes God is not dead, and that technology is changing everything, including religion: "I think we may end up with a far more expansive and inclusive sense of the sacred than we can possibly imagine right now. In fact, this century may be giving us the best chance humans ever had to create a global spirituality on enduring human values: compassion, justice, community, and the common drive to share and celebrate the wonder of our lives." [219] Sounds like another way of describing the Kingdom.

Wisdom is held to be the fruit of advanced years. Youth may be brilliant, but haven't weathered decades of experiences, haven't had the chance to distill insight and knowledge from daily living, as seniors have. Unfortunately, in a culture that devalues the contributions of the elderly, many are hesitant, reluctant, even intimidated to share their reflections.

In his play, *Zalmen, or the Madness of God*, Elie Wiesel describes a rabbi facing the dilemma of speaking out or remaining silent. He is to lead services in a Russian synagogue with American visitors present. Stalin has recently died and relations with the Soviet state are beginning to thaw. Everyone counsels the rabbi to refrain from speaking out—except the janitor, Zalmen. He advises him to "go mad and tell them the Torah is not free!" The rabbi rejoins that if he were younger, he would. Zalmen zings back, "You were younger and you didn't do anything!" If not now, when?

When younger, many would have liked to speak truth to power, but unless financially secure, they were impotent. Job insecurity is a check on most persons, especially those responsible for dependents. Country singer Johnny Paycheck's song, "Take This Job and Shove It," resonated around the world. Easier sung than done. Most persons are forced to stifle their true feelings.

Age, however, is a natural liberating agent. The window (and door) is closing. In a short time, we'll all be history (readers included), with no opportunity to speak the truth revealed through our experiences.

298

Those highly anticipated voices of the dead have never materialized, séances notwithstanding. It's now or never, sunshine.

More than bestowing material gains on the next generation, our richer legacy is sharing the fruit of life experiences. If it weren't for the words of those who preceded us, we'd be reinventing the wheel anew each generation.

I lament the unnecessary and unimaginable loss of life the institution of the RCC caused—so many were persecuted when their only crime was being true to themselves. Did the truth set them free? Does freedom only come through death, as it did for Jesus? Only truth will set the institution free, to become what Jesus envisioned in his brief lifetime, if it is willing to die to power. "Unless a seed falls to the ground and dies it remains just a seed, but if it dies it bears much fruit." (Jo 12:24) Only then is there the possibility of rising to moral integrity. There is a cost in speaking truth to power. If it valued "serving first," the RCC would welcome members' critiques. But the power virus of Constantine remains virulent and vindictive.

October of 2012 will mark the 50th anniversary of Pope John's opening of the II Vatican Council. The RCC is launching a "Year of Faith" to commemorate this event. Followers will be enjoined to read the Council's documents and study its *Catechism of the Catholic Church* (the production overseen by Cardinal Ratzinger and finalized by John Paul II at the Council's 30th anniversary). Fat chance many Catholics will crack open either book. But from that 1962 event blossomed a springtime of hope for a tired tradition in great need of opening itself to "the signs of the times." I am a victim of the rush of that spirit, which cannot be stifled.

But it is not for loss. As an intimate insider, I've been allowed a perspective beyond the realm of an outsider. I've been behind the curtain.

Aware of the dark side of tradition, I am fortunate to live in a day in which I feel less fear in expressing myself. In former times, I might have been subjected to intimidation, possibly torture, even death. Today, being "retired," the most that can happen in retaliation would be a loss of small "benefits." Besides, I've been stamped indelibly as a priest forever—I have the mark to prove it—and that can never be erased, even if I or the institution wanted it. And contemporary media protects individuals, when in previous times there was no investigative media. The RCC, nonetheless, does not hesitate to silence and sack any member it deems deviant. It's in the DNA since Constantine. It must retain power at whatever cost of elimination, suppression—even of members, even to those indelibly marked.

The unknown authors of the gospel accounts are united in their negative portrayal of the Jewish religious hierarchy. Jesus is positioned as the "devil's advocate" who challenges their accepted custom and tradition. He tries their patience. They view him as a threat to their interpretations. They hand him over to the authorities, who attempt to silence him and his followers forever. If we take to heart the message of the gospel writers, is it not incumbent for us to "go and do likewise," to "take up the cross" in real time?

Many Catholics revere tradition even when they bear the burden joylessly. It prevents them from rethinking childish things. The Devil surfaced in the campaign of Rick Santorum, extremely right-leaning Catholic who ran for the 2012 Republican presidential nomination, when he had to explain his 2008 claim (during a speech at a Catholic university) that Satan was attacking U.S. institutions. In defending himself, he talked about "taking on the forces around this world that want to do harm to America" and stated that America is a country "that when someone is in trouble, and forces of evil are moving, America would stand up and call evil by its name." [220] Rick, there is no Satan, no Devil, no minions. Rick and his own minions will remain defensive, however, toward any challenge of this unnecessary baggage, clinging to childish things.

Dissenting from doctrine or dogma is not as devastating as parting from practice. Jesus' objection to religious leaders stemmed from their failure to practice what they preached, not from their attraction to various abstract concepts or doctrines. Whether one believes there are three persons in the Trinity or three thousand won't affect the universe. (Anyway, many of us were told repeatedly from childhood that no one can understand the Trinity!) But failing to act in truth, justice, and love *does* affect the universe, and *will* have a profoundly negative impact.

Some reading my offering (or misreading it, or not even reading but defending an ideological position) will be quick to condemn me for denying various dogmas, doctrines.

First, for the record, I happily deny the existence of a free evil agent who goes about "seeking to devour," revered as the Devil and a legion of names. This dark personification is still a dogma of the RCC. [221] The Kingdom prayer petitions to be delivered from evil, but the RCC has morphed this into being protected from the character of Satan. I acknowledge evil exists, but not because of dastardly activities on the part of a cartoonish "Evil One." For rejecting belief in such an abomination, for denying the existence of a Devil who maintains an eternal firehouse of horrors, I think some would deem it appropriate that I be cast into a bonfire. But I should be judged not because I failed to hold dear dogmas such as the Devil, but because I failed to practice the commandment to love. St. John of the Cross believed, "In the evening of life, we will be judged on love alone."

Second, I reject the RCC's clinging to political power, attempting to maintain a secular state mimicking the kingdom of "this world." Our beloved planet would be embroiled in ceaseless wars if every religion was also a secular state. To reject the State of Vatican City is not based on any article of faith, or dogma. It's simply that Jesus would be aghast at its very existence, its current nature. Rejecting it acknowledges the RCC failed to witness to Jesus' position, "My kingdom is not of this world." In seeking to be aligned with secular political entities, the RCC demonstrates it is *absolutely* "of this world," the world of power and control. As long as it clings tenaciously to the apparatus of a state, it has no moral legitimacy. It cannot be, at one and the same time, both a political order and a moral order. Catholics, unfortunately, have long coexisted with this deviation from the Kingdom teaching without acknowledging the cognitive dissonance. And as part of the elimination of the State of Vatican City, the papacy needs to bankrupt its bank. The Vatican, where money lenders found a home, has been continually embroiled in financial scandals. For an institution with a mandate to "live in the light," it has preferred the darkness of questionable financial transactions. Otherwise, why is it struggling to be on the "white list" of banks above reproach in money laundering?

The devious papal position in wearing "two hats" is a ruse to evade responsibility (specifically moral responsibility) in claiming immunity through diplomatic cover.

A current case in point is the clerical sexual-abuse trauma in Ireland. One article referred to a recent Wikileaks release regarding the 2009 Murphy Report, and the RCC's response: "And one of the revelations from Wikileaks was that when the Murphy team approached the Vatican for information to help with its investigation it didn't receive a response—church authorities said that as it was a sovereign state it would only communicate with other governments." [222]

I offer my interpretations as one voice in a necessary dialogue that authentically only "comes from below." Many Catholics still cling to childish beliefs, backing off when hearing or accepting some unquestioned tradition, uncomfortable when forced to reexamine long-held assumptions, lest the house of cards upon which their faith is built collapses. Jesus warned about building a house on sand. Uncritical processing does not provide a firm foundation.

Many issues I have critiqued—fear, mortal sin, hell, torture, the Devil—still define the RCC's tradition. They are the foundation of the *Catechism* and will be passed on to the innocent and illiterate, "the little ones," who ask for bread and fish and receive a stone and a snake. (Mt 7:9) They need no additional burdens on their sagging shoulders. They need to hear the liberating news the gospel writers offered, to receive the potent seeds of the Kingdom proclamation. This is the tradition I would like to pass on.

That proclamation sought to empty the old wine and infuse the new wine of liberation and the praxis of love. The RCC desperately needs an exorcism to separate the old additives from the new if it hopes to move into the future not as an opulent, moribund museum but a lush, budding garden where "the head of household who brings out of his treasure things new and old." (Mt 13:52) Imposing only the old puts the message on hold.

The Kingdom offers fresh perspectives, seminal insights. When he was a lawyer in South Africa, Mahatma Gandhi, a Hindu, read the New Testament and was so profoundly moved, particularly by the

Sermon on the Mount, that he wanted to become Christian. He approached a Christian church, only to be turned away by members who directed him to a church for "colored people." Gandhi would become the Father of Nonviolence, deeply influencing Martin Luther King, Jr., Nelson Mandela, and others who devoted their lives, at severe personal cost, to nonviolently effect political change. Gandhi embodied the Kingdom unlike even popes by effectively putting into practice the Sermon on the Mount. Through nonviolent protest, he was instrumental in leading the Indian people to expel the British. There was no Gandhi at the time of the American Revolution, so colonists resorted to violence to expel the Brits here.

Jesus said "outsiders" would be entering the Kingdom before "insiders." (Mt 21:31) Apparently today, many outsiders are insiders, and insiders are outsiders.

The Kingdom of God remains a seed, awaiting fertile ground— inviting anyone, anywhere, anytime. "Still other seed fell on good soil." (Mk 4:8) The Kingdom's bottom line is compassion and care for "the least ones." Those who prefer the gospel of Ayn Rand (and similar ideologies) vehemently oppose solidarity and discipleship. Rugged individualism is about saving self, independent of others. That we are our brother's (and sister's) keeper is anathema to many American rugged individualists, many of whom also claim Jesus as their savior. But if they are rugged individualists, why can't they save themselves? Again, we are consistent in our inconsistencies.

Concern, solidarity, for "the least ones" remains central to Kingdom teaching. It is a reminder that we are *all* "least ones."

Gandhi revealed himself a true disciple of the Kingdom when he expressed these thoughts toward the end of his life: "I will give you a talisman. Whenever you are in doubt, or when the self becomes too much with you, apply the following test. Recall the face of the poorest and the weakest man [woman] whom you may have seen, and ask yourself, if the step you contemplate is going to be of any use to him [her]. Will he gain anything by it? Will it restore him to a control over his own life and destiny? In other words, will it lead to "*swaraj*" [freedom] for the hungry and spiritually starving millions? Then you will find your doubts and your self melt away." [223]

I end on a poor note. The RCC is obsessively focused on itself, narcissistic in too many ways to count. One embarrassing endeavor recently expended an enormous amount of energy worldwide on parsing language in a new rewrite of the liturgy, dragooning members to become consumed with this futile effort, which will not make one whit of difference, especially in affecting the poor. The pope preens more over a poor translation than the poor.

The primary focus of the Kingdom proclamation still remains "good news for the poor." The Kingdom will not be realized until "the least ones" have a mutual place at the table of equity and equality. Today, the plight of the poor is primarily ignored by the world media. Corporations control the media; their primary concern is profit.

But the media for "the least ones" is the gospels.

If the RCC were faithful to the gospels, the poor would have prominence in all its pronouncements and practices. It is not the prominent hierarchy that bears the eternal torch for the poor—it is the inspired "lowerarchy" that keeps the flame burning.

The disparity of wealth in the world today is unprecedented. "A study by the World Institute for Development Economics Research at United Nations University reports that the richest 1% of adults alone owned 40% of global assets in the year 2000, and that the richest 10% of adults accounted for 85% of the world total." (Wikipedia)

Even the Father of Capitalism, Adam Smith, indicated, "Wherever there is great property there is great inequality." Approximately 3 billion persons now struggle to subsist on less than $2 a day. Who hears their cry? Who gives a damn? Household pets often get better care than millions of persons.

Resolution will never be achieved solely by individual acts of charity, but by systemic change. Capitalism is content with a "trickle-down" solution. It lacks a moral conscience. There seems to be a universal acceptance that capitalism rules the world; hence, there is little appetite for systemic change to upend the status quo. So, the "wretched of the earth" are largely ignored—*save for* the Kingdom's proclamation, where they are the *top priority*. Would that the poor, and not abortion, be the primary focus of the RCC! After all, the mission statement of the Kingdom proclaims good news for the poor—not for the unborn. Only in these latter days has the papacy pushed abortion as its primary crusade, deflecting from itself conversion to simplicity of life and true solidarity with all on earth, like its vulnerable Jesus.

The kingdoms of this world divide and conquer by rejecting solidarity and emphasizing, at best, individual effort and response. This emphasis also divides and conquers, preventing solidarity of the many to coalesce, resisting true substantive change.

Dr. King said, "White people must recognize that justice for black people cannot be achieved without *radical changes* in the structure of our society. The comfortable, the entrenched, the privileged cannot continue to tremble at the prospect of change in the status quo." (Emphasis added) While there have been racial changes here, racism remains entrenched. The "war on drugs" first declared in 1971 became the "new Jim Crow" law, creating a permanent underclass of millions of people of color, locked in and locked out, barred from participating equally and equitably in this democracy. The 2008 election of a half-black president did not alter the power structure of the few over the many. Yet we continue, at best, with half measures.

The radical change in the structure of society here in America, as suggested by Dr. King, is one thing. But unless there is radical change across the planet, the poor will continue to exist in hell on earth. The prophetic message of the Kingdom is not simply to feed the poor, but to ask *why* they are doomed to be poor. And then mobilize in solidarity so the "least ones" have their rightful daily bread. Would that the RCC were true to the Kingdom and took this prophetic risk.

Mother Teresa demonstrated heroic involvement with "the least ones" but never questioned the structures of inequity that keep the poor poor. Gandhi knew change came only through mobilizing the masses when he inspired widespread protests against the British, who finally left peacefully. Dr. King sought to mobilize the masses through the Poor People's Campaign but tragically, the sudden removal of his vital guidance left a leadership void. With the loss of King, the poor lost.

Fundamentalist Christians look for a millennial kingdom on earth that will rise from a violent battle of Armageddon in the Middle East and a return of Jesus to reign on earth. This scenario is in stark contrast to the Kingdom of God, where change does not come from external force but internal will, conversion, the decision to be in solidarity with "the least ones."

And the Kingdom remains, awaiting spring to seed fertile ground.

EPILOGUE

This is my last testament, my last word, my last hope.

Writing this book has been an exercise in repudiating the theology of fear to which I was conditioned. If I were still its victim, I would have been reluctant to write.

I pray this ultimately proves to be a liberating experience for me and my readers, and a gift of "tough love" to my Roman Catholic Church, an urgent plea that it seek the Kingdom first.

On our last lap, with the days numbered and the eternal silence nearing, what can we possibly say? If we didn't seize the day when younger, the latter day seizes us. Then again, it's on the last lap that we might see the light at the end of the tunnel.

Carpe diem!

So in my life review, I look at the two institutions that strongly shaped my years here on earth. At birth I automatically became a citizen of the United States, and at baptism I involuntarily became a member of the Catholic Church—both because of others.

Now at the end, I have questions and concerns about both that I didn't have in the beginning. Both crave and maintain power. Both share an impulse for exceptionalism. Both aspire to be empires—one political, one religious.

307

I offer my critique of contemporary America —the political empire— to all who read this. I realize that the ideal of a democratic society remains subject to the demands of a nation-state in its drive for power, and that in the process, democratic values are threatened. Is the primary concern of American society to be a witness to a powerful democracy, or to a powerful vehicle for capitalism?

I fear that in coming years the majority of Americans will defend an economic way of life over a political paradise, and will accept violence as the only way to achieve this.

Have we progressed at all beyond our primitive ancestors who went to war with neighbors to ensure their economic advantage? The distressing difference today is that we support an enormous military with nuclear weapons and high-tech arsenals, and to keep our magnificent military-industrial complex running on all cylinders we willingly expend an amount equal to that spent by all other nations combined.

At the end of my days in this democracy of ours, the future looks bleak, not bright. Where does one go to get out of the reach of the empire?

I offer my exit interview to the Roman Catholic Church—the religious empire—in which I invested my life. Sometimes I wish I never had been part of this authoritarian establishment, especially as a priest.

I wouldn't have had to accept (and preach, and defend) a negative theology. I would have been open to explore religious beliefs without intimidation or conflict. As it was, I knew the drill, I understood the agenda. It was the theology of fear, not the praxis of love.

At the beginning of the journey I had no control over what was put before me, nor did I grasp the implications. If I knew then what I know now, I would not have been so enthusiastic about passing on what I now see as the institution's dark tradition.

Yet, as an insider I attained a perspective that I would have missed otherwise. Now I have laid aside childish thinking as I am about to be laid to rest.

308

Thy Kingdom come—on earth!

Meanwhile at the Vatican, as always, pure doctrine has priority over pure practice. As I was drafting this in February 2012, twenty-two clerics were elevated to the most exclusive male-only club in the world, the College of Cardinals, and were called princes of the Church.

The Roman Empire lives!

Benedict XVI asked his court of newly minted princes to pray "that I may continually offer to the People of God the witness of sound doctrine." [224] No reference to sound practice. I wondered ... how would the pope have these princes apply Gandhi's counsel? Were the least ones present in this papal panoply? Was the Kingdom proclaimed? Was it even mentioned?

Was anyone aware of the cognitive dissonance?

"And Jesus wept!"

REFERENCES

[1] Ratzinger, Joseph. 1987. *Principles of Catholic Theology.* Ignatius Press, San Francisco, CA.

[2] "Contraception Mandate Prompts Peoria Bishop to Instate St. Michael Prayer." Freerepublic.com, 1/28/12.

[3] "Quote of the Day (Cardinal Ercole Consalvi, on the Endurance of the Church Despite Its Clergy)." BoatAgainstTheCurrent.blogspot.com, 2/8/09.

[4] Brand-Williams, Oralandar. "Priest at Catholic Reform Mass Isn't Worried about Backlash by Archdiocese." *Detroit News*, 6/12/11. Posted on BishopAccountability.org.

[5] Farrell, Thomas. "Matthew Fox's Critique of the Roman Catholic Church." OpEdNews.com, 6/24/11.

[6] Oberman, Mira. "Child Abuse Scandal Cost U.S. Catholic Church $3 Bln." AFP, 4/4/10.

[7] Newman, John Henry. "Meditations on Christian Doctrine," Part I. Hope in God—Creator. 3/7/48. Posted on NewmanReader.org.

[8] Hall, Brian. 2008. *Fall of Frost: A Novel.* Penguin Books, New York, NY.

[9] Murphy, Cullen. 2012. *God's Jury: The Inquisition and the Making of the Modern World.* Houghton Harcourt Mifflin Publishing Co., New York, NY.

[10] Murphy, ibid.

[11] Robinson, Geoffrey. 2007. *Confronting Power and Sex in the Catholic Church.* Liturgical Press, Collegeville, MN.

[12] Boff, Leonardo. 1985. *Church: Charism and Power—Liberation Theology and the Institutional Church.* Crossroad, New York, NY.

[13] Prothero, Stephen. 2007. *Religious Literacy: What Every American Needs to Know—and Doesn't.* HarperOne, New York, NY.

[14] *U.S. Religious Knowledge Survey.* Pew Research Center, pewresearch.org, 9/28/10.

[15] "Fr. Benedict Groeschel: Pressures on the Christian Family and How to Respond to Them—Part II." CatholicFire.blogspot.com, 8/6/07.

[16] Boff, ibid.

[17] "Irish PM Slams Vatican 'Dysfunction' on Child Abuse." *The Telegraph,* 7/21/11.

[18] Fanon, Frantz. 1994. *Black Skin, White Masks.* Grove Press, New York, NY.

[19] Marcotte, John. "Top Five Republican Gay Sex Scandals." Badmouth.net, 8/31/07.

[20] Knox, Ronald. 1927. *The Belief of Catholics.* Sheed & Ward, London.

[21] Ehrman, Bart. 2009. *Jesus, Interrupted: Revealing the Hidden Contradictions in the Bible—and Why We Don't Know About Them.* HarperOne, New York, NY.

[22] Kinney, Monica Yant. "Cardinal's Absurdist Biblical Debate before a Grand Jury." *Philadelphia Inquirer Digital*, philly.com, 7/27/11.

[23] Roosevelt, Franklin Delano. "The Four Freedoms." Address to Congress, 1/14/41.

[24] Murphy, ibid.

[25] Marrin, Pat. "New Evangelization or Old Apologetics?" Review of Barron, Robert. *Catholicism: A Journey* (Image Books). *National Catholic Reporter*, ncronline, 2/1/12.

[26] Berman, Morris. In an interview with Nomi Prins, "Why the American Empire Was Destined to Collapse." AlterNet.org, 3/7/12.

[27] Nolan, Albert. 2001. *Jesus Before Christianity*. Orbis Books, Maryknoll, NY.

[28] Jenkins, John Philip. 2010. *Jesus Wars: How Four Patriarchs, Three Queens, and Two Emperors Decided What Christians Would Believe for the Next 1,500 Years."* HarperOne, New York, NY.

[29] Jenkins, ibid.

[30] Pope Benedict XVI. In the Regensburg Lecture, a speech at the University of Regensburg, Germany. Cited in "Pope's Islam Comments Condemned," CNN.com, 9/15/06.

[31] Westley, Richard. 1983. *Morality and Its Beyond.* XXIII Publications, Mystic, CT.

[32] Westley, ibid.

[33] Goldman, Gerard. "Church: Seeking First the Kingdom of God." In *Compass, A Review of Topical Theology*, posted on CompassReview.org, Winter 2010.

[34] Brueggemann, Walter. 2001. *The Prophetic Imagination*, Augsburg Fortress, Minneapolis, MN.

[35] Fuellenbach, John. 1994. *The Kingdom of God: The Message of Jesus Today.* Orbis Press, Maryknoll, New York, NY.

[36] Machiavelli, Niccolo. *The Prince.* Ch. XVII. Originally published circa 1515. Reprint of an unspecified previous edition.

[37] Kegley, Jr., Charles W. 2008. *World Politics.* The Thomson Company, Boston, MA.

[38] Vacant, A, Mangenot, E., and Amann, E. 1913. *Dictionnaire de Théologie Catholique, Vol. V.* Paris, Letouzey et Ané.

[39] Corbin Jane. 2002. *Al-Qaeda: In Search of the Terror Network that Threatens the World.* Thunder's Mouth Press/Nation Books, New York, NY.

[40] Halsey III, Ashley. "Fines Prompt Drivers to Drop Their Cellphones." *Washington Post*, 7/11/11.

[41] "Rome's Exorcist Gives Inside Look at Devil." Zenit.org, 4/11/08.

[42] Equale, Tony. "Resident Evil." Tony Equale's blog, TonyEquale.wordpress, 7/2/11.

[43] Cox, Sue. "What's a Fate Worse than Death?" Presentation to National Secular Society, 1/10/12.

[44] Berkowitz, Eric. 2012. *Sex and Punishment: 4,000 Years of Judging Desire.* Counterpoint Press, Berkeley, CA.

[45] Berkowitz, ibid.

[46] *U.S. Catholic Catechism for Adults. (CCA) 2006. U.S. Conference of Catholic Bishops, WDC.*

[47] *Catechism of the Catholic Church. (CCC)* 1995. Image Books, New York, NY, no.

[48] Eire, Carlos. 2003. *Waiting for Snow in Havana.* Free Press, New York, NY.

[49] Eire, ibid.

[50] *CCA*, ibid.

[51] Kowalska, Maria Faustina. 2000. *Diary: Divine Mercy in My Soul.* Marian Press, Stockbridge, MA.

[52] *CCA*, ibid.

[53] *CCA*, ibid.

[54] *CCA*, ibid.

[55] Filteau, Jerry. "Bishop Urges Change in 'Church Teaching Concerning All Sexual Relationships.'" *National Catholic Reporter*, ncronline.org, 3/16/12.

[56] *CCC*, ibid.

[57] Jamison, Peter. "Let Him Prey: High-Ranking Jesuits Helped Keep Pedophile Priest Hidden." *SF Weekly News*, 5/25/11.

[58] Doig, Matthew. "Teacher Says He was Fired after Seeking Priest Inquiry." *Herald Tribune*, 6/21/11.

[59] Graham-Dixon, Andrew. 2010. *Caravaggio: A Life Sacred and Profane.* Allen Lane, Penguin Press, Great Britain.

[60] Manahan, Kevin. "Two More Men Come Forward." The *Star-Ledger*, 1/24/12.

[61] Hecht, Jennifer. 2004. *Doubt: A History–The Great Doubters and Their Legacy of Innovation from Socrates and Jesus to Thomas Jefferson and Emily Dickinson.* HarperOne, New York, NY.

[62] Hecht, ibid.

[63] Smith, Daniel. "It's Still the 'Age of Anxiety.' Or Is It?" *New York Times*, 1/14/12.

[64] "Most American Christians Do Not Believe that Satan or the Holy Spirit Exist." Study conducted by The Barna Group, posted on barna.org, 4/10/09.

[65] Kowalska, ibid.

[66] Farrell, James T. 1935. *Studs Lonigan: A Trilogy.* The Vanguard Press, New York, NY.

[67] Nall, Merrie Ann. 2005. *Women of Hope: The Story of the Little Company of Mary Sisters in America.* Little Company of Mary Sisters, Evergreen Park, IL.

[68] *Breviary Office, II edition.* 1899. Ellis & Keene, London.

[69] Westley, ibid.

[70] Valentini, Mario. 2006. *Chewing Gum in Holy Water: A Childhood in the Heart of Italy.* Arcade Publishing, New York, NY.

[71] Vandenburg, Elizabeth. "New VA Law Gives Victims More Time to Sue Sex Predators." BurkePatch.com, 7/7/11.

[72] Westley, ibid.

[73] Ehrman, Bart. 2008. *God's Problem: How the Bible Fails to Answer Our Most Important Question—Why We Suffer.* HarperOne, New York, NY.

[74] Westley, ibid.

[75] Avalos, Hector. 2005. *Fighting Words: The Origins of Religious Violence.* Prometheus Books, Amherst, NY.

[76] King. Martin Luther, Jr. In a speech at Dartmouth, 5/23/62. Transcript posted on Dartmouth.edu.

[77] Grisham, John. 2006. *The Innocent Man: Murder and Injustice in a Small Town.* Random House, New York, NY.

[78] Kowalska, ibid.

[79] Tsai, Michelle. "The End of Limbo: What Happens to All the Babies Who Used to Be There?" Slate.com, 4/23/07.

[80] McCloskey, Pat. "Ask a Franciscan: A Question That Keeps Recurring." *St. Anthony Messenger.* Posted on americancatholic.org, June 2011.

[81] McCloskey, ibid.

[82] Haub, Carl. "How Many People Have Ever Lived on Earth?" Population Reference Bureau, prb.org, October 2011.

[83] Kowalska, ibid.

[84] Farrell, ibid.

[85] Harris, Sam. Untitled lecture at the Beyond Belief Conference. Salk Institute, La Jolla, CA, 11/7/2006.

[86] Dawkins, Richard. 2006. *The God Delusion.* Bantam Press, Great Britain.

[87] Cited by RDFRS on richarddaawkins.net.

[88] Cited on goodreads.com.

[89] Dawkins, ibid.

[90] Fuellenbach, ibid.

[91] Gabriel of St. Mary Magdalen. 1987. *Divine Intimacy, Volume III.* Dimension Books, Inc., Pittsford, NY.

[92] Hoffman, Edward. 2003. *The Wisdom of Carl Jung.* Kensington Publishing Company, New York, NY.

[93] Murphy, ibid.

[94] Filteau, Jerry. "Unusual Study Asks Former Catholics Why They Left Church." *National Catholic Reporter,* ncronline.org, 3/23/12.

[95] Ryan, Zoe. "Coalition for the Baptized Has High Hopes." *National Catholic Reporter,* ncronline.org, 7/5/2011.

[96] Berry, Jason. "Ratzinger Altered Canon Law to Soften Maciel Punishment, Book Argues." *National Catholic Reporter,* ncronline.org, 3/24/12.

[97] Posted on news-medical.net, 10/23/06.

[98] Ratzinger, Joseph. "Letter to the Bishops," 10/1/86.

[99] Keller, Helen. 1903. *The Story of My Life.* Doubleday, Page, & Co., New York, NY.

[100] Sheffield, Carrie. "A Mormon Church in Need of Reform." *Washington Post,* 1/29/12.

[101] Martos, Joseph. 2001. *Doors to the Sacred: A Historical Introduction to Sacraments in the Catholic Church.* Image Books, New York, NY.

[102] Kraybill, Donald; Bowman, Carl Desportes; and Bowman, Carl F. 2001. *On the Backroad to Heaven: Old Order Hutterites, Mennonites, Amish, and Brethren.* Johns Hopkins University Press, Baltimore, MD.

[103] Beardsley, Eleanor. "Off the Record: A Quest for De-Baptism in France." National Public Radio, npr.org, 1/29/12.

317

104 "Catholics in the World Grows by 15 Million." CatholicNewsAgency.com, 2/19/11.

105 "Disillusioned German Catholics: The Pope's Difficult Visit to His Homeland." *Der Spiegel*, Spiegel Online International, Spiegel.de.com, 9/20/11.

106 *The Catholic Telegraph.* Cincinnati, OH, August 25, 1904.

107 Gumuchian, Marie-Louise; Halpin, Padraic; and Gergely, Andras. "Special Report: In Irish Schools, Catholic Church Remains Master." Reuters.com, 7/8/10.

108 Conway, Jill Ker. 1994. *The Road from Coorain.* Alfred Knopf, New York, NY.

109 Donohue, William. 1991. *The New Freedom: Individualism and Collectivism in the Social Lives of Americans.* Transaction Publishers, Piscataway, NJ.

110 James, Frank. "Martin Luther King Jr. in Chicago. During His Stay in the City, the Civil-Rights Leader Faced a 'Hateful' Crowd." *Chicago Tribune*, 8/5/66.

111 Kirsch, Jonathan. 2006. *A History of the End of the World: How the Most Controversial Book in the Bible Changed the Course of Western Civilization.* HarperOne, New York, NY.

112 Tobin, Paul. 2009. *The Rejection of Pascal's Wager: A Skeptic's Guide to the Bible and the Historical Jesus.* Authors Online Limited, 2009.

113 Valentini, ibid.

114 O'Brien, Jon and Keenan, Nancy. "Mr. President, Catholic Women Use Birth Control, Too." CatholicsforChoice.org, 11/23/11.

115 Dodson, Lisa. 2009. *The Moral Underground: How Ordinary Americans Subvert an Unfair Economy.* The New Press, New York, NY.

116 Moynahan, Brian. 2003. *The Faith: A History of Christianity.* Doubleday, New York, NY.

117 Moskowitz, Eric and Russell, Jenna. "A Path of Destruction: With Storm Raging, a Mother Makes the Ultimate Sacrifice." *Boston Globe*, 6/3/11.

118 Jenkins, ibid.

119 Martos, ibid.

120 Martos, ibid.

121 Wan, William. "Gaining a Dose of Humility, One Washed Foot at a Time." *Washington Post*, 4/2/06.

122 Morris-Young, Dan. "Vatican II Priests Still Embrace Council's Model Despite Reversals." *National Catholic Reporter*, ncronline.org, 3/12/2012. Reply submitted by John Crepeau.

123 Martos, ibid.

124 *Boston Globe*, 6/15/11. Posted on BostonCatholicInsider.wordpress.com.

125 Pope Paul VI. *Humanae Vitae (On the Regulation of Birth): Encyclical Letter of the Supreme Pontiff Paul VI.* Section 14, Unlawful Birth Control Methods. Presented at St. Peter's in Rome, 7/25/68.

126 *CCC*, ibid., no. 2384.

127 John Paul II. *Familiaris Consortio (On the Role of the Christian Family in the Modern World): Apostolic Exhortation of Pope John Paul II.* Presented at St. Peter's in Rome, 11/22/81.

128 Carroll, James. *Boston Globe*, 5/13/97. Posted on SaveOurSacrament.org.

129 Newman, John Henry. In a "Letter to the Duke of Norfolk."

130 Myers, Ched. 1988. *Binding the Strong Man: A Political Reading of Mark's Story of Jesus.* Orbis Press, Maryknoll, New York, NY.

131 *CCA*, ibid.

132 Culver, Virginia. "Study: Religion No Divorce Preventive." *Denver Post*, 1/8/2000.

[133] Jaspers, Karl. 1967. *Philosophical Faith and Revelation.* Collins, London.

[134] Dupuis, J. and Neuner, J. 2001. *The Christian Faith: In the Doctrinal Documents of the Catholic Church.* (margin note) Alba House Publishers, Staten Island, NY.

[135] Berry, Jason. 2011. *Render Unto Rome: The Secret Life of Money in the Catholic Church.* Random House, New York, NY.

[136] Posted on BibleDiscovered.com, 3/1/2001. Also in "John Dominic Crossan's Blasphemous Portrait of Jesus," CNN.com, 11/18/2011.

[137] Myers, ibid.

[138] Myers, ibid.

[139] Hillman, D.C.A. 2008. *The Chemical Muse: Drug Use and the Roots of Western Civilization.* St. Martin's Press, New York, NY.

[140] Huxley, Aldous. 1963. *The Doors of Perception.* Harper & Row, New York, NY.

[141] *CCC*, ibid.

[142] Harline, Craig. 2000. *A Bishop's Tale: Mathias Hovius among His Flock in Seventeenth-Century Flanders.* RR Donnelly & Sons, Harrisburg, VA.

[143] *Worcester Telegram & Gazette*, 7/7/11.

[144] O'Conaill, Sean. *The Disgracing of Catholic Monarchism.* Posted on seanoconaill.com. First published in: Littleton, John and Maer, Eamon, eds. 2010. *The Dublin/Murphy Report: A Watershed for Irish Catholicism?* Columba Press, Dublin.

[145] Attributed to Deacon Greg Kandra. Posted on DiaryofaWimpyCatholic blog, 7/22/11.

[146] Ericksen, Robert. 1985. *Theologians Under Hitler.* Yale University Press, New Haven, CT.

[147] Ericksen, ibid.

[148] *Federalist Papers* No. 10.

[149] "Cato Institute Briefing Papers," March 2001.

[150] Moynahan, ibid.

[151] Ward, Maisie. 2008. *France Pagan? The Mission of Abbe Godin.* Kessinger Publishing, Whitefish, MT.

[152] Rizzo, Nick. "Is Pope Benedict XVI Gay? Wonders Andrew Sullivan." Mediaite.com news blog, 8/19/10.

[153] Tarico, Valerie. "How I Left My Christian Evangelical Faith." AlterNet.com, 4/25/12.

[154] Zizola, Giancarlo. "The Counter Reformation of John Paul II." *Magill*, 7/3/85.

[155] O'Malley, John W. 2010. *What Happened at Vatican II.* Harvard/BelKnap Press, Boston, MA.

[156] Huber, Robert. "Catholics in Crisis: Sex and Deception in the Archdiocese of Philadelphia." *Philadelphia* magazine, 6/17/11.

[157] Boff, ibid. Also in "The Power of the Institutional Church: Can It Be Converted?" Reprinted in Mannion, Gerald. 2003. *Readings in Church Authority: Gifts and Challenges for Contemporary Catholicism*, by Gerald Mannion. Ashgate Publishing Ltd.

[158] Berry, *Render Unto Rome*, ibid.

[159] "Scalia Blasts Death Penalty Ruling." The Associated Press. Posted on cbsnews.com, 2/11/09.

[160] *CCA*, ibid.

[161] Moynahan, ibid.

[162] Moynahan, ibid.

[163] Jenkins, ibid.

[164] "The Pope and the 'Perfidious' Jews." Fr. Milovan Katanic's blog, frmilovan.wordpress.com, 3/5/11.

[165] Walker, Jim. "Martin Luther's Dirty Little Book: On the Jews and Their Lies." Nobeliefs.com, 8/7/96.

[166] Wilson, Derek. 2006. *Charlemagne*. Doubleday, New York, NY.

[167] Chambers, David S. 2006. *Popes, Cardinals, and War: The Military Church in Renaissance and Early Modern Europe*. I.B. Tauris & Co., London.

[168] Chambers, ibid.

[169] *Storia d'Italia*, op. cit. Quoted in O'Malley, John. 2011. *A History of the Popes: From Peter to the Present*. Sheed & Ward.

[170] Brock, Rita Nakashima. 2009. Saving Paradise: How Christianity Traded Love of this World for Crucifixion and Empire. Beacon Press, Boston, MA.

[171] Brock, ibid.

[172] Milton, John. *Paradise Lost*. Book IV, Line 108.

[173] Moynahan, ibid.

[174] Moynahan, ibid.

[175] Moynahan, ibid.

[176] Parachin, Victor. 2011. *Eleven Modern Mystics: The Secrets of a Happy, Holy Life*. Hope Publishing Co., Pasadena, CA.

[177] Parachin, ibid.

[178] Whitehead, John. "The Military-Industrial Complex: The Enemy from Within." *Freedom Daily*, 1/11/12.

[179] Posted on Stockholm International Peace Research Institute website, sipri.org, 2012.

[180] Kirsch, Jonathan. 2008. *The Grand Inquisitor's Manual: A History of Terror in the Name of God*. HarperOne, New York.

181 Kirsch, ibid.

182 Drake, Tim. "Why Father Robert Barron Filmed 'Catholicism.'" *National Catholic Register*, ncregister.com, 9/22/11.

183 Murphy, ibid.

184 Boff, ibid.

185 "United States: Guns Facts, Figures, and the Law." Posted on gunpolicy.org.

186 Joyner, James. "Paralyzed Veteran Denied Home Permit." OutsidetheBeltway blogspot, 7/1/11. Citing the article, "Group Looks at Other Sites for Paralyzed Vet's Home," *Augusta Chronicle*, 2001.

187 Clark, Monica. "San Francisco Police Arrest Occupiers Who Took Over Archdiocesan Building." *National Catholic Reporter*, ncronline.org, 4/4/12.

188 Ehrman, Bart D. 2005. *Misquoting Jesus: The Story Behind Who Changed the Bible and Why.* Harpers, San Francisco, CA.

189 Podles, Leon. "The Agony of the Church in Chile." Leon J. Podles' Dialogue blog, podles.org, 4/22/11.

190 McElwee, Joshua. "Bishop: Total Re-examination of Catholic Faith, Culture Needed." *National Catholic Reporter*, ncronline.org, 3/28/12.

191 "An Interview with Regina M. Schwartz, author of *The Curse of Cain: The Violent Legacy of Monotheism.*" 1997. University of Chicago Press website, press.uchicago.edu.

192 "Thomas James Ball Self-Immolated in Protest of the 'Justice' System." *Keene Sentinel*, freekeene.com, 6/16/11.

193 Moynahan, ibid.

194 Wills, Garry. "Scientologists, Catholics and More Money Than God." *New York Times*, 7/21/11.

195 Hillar, Marian. "Liberation Theology: Religious Response to Social Problems." Center for Philosophy and Socinian Studies. In *Humanism and*

Social Issues. Anthology of Essays. 1993. American Humanist Association, Houston, TX.

[196] Allen, John L. Jr. "New Leader for Men's Orders Sketches Hopes and Fears." *National Catholic Reporter*, ncronline.org, 10/19/11.

[197] Erdely, Sabrina Rubin. "The Catholic Church's Secret Sex-Crime Files." *Rolling Stone* online, rollingstone.com,9/6/11.

[198] Harvey, Andrew. 2009. *The Hope: A Guide to Sacred Activism.* Hay House, U.K, Ltd.

[199] Harvey, ibid.

[200] McElwee, ibid.

[201] Chardin, Teilhard. 1936. "The Evolution of Chastity." An essay in *Toward the Future.* A Harvest Book, Harcourt, Inc., San Diego, CA.

[202] Posted on adherents.com, and on newworldencyclopedia.org.

[203] Robinson, Sara. "Atheism Rising, But God Is Not Dead Yet: 10 Ways Religion Is Changing Around the World." AlterNet.org, 3/29/12.

[204] Robinson, Sara, ibid.

[205] *CCA*, ibid.

[206] Fisher, Ian. "Benedict XVI and the Church That May Shrink. Or Maybe Not." *New York Times*, 5/29/05.

[207] Boyce, Mary. 1979. *Zoroastrians: Their Religious Beliefs and Practices.* Routledge and Kegan Paul, London.

[208] Meacham, Jon. "Pastor Rob Bell: What if Hell Doesn't Exist?" *Time* online, time.com, 4/14/11.

[209] *Religious Knowledge Survey*, ibid.

[210] Fuellenbach, John. "The Mission of the Church within the Context of Religious Pluralism." Posted on sedosmission.org.

211 St. Augustine. *Homilies on the Gospel of John*, 45, 12.

212 Paul, Gregory and Zuckerman, Phil. "Why Do Americans Still Dislike Atheists?" *Washington Post*, 4/29/11.

213 Tennyson, Alfred. 1854. *The Charge of the Light Brigade.*

214 Hall, ibid.

215 Hayes, Richard P. "Atheism in Buddhist Tradition." In *Philosophy of Religion,* by Roy W. Perrett. 2000. Garland Press, New York, NY.

216 Moss, Meredith. "Dayton Parish Embraces Traditional Latin Mass." *Dayton Daily News*, 4/18/11.

217 Robinson, Sara, ibid.

218 "Jesuit Officials Say America Editor Resigned After Vatican Complaints." *America Magazine*, 5/23/2005.

219 Robinson, Sara, ibid.

220 Walshe, Shushannah. "Rick Santorum on Satan Speech: 'I Will Defend Everything I Say.'" ABC News online, abcnews.go.com, 2/21/12.

221 *CCC*, ibid.

222 Garbutt, Nick. "Wounds Caused by Catholic Church Run Deep." Posted on newsletter.co.uk, 5/3/12.

223 Gandhi, Mahatma Gandhi. Last Phase, Vol. II (1958). Posted on mkgandhi.org.

224 "Pope Quells Speculation about Resignation Rumours." CathNews.com, 2/19/12.

Made in the USA
Charleston, SC
02 June 2014